The Politics
of Urban Planning

THE EAST ST. LOUIS EXPERIENCE

Dennis R. Judd
Robert E. Mendelson

UNIVERSITY OF ILLINOIS PRESS
Urbana   Chicago   London

Contents

Preface

The case studies which appear in this volume grew out of the authors' involvement and research in the planning politics of East St. Louis, Illinois. Over a four-year period, from 1966 to 1969, Robert Mendelson, as a staff member of Southern Illinois University's Regional and Urban Development Studies and Services Program, conducted studies on housing and relocation in East St. Louis, prepared urban renewal and planning grant applications, assisted in the creation of a housing development corporation, acted as an advocate planner for several neighborhoods seeking changes in city ordinances and practices, and served, for two years, as chief planner in the Model Cities program. Dennis Judd studied politics in East St. Louis as a Research Associate at the Institute of Government and Public Affairs at the University of Illinois and participated in the HUD evaluation of the East St. Louis Model Cities program. Working together on Model Cities projects resulted in this collaboration between a practicing planner and a professional political scientist.

We are grateful to the many people who assisted us in this project. Support by three individuals was particularly critical. William J. Tudor, Director of Regional and Urban Development

Studies and Services, Southern Illinois University, and his predecessor, Seymour Z. Mann, and Samuel K. Gove, Director of the Institute of Government and Public Affairs, University of Illinois, encouraged our involvement in East St. Louis. These individuals did not consider East St. Louis to be simply a research laboratory, but also were committed to the provision of tangible and useful services. That they did not withdraw support for our activity when participation meant controversy and risk is to their credit.

Other colleagues reviewed and analyzed our work: Jane Altes, Marguerite Bittner, and Alfred Kahn of Southern Illinois University at Edwardsville; Philip Meranto (now at the University of Washington) and Louis Gold of the University of Illinois; Jamie Cannon, Hellmuth Obata and Kassabaum, Inc., St. Louis (formerly Director of Department of Planning, East St. Louis); Mary Ellen Ross, Department of City Planning, New York City; Esley Hamilton, Model Cities Agency, East St. Louis; Charles Means, Director of Urban Renewal, East St. Louis; and Barry Phegan, Director of Development, East St. Louis Housing Authority. Their comments, though discouraging at times, provided direction and depth to our efforts.

Administrators and professionals who supplied information and guidance included Cannon, Means, Leroy Gruber, Harvey Henderson, Glenn Hendry, Fred Teer, and George Washnis. These competent people were often faced with difficult decisions in East St. Louis—a point not adequately stressed in our book. Choices of courses of action were continually clouded by the pressures from various groups and individuals. It is easy to employ hindsight to second-guess decisions which were made, but we have not forgotten the problems and constraints faced during the period covered in our case studies. The administrators and professionals were always under fire, and controversy surrounded every significant public issue. That they endured at all in their jobs was often remarkable.

Various elected officials endorsed our role in East St. Louis even though they did not always agree with our findings and conclusions. Former Mayor Alvin G. Fields and Commissioner

Dan Foley, in particular, gave us access to valuable data and a firsthand view of East St. Louis politics.

Ruben Yelvington, former editor of the *Metro-East Journal*, allowed us to use the files of his newspaper—a major source of information on history and planning activities. Many other people, both in and out of government, helped us—too many to mention individually. To them, our sincerest appreciation. We were trusted in East St. Louis and it is our hope that this trust was not abused.

Portions of Chapter 3 appeared in a monograph published by Regional and Urban Development Studies and Services of Southern Illinois University. Also, the original research for Chapter 2 was gathered and conducted by Mary Ellen Ross, formerly a planner for the City of East St. Louis. Portions of the chapter were included in her M.A. thesis for the Department of Urban and Regional Planning, University of Wisconsin. Permission to use the material for both these chapters is gratefully acknowledged. In addition, Chapters 1 and 4 were a substantial part of a doctoral dissertation completed for the University of Illinois by Dennis Judd.

Without typing and editing assistance from Sally Ferguson and Teri Thomas, much of this book would probably still be written in longhand on yellow legal pads. Sally reviewed content, reorganized chapters, and did the tedious job of checking punctuation and grammar. Teri typed, sometimes from barely legible script. Both of these very competent people made a difficult task much more pleasant and agreeable. We also appreciate the typing assistance provided by Lillian Ehrlich, of Washington University.

We are also grateful, of course, to our families for providing valued distractions from this project. Without camping trips, movies, children's art and music, and other family pursuits, none of this writing would have been worth doing.

Introduction

In the course of a discussion about the planning profession, an associate of ours related a conversation that he had engaged in with an executive of one of the nation's largest planning-engineering firms. They had been discussing the growth of planning activities, increasing federal support, and how, in the central cities, planning had rarely led to redevelopment. At one point the corporate executive, with evident seriousness, replied to a question concerning the gap between planning and implementation: "young man, you better hope this condition remains. In 1941, we did a water and sewer study for ——— city. In 1949 and 1953, we updated it. In 1959, we did the study again. In 1963, the city built the system and we haven't heard from them since."[1]

This statement might have been more humorous if it had not touched the heart of the matter so closely. For as this volume unfortunately illustrates, planning in the United States, as provided by public servants and private entrepreneurs, has tended to be encouraged and sustained as much to provide jobs and

[1] This conversation was related to one of the authors in an informal discussion in September, 1971. The quotation is paraphrased.

incomes for professionals as to reach social objectives. Our case studies of planning in East St. Louis, Illinois, which comprise the first part of this book, show the overwhelming influence of professional and bureaucratic autonomy and self-interest in the planning process. In the second part, we attempt to show that the East St. Louis experience is not particularly unique, for it reflects what is encouraged by the values and ideologies of the planning profession.

From 1960 to 1969, over 125 studies were produced which related to East St. Louis's problems, many of them prepared by outside consultants. During the same period, the professional component in East St. Louis steadily grew. The planning staff of the city increased from four to fifteen persons between 1966 and 1969, while planning activities expanded from zoning regulation and administration to technical responsibility for a Community Renewal Program and a General Neighborhood Renewal Plan (GNRP) and assistance in urban renewal and Model Cities planning. Growth of professional activity was directly attributable to an enlarged federal presence in the city.

Despite the proliferation of planning activities, there were few signs of physical improvement or social renewal in East St. Louis. In explaining the gap between planning and implementation in the city, it would have been natural to regard the social and political environment as too hostile for planned allocation of resources to take place. At first glance this explanation would seem logical and persuasive. East St. Louis had historically been governed by a political organization which held tight control over the community. Perpetuation of this control was given higher priority than the provision of basic municipal and educational services. The machine had traditionally failed to reduce organized crime in the city and illicit profit-taking from public office. City government, the labor unions, and the business community had, over a long period of time, devised a closely tied, mutually beneficial political organization. Public action to upgrade the community coincided with increased availability of federal funds in the 1960s and from pressures within and without the community to take advantage of these funds.

Blame for the failure to implement planning could easily have been assigned also to the social heritage of East St. Louis. The city had not traditionally attracted populations or political groups committed to and supportive of those values (efficiency, rationality, and objectivity) which are, according to conventional wisdom, associated with middle-class government and planning efforts. Almost from its inception, East St. Louis had been populated by an extremely large proportion of poor residents. Waves of new arrivals settled there in search of job opportunities in the labor-intensive industries located in, and adjoining to, the community. Irish immigrants were joined by Eastern Europeans in the late nineteenth century and by Blacks shortly after 1900. A rapid influx of Blacks from the south occurred when many of those en route to northern destinations such as Chicago and Detroit stopped along the way. Competition for jobs and manipulation of race issues by politicians and businessmen led to the 1917 race riot in East St. Louis—one of the bloodiest of this century. A legacy of racial discord and political control over Blacks persisted for many years, but the Black in-migration continued, with Blacks reaching a majority in the city by 1960. Massive poverty, unemployment, low education, poor health conditions, and a substandard physical environment characterized East St. Louis. In the 1960s these conditions still persisted, despite growing unrest and militance by Blacks. Thus, one seemingly had to look no further than the city itself for an explanation as to the futility of planning efforts.

Our involvement and research on planning in East St. Louis, however, made us skeptical about the environmental explanation. It was not only too simplistic but also failed to account for the continued persistence and growth of planning in the 1960s and for the actions of the professionals themselves. Many residents felt that professionals were almost as aloof from the community as the machine politicians had been. Plans and studies had been carried out with no consultation from local groups or individual residents. As the book unfolded our views tended to join those of resident critics who argued that something appeared to be wrong within the planning process as it had been carried out locally. One incident particularly illustrated that the

professionals could not be held blameless for the lack of redevelopment in East St. Louis.

In 1968, East St. Louis Representative Melvin Price approached the Allied Mortgage and Development Company and
its partners in housing projects, John Hancock Life Insurance
and United States Gypsum, about the possibility of building
federally subsidized housing in East St. Louis. Allied subsequently proposed to construct 5,000 turnkey housing units over
a five-year period in the city. East St. Louis's downtown business
organization, PACE (Progress and Action by Citizens Efforts),
immediately became interested, and instructed its consultant,
a professional in urban redevelopment and planning, to coordinate efforts to get the project started. PACE subsequently
presented the Allied plan to the local housing authority and to
the city council, which gave their support. Black leaders and
residents learned of the plan through the newspapers, television,
and at later meetings.

A newly formed coalition of groups called Black Unity reacted vociferously against the proposal, feeling that outsiders
were foisting plans upon the community, just as had occurred
in the past. They were not opposed to new housing; everyone
knew that housing was needed. Their objections concerned the
fact that no representatives of the Black community could speak
knowledgeably about Allied or its intended use of the Turnkey
III federal housing program. Why had PACE, which was primarily White, been selected to introduce the plan to East St.
Louis? Many Blacks believed that the principal beneficiaries
would be bankers and businessmen rather than low-income
residents.

Black exclusion was the main issue, not the merits of the
Allied scheme. There was, in fact, general agreement, especially
among Black and White professionals in city government, that a
proposal of this size was the only realistic way to raise housing
quality in the community.[2] Four or five months later, when
tempers had subsided and a mechanism for resident involve-

[2] For additional information see the component on Citizen Participation by
Mary Ellen Ross, Model City Agency, *Model Cities—Phase I* (East St. Louis,
Ill.: City of East St. Louis, 1968).

ment and coordination of new housing had been created, the Allied plan received a degree of community support. Once the program was completely explained, it was apparent that there would be not only housing advantages but also employment in a prefabrication plant which was to be erected with proposed advances from the Department of Housing and Urban Development (HUD).

By fall, 1968, the initial controversy was resolved sufficiently to achieve reasonable consensus on the merits of the Allied proposal. Considerable activity by residents, planners, and federal officials to implement the Allied proposal followed. One team after another was sent to East St. Louis by HUD to evaluate community need, market feasibility, and local competence to administer the program. As each group left, another followed closely behind. In January, 1969, the new national administration came into office. Suddenly, there were new HUD officials talking about different kinds of housing breakthroughs, and the fate of East St. Louis was being discussed from different perspectives. Throughout February and March, each day brought expectations that a decision on the 5,000 units would be reached. By summer, when no official word had been given, it was generally conceded that East St. Louis had been eliminated from HUD's plans and the Allied proposal was dead.

In the Allied case, the professionals' autonomy from the Black community had led them to seriously underestimate—if they thought of it at all—the political changes which were taking place in East St. Louis. Moreover, they viewed housing and redevelopment as self-evidently good. Justifiably, they felt that East St. Louis was in critical need of federal aid. Their reaction to the controversy which surrounded the announcement of the Allied plan was that the opposition was self-serving and politically motivated. They simply could not understand why anyone would oppose the project. It did not occur to the professionals that opposition might be connected to past bulldozer projects, such as the clearing of residential areas near downtown with little subsequent redevelopment, or the construction of a spaghettilike system of interstate highways and ramps through and over residential areas. From the professionals' perspective, opposition delayed and ultimately killed a critically needed housing project; from the residents' perspective, opposition meant a chance for them to have something to say about types of housing for their community, who would build it, and who would live in it. And it also gave local Black leaders power to give their preferences greater credence than the preferences of those who did not live in their neighborhood or even in their community.

That planners were unable to understand the legitimate claims of other groups on the planning process was evident in the case of the Allied controversy. There were other instances, too, in which this tendency, and the self-interest of the professionals, intruded into planning. Job security, prestige, and agency prerogatives were given paramount consideration in the three case studies included in this book. East St. Louis urban renewal planning largely represented professionals' stakes in protecting their positions and programs. In the attempts at master planning implementation through redevelopment of the Mississippi River waterfront, professional proponents sketched visions of community renewal and enrichment while pursuing very individualized aims. And Model Cities, despite its great potential for redevelopment and community mobilization, eventually became dominated by planners attempting to satisfy endless federal bureaucratic requirements. Chapters 2 through 4 describe these planning efforts in detail.

Rapid expansion of the federal role in East St. Louis between 1966 and 1969, described in the latter part of Chapter 1, represented primarily an attempt by federal officials and local professionals to build a professionalized administrative capacity in local government. Even program implementation was, if necessary, sacrificed to achieve the growth of professionalism. In urban renewal planning (related in Chapter 2), the primary purpose for much activity and federal funding was to increase the number of hired professionals. Attempts to create individual professional autonomy and larger local bureaucracies often came at the expense of engaging in activities to translate plans into operating programs.

Similar tendencies appeared in planning for development of the East St. Louis riverfront (Chapter 3). For years, plans for the area were prepared without any attempt to go beyond the publication of aesthetically pleasing booklets. Even though no programs resulted, the cost of planning escalated, amounting to approximately $400,000 from 1960 to 1970. An illusion of imminent redevelopment was maintained with the promise of immediate action following the publication of each new proposal. Planning, however, remained detached from those political interests which may have been able to supply the necessary resources for effectuating redevelopment. Perhaps for that reason, riverfront planning was uniformly abstract and grandiose.

In recent years pressure for Black community involvement added a new dimension to planning in East St. Louis. Black influence in local politics increased with civil rights gains in the late 1950s and early 1960s. By 1966, when East St. Louis received a Model Cities grant, city officials and professionals could no longer work in isolation. As indicated in Chapter 4, local officials and university professionals drew up East St. Louis's Model Cities application in relative isolation from groups and residents in the community. Not long after East St. Louis received approval for a Model Cities program, however, Black insurgents led a take-over of the city hall–dominated Model Cities Agency. Though a few White professionals were willing to cooperate with these insurgents, they did not alter their belief that the program was designed to improve the delivery of physical and social services and bring efficient administration to local government. For a few months, local residents gave community organization the highest priority in the Model Cities program, but federal pressure to produce planning documents, along with the expression of other priorities by the professionals, gradually transformed Model Cities into a professionalized, bureaucratized program which accomplished few of its original aims. Many of the professionals who were involved in Model Cities were disturbed first by the conflicting goals between the residents and themselves and then by the bureaucratic tendencies of the program, wherein substance was often replaced by form. But their understanding of how the program changed from community involvement to bureaucratic control was extremely limited.

While the performance of the professionals in East St. Louis could be criticized, they seemed, to us, no less competent or capable of insight than their counterparts in other American cities. On the whole, they possessed the skills which were expected for their jobs. Some were trained in planning; others in allied professions such as architecture, public administration, and sociology. Further, if the case-study literature about planning is any criteria, then planning in East St. Louis appeared to be generally no poorer in performance than that of other cities. Our strong suspicions that the East St. Louis experience was, in many ways, typical of planning elsewhere led us to the review of professional planning literature which appears in Chapter 5.

Our review of the literature in planning revealed that what happened in East St. Louis rather accurately reflected the norms and doctrines of the profession. Traditional planning doctrine in the literature characterized planners as neutral experts, independent and superior to laymen or even other professionals. Moreover, the literature rarely went beyond a thinly veiled attempt to enhance, justify, and preserve the profession. Planners had developed a self-enhancing ideology which extolled the profession more than it described the tasks and roles of its practitioners. Claims that planners were uniquely rational, that they viewed the whole and not its parts, that they presided over ordered change and often championed the interests of the poor and disaffected, read more like religious statements of faith than like descriptions and prescriptions of actions which could be taken in the present rather than future life.

We found in the literature, however, strong dissent from the values traditionally expressed by planners. Advocate planners have charged the profession with representing powerful political interests to the exclusion of the underclass in American society, citing programs in urban renewal, public housing, and highway building as examples. Advocates see themselves as attempting to change the "present distribution of public and private resources in American cities (which) favors the haves, not the have-nots."[3] With reference to powerless groups, the advocate planner's "role is (proponents assert) to defend and

[3] Marshall Kaplan, "Advocacy and the Poor," *Journal of the American Institute of Planners*, XXXV (March 1969), p. 97.

prosecute the interests of his clients. The planning advocate links resource and strategy alternatives to objectives and joins issues at the request of his client when others' interpretation of facts overlooks, minimizes, or negatively affects his client's interests."[4]

Unfortunately, this formulation does not explain or define tasks and responsibilities more adequately than traditional doctrines. Some of the reasons for this are discussed in Chapter 5, but it is sufficient to say here that the professional's training and values and his self-interests often lead to manipulation, rather than representation, of clients.[5] Given the insulated and autonomous position of planners, advocacy planning can only be marginally successful at best. In many ways, advocacy planning has been a relatively conservative response to the political changes of the 1960s. Faced with large segments of the population, especially in the central cities, who rejected planners' values and services, a rationale was developed to appeal to the new constituency and make planners relevant in a changing political order. Thus, the profession received added legitimacy through the new doctrine. But advocate planners were not the vanguard of change. They reacted to change, using it often as a way to enhance the prestige and advantages of their professional positions.

Consequently, it is not likely that advocates or traditionalists will alter what have been the effects of their work as long as the autonomy of the planning profession is not challenged. The maintenance and enhancement needs of the profession militate against basic change. Planning is not unique in this respect; other professions show comparable tendencies. Organizing people who provide similar services or possess similar skills introduces restraints on the range of activities and viewpoints of the members, and also offers inducements to conformity such as financial and job security, status, and favorable work conditions. Professionalizing a skill or service usually has the effect of insulating the practitioner from the recipients of the service, and it

[4] *Ibid.*
[5] Lisa Peattie, "Reflections on Advocacy Planning," *Journal of the American Institute of Planners,* XXXIV (March, 1968), Ch. 5.

introduces a set of group self-interests which may reduce the quality and utility of the professional's service. Thus, the American Medical Association has vigorously resisted attempts to provide equitable health delivery systems, and has coerced doctors to abide by AMA policies.[6] Partly as a result of the power and self-interests of the AMA, doctors have not exerted leadership in studying the effects of environmental pollution on health, have not attempted to prevent rather than simply treat disease, and have continually tried to enhance their incomes through the perpetuation of an elitist and exclusionary system. Likewise, the American Bar Association has often served as a barrier between equitable application of the law and the needs of clients. In the past the ABA has not facilitated and has often resisted legal representation for indigents and reforms which would reduce the necessity for litigation. The professionalization and training of social workers has done little to increase bureaucratic responsiveness to the needs and demands of the poor. In fact, the professionalization of social welfare workers appears to have had the effect of increasing bureaucratic rigidity and arbitrary conduct in welfare agencies.[7]

The point is this: professional autonomy and power encourages manipulation and intervention by the professionals; few of them are willing to voluntarily give up job security and status. Professional responsiveness has been primarily induced by pressures from outside, not inside, the professions. Advocacy planning shares these limitations.

In the last chapter, a professional role is sketched which seeks to avoid these liabilities. Professional autonomy partially accounts for what occurred in East St. Louis. Only when the clients of planning can share in determining what the professional role is and ought to accomplish will planning be basically changed. If "effective" planning is that which pursues the public interest, then the several interests which make up the public presumably would have to be included.

[6] See, for example, *The American Health Empire: Power, Profits, and Politics*, A Report of the Health Policy Advisory Center (New York: Random House, 1970).

[7] Frances Fox Piven and Richard A. Cloward, *Regulating the Poor* (New York: Pantheon Books, 1971), Ch. 5.

The Politics of Urban Planning

Acronyms Used in Text

AIP	American Institute of Planners
CAA	Community Action Agency
CBD	central business district
CEP	Concentrated Employment Program
CPI	Community Progress, Incorporated
CRP	Community Renewal Program
EOC	Economic Opportunity Commission
GNRP	General Neighborhood Renewal Plan
HEW	Department of Health, Education, and Welfare
HUD	Department of Housing and Urban Development
LPA	local public agency (HUD, urban renewal)
MCA	Model Cities Agency
NDP	Neighborhood Development Program
OEO	Office of Economic Opportunity
PACE	Progress and Action by Citizens Efforts
S and P	Survey and Planning (HUD, urban renewal)
SIU	Southern Illinois University

The Context for Planning
in East St. Louis

1

On April 6, 1971, James E. Williams defeated Virgil L. Calvert for mayor of East St. Louis, Illinois, by winning 10,813 votes to Calvert's 8,202. The election outcome marked a dramatic break from the past. Williams, labeled a reformer by himself and his supporters, upset the bipartisan machine's candidate. Centralized control by a few politicians had been a fact of life in East St. Louis for more than fifty years. For much of that period, and before, the East St. Louis political culture had nurtured an oligarchic and often venal politics.

Political Heritage

Two factors have played major roles in determining East St. Louis's growth pattern: the proximity to St. Louis, Missouri, and the advent of the transportation industry. East St. Louis served as a crossing point for produce, goods, and people to St. Louis, and its original land uses were defined in relation to the larger city on the opposite bank of the river. To the extent that it was independent, as a transportation crossroads, East St. Louis served as a way station to other points in the west and midwest. Much of this can be explained by reference to geographic features. St. Louis provided an ideal location for residential settlement. Rolling hills provided protection from river flooding and afforded good drainage while, in contrast, East St. Louis was located on a low, marshy flood plain. Before extensive landfill raised the downtown area by about ten feet at the turn of the century, some of it was actually below the normal level of the Mississippi River. Though unfavorable for settlement, the abundant flat land was ideal for the building of a railroad terminus and, later, for industries requiring large land areas.

East St. Louis began its institutionalized existence as a transportation center when Captain James Piggott completed construction of the first bridge spanning Cahokia Creek in 1795 (ending East St. Louis's island status between the Mississippi River and Cahokia Creek) and shortly thereafter built a hand-operated ferry to carry merchants and produce across the Mississippi River. In 1819 the hand ferry was replaced by a horse-operated one and then, nine years later, by a steam-operated model.

Long after the ferryboats stopped running across the river, East St. Louis continued to perform critical transportation functions for the entire region. First the railroads then the highways played a major role in the community, influencing social and economic conditions and shaping land-use activities. Since 1836 when the first railroad line was laid in the city, railroads have occupied a sizable portion of acreage and determined the community's street and circulation systems. East St. Louis now ranks second nationally to Chicago in land devoted to railroad usage. It also serves as a focal crossing point for highways from all parts of the eastern and central United States. Six interstate highways pass through the city, as do other federal and state roadway systems. Traffic between St. Louis and East St. Louis is carried over the Mississippi by three toll bridges and a six-lane free bridge which is part of the interstate system.

Abundant flat land on the east side of the river was also favorable for the location of heavy industry supplying St. Louis and other midwest cities. When the National Stockyards opened in 1873, East St. Louis became known as one of the biggest pork-producing areas in the world. Railroad development, the stockyards, and industrial development led to a boom that carried through World War I and into the 1920s. There was so much heavy industry located near East St. Louis during that period that employment opportunities abounded.

East St. Louis became surrounded by company towns which were industrial satellites to St. Louis. Often consisting of several blocks of company-owned houses along with the company's industrial facilities, these municipalities protected a particular industry or set of industries from the tax burdens of residential municipalities. These so-called cities were characterized by absentee ownership, unfair labor practices, no municipal services or levies, and under-assessment for school taxation purposes. These patterns are still primary aspects of the political scene of East St. Louis. Although industrial development slowed following the 1920s, especially during the Depression and World War II, chemical plants, power plants, refineries, auto junk-yards, and other land-consuming and polluting industries have developed in great abundance in the area, often leaving residential enclaves among the transportation and industrial enterprises.

This pattern of economic development resulted in the re-cruitment of an especially homogeneous population to East St. Louis, consisting of ethnic White and southern Black immi-grants who were often manipulated by business and political interests. While most established American cities were experi-encing a decline in the numbers of immigrant populations due both to the strict immigration laws of the 1920s and to the im-proving economic status of certain immigrant groups, East St. Louis showed a continuing influx of a highly dependent popula-tion. During the 1870 to 1920 boom period large numbers of unskilled workers came to the city. By 1910 nearly 6,000 Blacks, more than 10 percent of the total population, were living in East St. Louis; seven years later, just before the 1917 race riot, the number had grown to more than 10,000 (about 16 percent). Racial antagonisms were inflamed by politicians running racist campaigns and companies threatening union organizers and strikers with replacement by Black workers. Deep fear and sus-picion of Blacks by Whites, combined with widespread lawless-ness and corruption in East St. Louis, culminated in the bloody race riot of July 2, 1917, which took forty-six lives, thirty-nine of them Black.

Conditions encouraging violence and social instability were not tempered by the presence of a reformer middle-class population. Unlike other American cities where business and civic elites, under the guise of reform, mobilized to protect their own self-interests, those who might have led reforms benefited from and encouraged corruption and lawlessness. A pattern of absentee ownership lessened the interest of company owners and managers in encouraging favorable living conditions. But far from having no impact on local politics, company interests pervasively intruded into East St. Louis politics.

Industrial and business concerns located in and near East St. Louis narrowly confined their span of attention to tax benefits, cheap land, and low labor costs. In collusion with political leaders at the state, county, and local level, they were notoriously successful in maximizing profits and minimizing costs. A common strategy of the companies was to stake their own legally separate fiefdoms where they could control tax rates, property assessments, police forces, and the like. The meat-packing industry became the first to seize upon this device by incorporating a municipality in 1907 called National City. This village, with only a few hundred residents living in company-owned property or transient hotels, had a mayor, board of aldermen, and tax assessor, each of whom worked for one of the companies. Swift, Armour, and Morris were assessed cumulatively for $177,201 in 1915 by the municipality. Although this figure was subsequently raised by the St. Clair County tax assessor to $1,256,603, still only a small fraction of their actual worth, the St. Clair County board of review reduced it back to $162,810. The judge who had appointed the majority of members on the board had close connections and sympathies with the corporate interests, and the companies had once hired his son to argue before the board for tax reductions.[1]

Actually, the meat-packing companies need not have gone to such elaborate lengths since other companies in the area also

---

[1] Elliott M. Rudwick, *Race Riot at East St. Louis, July 2, 1917* (Carbondale: Southern Illinois University Press, 1964), pp. 193–194.

enjoyed the benefits of close collusion with politicians. In 1913 six East St. Louis city councilmen each accepted a $500 bribe for passing an ordinance favorable to the East St. Louis Interurban Railway Company.[2] Several councilmen were also paid $3,000 to grant a franchise to the Alton and Southern Railway which the Aluminum Ore Company reportedly helped "finance." Downtown merchants also enjoyed close relations to city hall in the early twentieth century, and open vice in the downtown area was seen as a boon to legitimate business. Since license fees were a major source of city revenues, the taverns flourishing with gambling and prostitution brought considerable tax income to the municipal treasury.[3]

As industry prospered through the 1920s, corporate managers and downtown businessmen became satisfied with the vice and politics of East St. Louis. Those corporations in the city and those just outside the city limits were typically assessed at very low rates. City real property appraisals were usually cut by the St. Clair County Board of Review. In 1951, for example, the Aluminum Ore Company's assessment was reduced more than two-thirds from the original figure, and Missouri Malleable Iron Company enjoyed a 72 percent cut.[4] Like their larger brothers, downtown businessmen were also able to escape fair taxation through nonpayment and by forcing the taverns to carry the load by paying the going rate for protection of their lucrative gambling and prostitution operations.

Besides keeping the city in a constantly bankrupt state, the companies intruded into local politics through their antiunion and low-wage policies. Companies not only refused to bargain with workers, but also threatened to use Blacks as strikebreakers. Armour actually attempted to import Black and White workers from other cities during one strike, and the company's threats to use Black labor and the refusal to grant minimal job security helped inflame racist sentiment leading to the 1917 riot.

If the corporate and business interests had little incentive to seek reform, the politicians had even less. Since the incorpora-

2 *Ibid.*, p. 177.
3 *Ibid.*, pp. 191, 197–198.
4 *Ibid.*, p. 193 (see Table 4).

tion of the city, the main inducements for many to seek public office had been immediate personal power and/or monetary gain through control over the public purse and manipulation of public office for favors. Holding a political position often brought benefits so lucrative that intense and sometimes violent competition for official positions was encouraged.

For twenty years after its official incorporation in 1861, East St. Louis experienced the most violent form of politics. At one point the city was racked by a bloody riot that broke out during the final stages of an election campaign, and it took the Illinois militia to restore order. It was not hard to identify the reasons for fierce competition for public office. In the 1880s, elected city officials absconded with the city treasury and burned down city hall to destroy the municipal records.[5] Shortly after the building was reconstructed, its vault was dynamited to make it appear as though the treasury had been robbed, when, in actuality, most of the city's money and bonds had been stolen. Soon after, in 1885, a former mayor who had advocated honest government was assassinated. His death catalyzed the election in 1887 of one of his followers who for a brief period brought honesty and a semblance of order to East St. Louis government.[6]

This pause in governmental antics was only temporary. Several years later it was business as usual, except that the inducements and rewards had become richer. Every public office, from the highest to the lowest, provided opportunities for financial benefit. City and school treasurer positions were especially rewarding since the meager salaries could be multiplied many times over by the pocketing of interest on bank deposits and skimming off the top of tax collections. Such chicanery was easily protected by insuring that judges, prosecutors, police forces, school trustees, and other officials responsible for overseeing and enforcing the laws were included within the privileged circle. Somehow the office of State's Attorney of St. Clair County fell into the hands of an uncorrupted person in the election of 1912, but he was defeated in his bid for reelection in 1916 at a critical time in the prosecution of several city officials for

[5] *Ibid.*, p. 175.
[6] Tony Canty, article in the *East St. Louis Journal*, May 21, 1961, p. 8-F.

fraud and bribery. His replacement was considered far more cooperative.[7]

An illustration of the extent of corruption occurred in 1913. In that year the city council took the unprecedented action of recommending that all financial records of Mayor Lambert's administration be destroyed, on the ground that all funds were legally accounted for and records were no longer needed on past transactions. Newspaper publicity forestalled destruction of the records, and a subsequent investigation revealed chaotic record keeping and fraudulent practices. Shortly thereafter financial records disappeared from the city comptroller's vault.[8]

While the political practices of the city contributed to East St. Louis's image, its reputation for vice was even more widespread: "During the 100-year history of East St. Louis if there ever was one word which spread the city's fame, or ill fame rather, around the country and even to some remote corners of the world, it was the word 'Valley.' The 'Valley' was the term used to cover the area of the city in which prostitution flourished and was cultivated through pay-offs to politicians and police."[9]

Vice operations began around 1900 and reached an apex during Prohibition (1919 to 1933) and for about ten years after. At its height many hundreds were involved in plying their trade in the taverns and "houses" in neighborhoods adjoining city hall and the downtown business district. Legitimate business was stimulated by the steady flow of patrons and sightseers to the area. City fathers terminated the boom when they closed the "Valley" during World War II under pressure from Scott Air Force Base officers who threatened to place East St. Louis off-limits. Construction of an interstate highway in the 1950s erased the memory of the bumpy roads, the rundown shacks, the taverns, and huge crowds which characterized the "Valley."

As large-scale prostitution was closing down in the 1940s, organized crime moved into the city and surrounding communities. Late-hour tavern closing and Missouri's "blue-sky" laws had traditionally made East St. Louis a favorite spot for night-

---

[7] Rudwick, *Race Riot*, 184.
[8] *Ibid.*
[9] *East St. Louis Journal*, May 21, 1961, p. 6-H.

clubbers. Gambling became an added inducement. Slot machines, hand books, and plush casinos featuring expensive entertainment became located in and around East St. Louis. By the early 1940s, members of the Capone gang had moved south and established themselves in East St. Louis. Through violence and other softer methods, they gained undisputed control over the taverns, casinos, and other bases for gambling. About a decade after prostitution was curbed, organized and blatant gambling was also curtailed.[10] By this time, however, the reputation of East St. Louis as "sin city" had been firmly established.

In the summer of 1950, the image of the city was spread through the televised hearings of the U.S. Senate special committee to investigate organized crime in interstate commerce. After several unsuccessful attempts to obtain testimony from the East St. Louis police commissioner, who was a prominent Democratic politician, the Senators, led by Estes Kefauver, were finally able to question him. They asked him about the operations of one of the largest bookmaking enterprises in the country, which was within a block or two of city hall and the police station. He said that he hardly knew anything about it; and, when queried whether he was concerned about the gambling, his response was that "at one time, like I testified, we investigated after we seen it in the paper and the place was locked. The police officers were sent up there by the orders of the chief of police and the establishment was locked."[11] When pushed by the Senate committee about the possibility that he might have been lax in fulfilling his police duties, his reply was that he sent his men over to "investigate" after he read the newspaper accounts of large-scale betting, but he really did not know too much about either the owners or what they were doing.[12]

In the early twentieth century, the working relationship between local authorities and vice became increasingly organized

[10] *Ibid.* East St. Louis was only one of many midwestern cities with "red light" districts. However, the extent of these activities was unusual.

[11] U.S. Congress, Senate, Special Committee to Investigate Organized Crime in Interstate Commerce, *Investigation of Organized Crime in Interstate Commerce, Hearings,* before a Special Committee to Investigate Organized Crime in Interstate Commerce, Senate, 81st Cong., 2nd Sess. and 82nd Cong., 1st Sess., pursuant to S. Res. 202, Part 4A, Missouri, June 13, 1950–Feb. 24, 1951, p. 604.

[12] *Ibid.,* p. 603–606.

in both pay-off arrangements and in overlapping personnel. A Democratic victory at the polls in the 1915 election brought increased centralization in local politics, and intense competition for local office declined. This trend was accompanied by the centralization of vice and crime activities into a two-county syndicate by the early 1920s. Nepotism in both politics and organized crime helped to bring a degree of stability to both enterprises, although interfactional peace was by no means assured. Violence within organized crime in the late 1920s and 1930s on the national level was also reflected in the local syndicate.

By the end of World War I, East St. Louis political elections were becoming less and less competitive. This was due more to lessening factionalism than to the weakening of either political party. At least since the turn of the century, and probably before, party affiliations had meant much less than the willingness to "go along" with profitable political arrangements. Coalitions fighting for public office did not respect party lines; the competition continued because the factions had relatively equal resources. By 1915 Locke Tarlton, a Democrat, had become the political boss in East St. Louis. Much of his power came from his willingness to spread the rewards of politics liberally. His positions as chairman of the St. Clair County Democratic central committee and the East Side Levee and Sanitary District (a large patronage source) gave him control over money and jobs. In the 1916 election Republican and Democratic leaders united in support of Tarlton against a Democratic prosecuting attorney who had the impudence to investigate election frauds and misuse of public office. A bipartisan Republican who would make more discrete use of his prosecution powers replaced him.[13]

Centralization of political power was given an official stamp of approval when the city government was converted to the commission form in 1919. Under the commission form, five men are elected by popular vote in an at-large, nonpartisan election to carry out the legislative, executive, and administrative functions of the city. Originally conceived as a political reform to promote efficiency through the linking of policymaking and administration in East St. Louis, the commission structure facili-

13 Rudwick, *Race Riot*, p. 184.

tated the concentration of power in the hands of a few people.

Republicans often dominated the politics of both St. Clair County and East St. Louis prior to 1932. A combination of Roosevelt's election and a trend toward the Democrats which was already underway combined to effectively destroy Republican leadership until their recent participation in the Williams election. One of the significant acts of the Republicans while in power was the establishment of the East Side Levee and Sanitary District which they made into an effective vehicle for dispensing jobs and favors.

For the past fifty years, however, no matter which party was in control, the power in East St. Louis has actually been bipartisan, transcending both political parties. From the mid-1930s and for two decades, Dan McGlynn headed the Republican party in St. Clair County. Not only were his connections with Republican governors sources of strength but also his alliances with Democratic politicians—one of which resulted in the ouster of Alvin G. Fields, Mayor of East St. Louis from 1951 to 1971 and present leader of the bicounty Democratic machine, from the office of city clerk in 1940.

While the machine power after 1932 was ostensibly based in the Democratic party, it also controlled many Republican candidates. In fact, when it was to the machine's advantage it would support Republicans. One of the East St. Louis commissioners from 1951 to 1971 was a Republican, and Republicans and Democrats traditionally courted the favor of Mayor Alvin Fields. Because city elections are nonpartisan it has traditionally been impossible to be elected mayor or commissioner without support from both parties. Until very recently, outsiders have simply been unable to compete. Mayor Fields controlled both Republican and Democratic precinct committeemen through most of his twenty-year term in office.

Endurance of machine-style politics in East St. Louis can be traced directly to a history which included a continuous influx of dependent populations, the absence of a reformer class, and the often close ties between politicians, organized crime, labor unions, and business leaders. The pervasiveness of the machine gave it a virtual monopoly over most avenues to financial and political success and even survival. This meant that no independent political leadership could develop in the White or Black communities. Ambitious individuals nearly always became a part of the machine. Machine politics had the effect of reducing competition and tied elections to the individual politician's pursuit of power, prestige, and money. Favors dispensed through the machine were richest at the highest levels, of course, but voters, too, felt that their survival required allegiance. Many residents, especially Blacks, became thoroughly convinced that their very existence depended on city hall generosity: "We are at the brute level, the pure level of existence, so politics means money, a job, or placement on relief. The politicians have exploited us and our fears, so Negroes do as they are told. . . . The machine has the power to stop progress by threatening people with loss of jobs. (It) can get almost every family in East St. Louis. Somebody (in the family) has a job."[14] In addition to this psychological grip on the Black community, the machine provided a $5 pay-off to loyal voters on election day. Competition against the machine in elections was made virtually impossible, so that even if elections had been honest, the machine could be expected to win easily.

Whichever party was in power, the Republicans before 1932 and the Democrats after, machine strength was built on an ability to consistently produce sizable margins at election time. Large majorities were delivered not only in local elections, but also in state and national voting. At issue was not whether machine candidates would win, but by how much. Of course the larger the majority, the greater the favors to the machine in jobs and contracts from state and national winners. In 1967, for the first time since his election in 1951, Mayor Alvin Fields's slate was opposed for election. Though two-thirds of the East St. Louis population in 1967 was Black, the all-Black slate opposing the Fields group, which had only one Black on its ticket, was smashed, receiving only 25 percent of the vote.

One account of the 1967 election cites reasons for the defeat of the all-Black slate in addition to those mentioned in the pre-

[14] Quoted by Philip Meranto, "Negro Majorities and Political Power: The Defeat of an All Negro Ticket in East St. Louis."

vious discussion. These reasons include distrust for Black leadership within the Black community, control of the Black submachine by the White machine, and almost total penetration of politics into the Black community.[15]

That Blacks distrusted Black political leadership was a rational response to past history. Black leaders were almost invariably bought off by the machine. The more threatening a new leader appeared to the machine, the greater the rewards offered for his cooperation. Even after the 1967 election many Blacks believed that some of the candidates had secretly conspired with the machine, especially since one of the candidates was given an advancement in his position with a public agency after the election. These suspicions and speculations may have contributed to the defeat.

Rather than providing an alternative for advancement, the Black submachine has been carefully controlled by White politicians. Black machine politicians have had a far greater stake in the machine organization than in the community, have jealously guarded their power, and have strongly resisted challenges to their leadership. Their jobs and status have been dependent on controlling the Black community, not encouraging independence. Often they were caught directly between allegiance to the machine and personal and ideological preferences, such as illustrated by an editorial written in the Black community's largest newspaper. Faced with a tormenting choice, the publisher reached the following conclusion in the 1967 election:

> To this point, I've deliberately refrained from personally commenting on the city election to be held Tuesday because to be perfectly frank, I've had mixed emotions. It generally is known that I'm employed at the East St. Louis City Hall as administrative aide to Mayor Alvin G. Fields, who is seeking re-election.
>
> It is also no secret that Elmo J. Bush, who is opposing Mayor Fields, is my close personal friend. Bush and I were former business partners—in fact, he and I founded *The Monitor*. We have worked closely together in various civil rights, civic, social and political activities. Another all important fact is that Bush is a Negro and I've said time and time again that the Negro citizens

15 *Ibid.*, pp. 35–40ff.

of this community definitely need more competent representation on all levels of government. . . . There is no question in my mind that Elmo Bush would make a good mayor.

During the fourteen months I've worked as administrative aide to Mayor Fields, I have found the mayor to be a real understanding man with innate ability and intelligence. I myself believe that Mayor Fields has done a good job as chief executive of our city. I write this not because I work for him because I know of many of his actions and decisions that are not known to the general public. I disagree with those who have questioned the Mayor's honesty and integrity.

I can say nothing but good about either the Mayor or Bush . . . I sincerely regret that I cannot vote for both Mayor Fields and Bush. I personally shall vote for Mayor Fields because I work as his administrative aide and I believe in the age-old philosophy of loyalty. He has been my friend and has done so much for me that I would be less a man to do otherwise. I think my friend Bush understands this better than anyone else.[16]

Practically no individuals or groups existed in the Black community who could afford to put other interests ahead of the machine.

Pressures for Change

Mayoral and council primary elections in East St. Louis in the spring of 1971 were unique in the history of the city. The White-controlled machine was effectively challenged by the Black sub-machine, and this machine, in turn, was effectively challenged by Black and White reform candidates. On the basis of the previous discussion, how was it possible for such rapid changes to take place? Four major factors encouraging change may be identified: worsening economic problems for the city government and the machine, increasing visibility of local conditions as urban problems were put on the national agenda, civil rights pressures, and the introduction of new constituencies into the city—new Black leadership, local and university professionals, and federal officials.

[16] Quoted in *ibid.*, p. 15.

Until recently it could be argued that East St. Louis's fiscal problems were worse than those of most American cities. It now appears that East St. Louis's long-standing courtship with bankruptcy was only a bellwether for the nation's large cities. A well-known central city syndrome—emigration of middle- and upper-class populations, loss of industries and businesses, the concomitant decline in tax base and rise in demands and cost of public services—has long been evident in East St. Louis. These conditions were exacerbated by imprudent administration of public funds.

Since 1951, the city has been forced to borrow under judgment funding procedures to meet its current operating expenditures. Borrowing has become an increasingly important aspect of East St. Louis's fiscal life, not merely to spread large capital improvements over a long period of time or to allocate the cost of projects to future as well as present taxpayers, but to finance day-to-day operations of the city. Over 90 percent of East St. Louis bonds are judgment-funding bonds used to meet deficits in current expenditures. In 1969 over 42 percent of the revenue from property taxes was used for principle and interest on bonds. Payment on the bonds comes through the property tax, over half of which will be used for borrowing by 1975, based on present trends. Judgment funding has hurt the city's credit rating to the point that the issuance of general obligation bonds for large-scale capital projects is out of the question. East St. Louis bonds are not rated by standard rating services; if they were, the ratings would be so low as to prevent marketability. Local banks and institutions avoid the city's bonds, even though discount rates have been raised and the term of payment has been drastically reduced from fifteen- and twenty-year periods to three years. These problems forced the city to pay material and service creditors for 1968 and 1969 in judgment funding bonds. Cash is strictly reserved to meet monthly payrolls. In 1970, there were no local buyers at all for the bonds.

Even recent state legislation has made little difference. New tax legislation enabled the city in 1970 to receive approximately $800,000 in new revenues—$500,000 in a "no strings" block grant from the state income tax, $300,000 from other taxes. Nevertheless, debt continues to increase, property taxes to rise. Stop-gap measures have not solved the crisis.

For most of its history, the city has been nearly bankrupt. While the fiscal squeeze affected the quantity and quality of public service, the lack of funds also had a negative effect on the political machine. Sources of money for the machine dried up. Public funds declined due to the drop in tax assessments; important contributors such as downtown businessmen felt the loss of purchasing power in the city; and organized crime suffered from more diligent law enforcement. The consequences were evidenced in the 1971 elections. When asked for a prognosis of the 1971 election in a 1968 interview, a Black precinct committeeman allowed that "there just isn't much money left. Last time they had $5 a vote. Next time around they might have only $1 or $2. When it gets that low, you might have an honest election!"

Declining patronage had also hurt the machine. Few city hall cutbacks were implemented by Mayor Fields since so many employees were patronage. Hiring practices changed somewhat with the passage of a civil service law in 1967. In addition, the opportunities for pay-offs through contracts all but disappeared even before the 1971 election. In early 1970 a leading political figure in East St. Louis claimed that he did not know where money was to be had in the city—anywhere.[17]

During the last decade, East St. Louis's problems and those of other urban centers have become highly publicized, and this has constituted a pressure for change. While adverse conditions in the city (except for employment) have persisted for most of its history, extensive publicity from the local and national media has drawn attention to them only in the past decade. Blame for the city's conditions was directed at machine politicians. Interpreting the socioeconomic conditions as political exploitation made for colorful reporting.

As has already been noted, East St. Louis has historically attracted highly dependent populations to work in the meat packing, transportation, and heavy industries. For the past five

---

[17] This story was related to the authors by a high official in the East St. Louis government during an informal conversation in March, 1971.

decades, issues of power and economic dependence have been closely linked to race. White immigrants began leaving the city after World War I, being replaced by destitute Blacks. Traditionally, the city was the first stopping point for Black families coming north from Mississippi in search of jobs and improved living conditions. A large number went across the river to St. Louis, or on to Chicago and Detroit, but many stayed in East St. Louis. In the 1930s the immigration accelerated, especially when defense plants in the city offered employment opportunities. By 1940, 22 percent of the East St. Louis population was Black. In the years following World War II Black immigration pushed the proportion to 34 percent by 1950 and 45 percent by 1960. Although Black movement into the city slowed considerably in the 1960s, there was an increase of about 10,000 Blacks in the decade, more attributable to birth and death rates than in-migration. On the other hand, White emigration reached a floodtide that had been started in the 1950s. Between 1960 and 1970, the White population fell 26,000. By the end of the decade, the Black population had increased to 70 percent, and the city's total population had declined from 81,712 to 69,996. Many of those who remained were too poor or too old to move or perceived few opportunities elsewhere.

Diminishing employment opportunities are, no doubt, primarily responsible for the slowdown of Blacks coming to the city. Until 1950, jobs were plentiful in the labor-intensive industries of the East St. Louis area. Technological changes and a series of labor disputes, however, resulted in a loss of about 10,000 jobs over the last decade, leaving a critical shortage of jobs and a huge supply of unskilled labor. In 1969, the *St. Louis Post-Dispatch* described conditions as follows:

> Unemployment in East St. Louis has been estimated to be as high as 20 percent; nearly 30 percent in the Model Cities target area.

> The Aluminum Company of America (Alcoa) in World War II employed about 2,000 persons, averaged about 1,500 persons employed in the mid-1950's and, in October, 1963, closed its East St. Louis plant.

The East St. Louis economy suffered a series of setbacks with other plant closings: 1,400 jobs were lost when Armour and Company shut down its slaughtering operations in 1959, Swift and Company closed out 600 jobs in 1967 and 1968, 200 jobs were lost when American Zinc closed its Fairmont City Plant, 100 jobs were lost when Darling Fertilizer Company closed in 1967, 365 jobs went up in smoke with a warehouse fire at Norfolk and Western Railroad facilities. East St. Louis is part of the nation's second largest railroad complex, and suffers as area industry is buffeted by changing trends in transportation.[18]

In 1963 a Southern Illinois University study found 21 percent of the East St. Louis labor force unemployed (defining the rate of unemployment as the percentage of those in the labor force unemployed but looking for work).[19] Resurveying again, five years later, the author of the original study found that the figure had dropped to 10 percent—at first glance, employment conditions had improved remarkably, contradicting the *Post-Dispatch*'s analysis. But this was not the case at all, for many people had simply quit looking. In fact, 36 percent of the households had no one employed and 43 percent of the household heads were not working in 1969. These high percentages are attributable to a large number of household heads, especially White, who are retired and to the fact that women head many households. Forty-six percent of the households in East St. Louis do not have both a husband and wife.[20]

Employment characteristics in 1969 showed a very low percentage of the employed household heads in the management and professional categories. Most of the operatives, service personnel and laborers, which comprise 78 percent of the employed household heads, work in durable-goods industries which require limited job skills. Despite a considerable decline in railroad employment, 12 percent of employed household heads are

[18] *St. Louis Post-Dispatch*, March 23, 1969.

[19] Jane Schusky, *Employment and Unemployment in East St. Louis* (Edwardsville: Southern Illinois University, Public Administration and Metropolitan Affairs, 1964), pp. 23–24.

[20] Jane Altes, *East St. Louis, the End of a Decade* (Edwardsville: Southern Illinois University, Regional and Urban Development Studies and Services, 1970), pp. 30, 35–36.

in transportation, communication, and public utilities. About 11 percent are in public administration working for city, state, and federal governments, and this figure does not vary for Blacks and Whites. Another 11 percent of Black household heads are in the professional and related services category, being employed by the school district and the numerous welfare agencies in the city.[21]

Both the high rate of unemployment and the types of jobs available contribute to the extensive poverty of the city's population. Incomes are very low, especially for the Black majority. Median income for the household heads is $3,600 per year; for entire households, $4,400. Seventy-two percent of annual family incomes is less than $7,000. Not only are incomes low, but also the sources of income leave few in the population financially independent. Almost as many families receive their money from (1) retirement income and social security, (2) unemployment insurance, and (3) public assistance or welfare, as from wages, salaries, and commissions. There is such a high dependence on welfare that half of the families with female heads and approximately one eighth with male heads get aid in some form.[22] St. Clair County, in which East St. Louis is the largest city, ranks second in Illinois to Cook County (Chicago and suburbs) in the number of persons receiving public assistance. No other counties even approach the income and welfare requirements of these areas.

Many facets of community life are predictably encompassed by the poverty syndrome, including housing, education, health, and public administration of services. A 1964 comparison with other Illinois cities over 50,000 population ranked East St. Louis first in the percentage of families with income less than $3,000, first in the percentage of unsound housing units, first in the percentage of adults with less than eight years of education, and second in the rate of criminal offenses.[23]

Housing reflects the low family income of the community.

[21] *Ibid.*, pp. 40–41.
[22] *Ibid.*, pp. 49–60.
[23] Robert E. Mendelson and Paula Parks, *Why East St. Louis, Illinois, Needs to Be a Demonstration City* (Edwardsville: Southern Illinois University, Public Administration and Metropolitan Affairs Program, 1967), p. 39.

Existing housing is not being replaced, and large segments of the housing inventory are beyond repair or rehabilitation. In the 1960 Census of Housing only 57 percent of the dwelling units in the city were classified as sound with all plumbing facilities. Seven years later surveys of the Model City area, which comprises one-fourth of East St. Louis, found that no more than 33 percent of the units were in the sound category.[24] Despite these conditions, and an abundance of land, there is virtually no residential construction based on market rents and interest. Private enterprise's involvement in new construction is only with federal assistance—especially under the risk-free Turnkey public-housing programs. This void of private enterprise in construction and rehabilitation has not been filled by nonprofit groups utilizing federal programs. In the past four years (1966 to 1969) only two projects of slightly over 100 units have advanced to the point of construction in East St. Louis. Both are being financed under Section 221 (d)(3) at below-market interest with rental supplements. A national inability to provide low- and middle-income housing is exemplified in East St. Louis where the private market is inoperative and federal assistance meets only a fraction of the need.

Incompatible land uses and homemade structures are common, especially in the older areas surrounding the central business district. Today, if codes were vigorously enforced, approximately 25 percent of the population would be dislocated—most of them low-income Blacks with few other housing alternatives. A 1966 housing study by Southern Illinois University estimated that about 1,300 new or rehabilitated units were needed annually for five years to correct serious deficiencies in the city's housing inventory.[25] In the succeeding two-year period, thirty-five new housing units were built while 670 vacant, vandalized, and substandard units were demolished.

Since family incomes in East St. Louis cannot be matched with the amortization of conventional housing costs and market

[24] Model City Agency, *Model Cities—Phase I*, pp. B8–B10.
[25] Robert E. Mendelson, *Housing—An East St. Louis Challenge* (Edwardsville: Southern Illinois University, Public Administration and Metropolitan Affairs Program, 1966), pp. 50–55.

interest rates, the city has turned to public housing over the past two decades. With public-housing units now accounting for about 15 percent of the city's housing stock, the effect on the tax base of East St. Louis local governments has been extremely negative. Payments from the housing authority constitute 10 percent of gross rents in lieu of property taxes; hence they are probably no more than 25 to 33 percent of the revenue that could be received from privately owned units. In fact, required school and municipal expenditures to service the occupants of those units far exceed revenues from the local housing authority.

Housing conditions comprise only one aspect of the adverse physical environment. Streets, sidewalks, school buildings, and recreational facilities are also seriously deteriorated. Four hundred acres and 2,100 households are without sanitary sewers. Of the 14.7 miles of alleys in the Model City neighborhoods, none are paved. They are hardly passable and are strewn with rubbish. Oil and chip streets are numerous and there is a widespread absence of curbs and sidewalks.[26]

Urban renewal has helped little. One project, begun in July, 1959, remained largely undeveloped for eleven years. In February, 1971, announcement was made that 247 units of public housing modeled after a highly successful project in St. Louis would be constructed under the Department of Housing and Urban Development's Turnkey program.[27] While the project will have only limited impact, it represents an advance over past stagnation in generating construction on urban renewal land.

Severe economic dislocations and increasingly publicized conditions in East St. Louis stimulated the downtown business interests to push for moderate reforms a little more than a decade ago. In the early 1960s, limited civil rights activities were also taking place. While it is difficult to assess accurately the effect of the civil rights movement on local government, it did increase Black employment at the banks and merchandising establish-

[26] See the components on Physical Development and Transportation in Model City Agency, *Model Cities—Phase I.*
[27] *St. Louis Post-Dispatch*, February 24, 1971.

ments. Nevertheless, the two forces combined together to bring about a response from the city.

In 1957, a group of neighborhood associations was formed into Community Progress, Incorporated (CPI). It was called a "grass-roots" effort, but there was considerable technical support from Southern Illinois University and financial assistance from businessmen and bankers. This coalition was formed at a time when a sizable number of middle-income residents, mostly White, were leaving the city. Loss of purchasing power and growing physical deterioration encouraged formation of CPI.

While there are conflicting stories about the reasons for its demise in the early 1960s, CPI did bring together enough political leverage to stimulate limited planning efforts and modest government reform in East St. Louis. A move in that direction came in one of the group's first actions, which was to push for an urban renewal project adjacent to the central business district (CBD). One year later, in 1960, CPI requested the mayor to initiate several reforms in city government, to use tax monies more efficiently, and to revitalize the CBD. Faced with a deficit budget and a continually declining tax base, Mayor Alvin Fields could not afford to ignore these requests from the neighborhood groups and the downtown bankers and merchants who had given long-time support to the machine. (The banks provided temporary financing and cash flow to the municipal administration and many downtown interests contributed to election campaigns.)

On April 20, 1960, the mayor and council passed a resolution requesting the Local Government Center of Southern Illinois University to make an evaluation of the financial practices of East St. Louis. Financed by Southern Illinois University, this study contained fourteen major recommendations including professional administration, aldermanic government, a new budgetary program, enforcement of the housing ordinance, reform in the police department, and extensive urban renewal. A reformer sentiment stressing administrative structure and efficiency can be gleaned from the recommendation for a professional administrator:

... where is the top level in East St. Louis government? At present, it exists in the personal and political authority of the Mayor. In terms of broad policy formulation this authority can be felt. ... In terms of administration, however, the Mayor's power is not really effective because there is no formal machinery for making it. .... An essential element of good administration is a professional administration for that government. This requires an administrative office and a competent person to fill this office.[28]

Reacting to continued pressure for efficiency from the businessmen and CPI, Mayor Fields, in 1963, advertised widely for an administrative assistant. George Washnis, personnel manager and assistant administrator in Evanston, Illinois, accepted the newly created office of administrative assistant to the mayor. His powers were never legally expressed and were dependent upon the willingness (or unwillingness) of the commissioners to delegate responsibilities. Washnis soon became a leading figure in city hall, directing fiscal, management, and development activities. Another recommendation to return the city to an aldermanic government was ignored. Of the fourteen suggestions, few were reflected in subsequent actions.

Washnis's power came through a differentiation of himself from the five commissioners' prerogatives. He became a quasi city manager while the mayor concentrated his efforts on politics and conflict resolution. He also mediated between competing groups while the mayor legitimatized the outcomes. Washnis was extremely effective as a buffer between young Black activists, bankers, businessmen, and politicians in city hall. Washnis sought out new revenue sources and pursued federal and state assistance.

In 1964 Washnis was instrumental in bringing an antipoverty program to the city, administered by the St. Clair County Economic Opportunity Commission. Through limited employment and training benefits, it demonstrated that low income residents, especially Blacks, could obtain information, advice, and, in a

[28] *Organization and Management of the Government of East St. Louis,* report to the City Council of East St. Louis, Ill., February, 1961 (Carbondale: Southern Illinois University, Local Government Center, 1961), p. 7.

few cases, jobs from an organization other than the machine.

Washnis pushed hard for the creation of a management capacity to attract and administer federal funds for redevelopment. From 1963 to 1970, Washnis's job tenure, over thirty-five professionals were placed on the city's staff. Many had master's degrees and a sizable proportion were paid with funds from federal programs. Relying on a reorganization proposal prepared in October, 1966, by the Public Administration and Metropolitan Affairs Program at Southern Illinois University and pressure by federal officials for administrative changes as a condition for further federal assistance, Washnis was able to secure approval for revamping the planning and urban renewal departments. In March, 1968, Washnis hired Jamie Cannon, an architect, to direct the planning department. Rapid expansion of planning activities quickly followed federal grants for the Community Renewal Program and the General Neighborhood Renewal Plan. Soon after, a new urban renewal director was also appointed. During the same year an industrial development department was lodged in city hall with assistance from the Economic Development Administration of the Department of Commerce. All of these activities helped to develop a base for a new political constituency made up of professional administrators. It also enhanced the ability of federal administrators to affect the politics of the city. Especially in the Model Cities program, the development of new political constituencies was quite dramatic.

Professionals from Southern Illinois University (SIU) first became interested in a Model Cities grant for East St. Louis. During the summer of 1966 they approached Washnis about the idea and found him quite receptive. Following the passage of the Model Cities legislation, SIU planners and Washnis laid the groundwork for a Model Cities application. A group was formed to help prepare and to support the application. In November, 1967, the federal government announced that East St. Louis would be included in the program.

Up to that point the Model Cities activities had been in the hands of a few professionals. In December, 1967, however, a group calling itself Negro Unity Planners took over a meeting of the Model Cities professionals, and declared their intention to run the program in the interests of the grassroots citizens of East St. Louis. Black leaders quickly consolidated their hold on the program by hiring paid staff of the Model Cities Agency primarily from the target area, by dominating the agency board, and by insuring policy and direction of the program from Blacks not dependent upon the political machine.

Model Cities became a rallying point for emergent Black leaders. Joining with federal officials, whose main concern was administrative reform in East St. Louis, the two groups advocated hiring practices other than loyalty to the political machine. In December, 1968, Mayor Fields clashed with Model Cities leaders over the appointment of six resident assistants in an urban renewal program. Though precinct committeemen fought for the jobs, the Model Cities group won, and an agreement was reached to establish quasi civil service procedures for all federal programs. After this loss, Black politicians seemed less and less willing to accede to Fields's leadership.

A combination of local Black leaders, university and newly recruited city professionals, and federal officials had challenged the hold of the machine on public employment. Combined with the city's fiscal bankruptcy, which further diminished the machine's ability to provide cooptive rewards, the White machine's control of the Black submachine deteriorated. Patronage jobs declined. A local referendum held in 1967 brought civil service to the community. Public employment from federally assisted programs was, for the most part, unavailable to the old-style politicians. Groups which were formed to participate in and control funded projects effectively isolated machine politics from the dispensation of jobs.

Also important in weakening the machine were activities of reporters and federal law enforcement officials in uncovering illegal activities and election discrepancies. Smooth and routine functioning of the machine was seriously disrupted by public revelations of wrongdoings and criminal indictments. On March 19, 1970, all four members of the East Side Levee and Sanitary District Board were indicted by a grand jury as a result of stories published a few months earlier in the *St. Louis Globe-Democrat*.

These newspaper accounts described unlawful contract awards, overpayments to attorneys, and patronage by the levee board, long a center of power for the county machine. After the indictments and through the trial and convictions, St. Louis and East St. Louis newspapers kept the story prominent. Also kept in the public focus was the April, 1970, indictment of all but one member of the East St. Louis school board by the same grand jury. Misconduct in office was alleged. A contract had been awarded without competitive bidding and the board had failed to require a performance bond from one contractor. Charles Merritts, the school board president, maintained that the indictments were politically inspired: "They're after me because I showed strength in the last (school board) election," he asserted, claiming that Virgil Calvert and the Paramount Democratic Club were out to get him.[29] When indictments were later dropped a few months before the February, 1971, primary election for mayor, opponents of Merritts charged political collusion with the state's attorney's office.

In March, 1970, the U.S. Department of Justice assigned an organized crime task force to an area including East St. Louis. Its chief assignment was to investigate the election system in St. Clair County, with an emphasis on East St. Louis. The U.S. attorney announced that a federal grand jury would be selected as a preliminary to a full-scale investigation of local elections.

Federal intervention into East St. Louis elections upset a long-established, stable pattern of machine electoral control. Questionable practices had always characterized East St. Louis electoral politics. It was traditional for the levee board to hire large numbers of part-time workers just before each election, and to no longer need their services afterward. For example, men laid off early in 1968 were put to work just before the 1968 elections, supposedly to catch up on maintenance.[30] As part of the

[29] *Metro-East Journal*, May 1, 1970.

[30] *Ibid.*, December 19, 1968. According to a November 15, 1971, interview with a *Metro-East Journal* reporter who was familiar with the activities of the levee district, there were, traditionally, insufficient funds to support full-time jobs for many employees. Peak workload came at certain periods in the spring and fall when the crest of the river was high. Added employees were needed at

county machine, the board of election commissioners had also been able to provide short-term patronage, and had always been reticent in investigating charges of election fraud. Until 1964 the three board members were appointed by the county judge, with two of its members traditionally belonging to the same political party as the judge. In 1955 a tavern operator who had just completed one term as an assistant township supervisor was appointed, reportedly as a consolation for Mayor Fields's support of another candidate to succeed him as supervisor. In 1963 Alvin Fields, Jr., son of the mayor, was appointed to the board. The board clerkship positions are also patronage appointments and include some employees who have previously worked for the levee district. Finally, patronage is available through the appointment of election judges for the city's fifty-one precincts. All of these perquisites were threatened by the federal action.

Challenges to the election commissioners mounted in other quarters, too. On March 2, 1970, the *Metro-East Journal* claimed that a petition to nominate Dakin Williams, a Collinsville, Illinois, attorney and brother of author Tennessee Williams, for the 1970 U.S. Senate race contained forged and duplicated names. Seven-hundred names on Williams's petition had apparently been signed by sixteen people. The president of the levee board had been paid $1,010 to circulate the petition, and had failed to notice the changing rules of the game in East St. Louis. He was subsequently indicted for perjury in an investigation of the case by a St. Clair County grand jury.

In another instance, on March 3, *Journal* reporters uncovered voter list irregularities. Two weeks later the *Journal* ran an article on the exceptionally high number of absentee ballots that had been cast in the city in the spring primaries. Pressure was put on the election commissioners to give the newspaper a list of the absentees. A list, with 249 names—four times the normal number of absentees—was published on March 22. Several people whose names appeared on the list denied having voted; some no longer lived in East St. Louis. In mid-March Charles Kolker,

---

these times, but the machine used it as a rationale to hire even larger numbers of workers. Seasonal maintenance work coincided conveniently and fortuitously with election dates.

chairman of the aldermanic government committee, a reform group, asserted that 1,700 voters listed as registered had moved or died. He called for prosecution of the election board members. After school board elections in April, State's Attorney Robert Rice asked the election board to investigate election irregularities in the school board elections. Charles Merritts, the winning candidate for school board president, called for an investigation, accusing the Paramount Democratic Club of turning the election into a start on the 1971 mayoralty race. In this atmosphere—in March and April the levee board and the school board members had been indicted—the election board decided to instigate its own probe into election irregularities. This investigation was begun almost simultaneously with the beginning of federal grand jury investigation in which some of the first witnesses were election board members.

Reform efforts were also encouraged by the changing political environment. In March, 1969, petitions were filed with the board of election commissioners for a referendum to change the commission government of East St. Louis to an aldermanic form. After some signatures were disallowed, the petition was disqualified. Thirty days after the petition filing, the president of the aldermanic government committee mysteriously left East St. Louis. It took ten days for the *Metro-East Journal* to find him in Ohio, where he claimed that he had been threatened in East St. Louis with physical harm. Under new leadership, efforts were renewed, and new petitions were submitted in December, 1969. When the court dismissed early objections to the petitions, it was assumed that the referendum would soon be forthcoming. While professionals and the local daily newspaper endorsed the change, the machine resisted and won again. Delays by the board of election comissioners and a subsequent court ruling effectively blocked the setting of an election date.

Another attempt to stimulate reform occurred when George Washnis resigned in March, 1970, to take a high post with a private governmental research center. Among other things, he recommended the hiring of a full-time attorney to replace the four who then served the city part-time, one of whom was the mayor's son-in-law. Washnis's contention was not that the city was overstaffed, but rather that some city employees were not producing in their jobs. In particular, he claimed that many of the building inspectors were simply not working at all.[31]

Among the administrative assistant's other proposals were that the city eventually adopt the council-manager form of government, and that if this were not possible, it should move immediately to the aldermanic form, with strong administration provided by a professional city manager. However, Washnis added, even if all his suggestions were followed and if the city were completely efficient, it would be impossible to eliminate the city's deficit. At best, only several hundred thousand dollars could be chopped off the $1-million plus revenue gap.[32]

Mayor Fields glossed over the charges of patronage and governmental inefficiency, feeling, no doubt, that public pronouncements by professionals were not especially damaging. Conforming to his usual style, Fields reacted without hostility. Washnis's constituency was limited. Further, Fields had developed a cordial relationship with Washnis over the years. Both men respected the skills of the other; Washnis the professional administrator, Fields the arbitrator and conciliator.

Building Commissioner Virgil Calvert responded differently. As head of the powerful Paramount Democratic Club (the Black submachine in the county machine) and as a leading contender to replace the mayor in 1971, he saw this as a significant public issue. For one thing, Washnis's negative comments on the building department reflected adversely on him, since the department was under his jurisdiction. Second, if elected mayor in 1971, Calvert would be in a position to distribute jobs and favors to party regulars. At every opportunity he wanted to retain their support by being their public defender: "George Washnis, administrative aid to Mayor Fields, will not make me a scapegoat for his blundering errors or any other black people. It seems strange that most of what this individual has to say relates to black people. I resent his implications. I resent his prejudiced stand and he has proven what kind of an individual

[31] St. Louis Post-Dispatch, December 15, 1969, and January 8, 1970.
[32] George Washnis, interview, East St. Louis, Illinois, January 20, 1970; and St. Louis Globe Democrat, January 20, 1970.

he really is. I have told Mr. Washnis this to his face many times."[33]

Throughout his long tenure in the machine Alvin Fields had known conflict like this. Time after time he had successfully mediated between conflicting groups. He was an acknowledged master in the brokerage role. Facing trade unionists, militant Blacks, politicians, toughs, downtown businessmen, professionals, irate residents, he rarely became flustered. Even in situations where violence seemed imminent, he appeared composed and strong. One of the city commissioners, Fields's political ally for thirty years, stated that he had never seen the mayor mad.

Partly because of his great facility at reaching compromise and responding to many different interests, Fields's leadership in the bicounty and East St. Louis organization went undisputed. But his penchant for always seeking the middle ground may have hastened the demise of his organization. Far from filling the stereotype of the ruthless machine leader, he was committed to give-and-take politics. Thus, he permitted George Washnis to bring into the city many professionals who asserted their independence from machine politics. He maintained a hands-off attitude toward the city's antipoverty, urban renewal, and Model Cities efforts. As the local and federal professional base grew stronger, he was willing to reach accommodations based on the relative strength of the contending forces. When the machine lost in these confrontations, those vying for the jobs and favors—mostly Black precinct committeemen in the city—became increasingly convinced that their interests were not being adequately represented.

Fields's failure to consistently protect the interests of the Black precinct committeemen led to resentment. In addition, Calvert's ambition to become mayor caused him to extend his influence over the Paramount Club. Calvert could not expect Fields's support in his election bid. Though Fields had been close to Saverson, the Black councilman who preceded Calvert (Calvert had been named after Saverson's death in 1968), the mayor had dealt at arm's length with Calvert. Under these circumstances, Calvert had to build his own support. In the fight

[33] Virgil L. Calvert, article in the *East St. Louis Monitor*, January 8, 1970.

with the Model Cities group for the General Neighborhood
Renewal Plan (GRNP) jobs, Calvert had led the Black committeemen's fight. When he made a bid for the mayoralty
position, Calvert found ready support in the same group. The
committeemen saw little to lose by opposing Fields, who, they
felt, had not fairly cut them in on jobs and favors. Possibly there
was much to gain; their opposition might end the inferior status
of the Black submachine.

The 1971 Mayoralty Election

In early January, 1969, Calvert and Morris Campbell, president
of the East Side Levee and Sanitary District, led members of the
Paramount Club in demanding more jobs and better pay for
Blacks in St. Clair County government. Six months later Calvert
publicly split with Fields over a dispute in the police department
between twenty-three Black policemen and the White director
of public safety, Ross Randolph. Later, in early March, 1970,
Fields's diminishing ability to command allegiance was shown
when the city council could not reach an agreement on a replacement for Commissioner Robert Keeley, who had died on
February 3. Calvert held out for Welbon Phillips, a long-time
member of the Paramount Club, while Russell Beebe, the lone
Republican on the council, pushed for Willie Nevills, chairman
of the Republican precinct committeemen in East St. Louis.
Fields hesitated to force a decision, especially at the price of
antagonizing Calvert and Black committeemen. If Fields had
called a special election to fill the vacancy, the conflict within
the machine might have been brought out into the open. Keeley's position was left unfilled.

Speculation as to whether Fields would run for reelection in
1971 began soon after his slate's victory in 1967. It appears that
Fields was inclined to run and changed his mind only a few
weeks before the 1971 primaries. Anything less than the traditional landslide victory would be unacceptable; not only would
it show the vulnerability of the machine and weaken it still
further, but a close election would also make it difficult for him
to play the mediator role. Governing would become an oppres-

sive burden. Until relatively late, Fields thought he could pull the machine together. On March 26, 1969, he told the *Metro-East Journal* that, barring health problems (he had been disabled since a knee operation the previous August), he would run for reelection "regardless of what form of government we have."[34] An open challenge by Calvert and the Black submachine might have affected Fields's decision.

On September 17, 1970, Reverend Foster Calvert, Virgil Calvert's brother and a precinct committeeman, led a delegation of twenty-one Black committeemen to see the mayor. All of the committeemen were members of the Paramount Democratic Club. Bearing a petition signed by thirty committeemen (there are fifty-one precincts in East St. Louis) which supported his brother for mayor, Calvert told Fields that the Paramount Club would not support him if he tried for reelection. One of their primary complaints was that the mayor had not dispensed enough jobs to the Black machine.

Though Calvert's challenge was strengthened by the claim that Fields ignored needs of Black politicians, Virgil Calvert was no political amateur. He had waited a long time for this opportunity. For twenty-five years he had been a precinct committeeman, and had diligently worked his way up through the machine. He was a deputy sheriff eleven years, and was later appointed as police magistrate, circuit court magistrate, and city license supervisor. With Fields's help he was elected justice of the peace in 1961. He helped to organize the Paramount Democratic Club, an organization of Black precinct committemen, in the early 1960s. His strength in the club grew until he felt strong enough to challenge Fields. In November, 1966, the *Journal* reported that Calvert might replace one of the White commissioners on the machine ticket in the 1967 election. It was rumored that this move would strengthen the machine's electoral position in relation to an all-Black slate that was being organized. With Calvert added to the machine ticket, two Black leaders of the Paramount Club would be candidates (Ester

[34] *Metro-East Journal*, March 26, 1969. The reference is to the publicized efforts of the aldermanic government committee to change the system of government from the commission form.

Saverson, a Black, had been included on the ticket in 1963). By the end of 1966 Calvert announced his own candidacy for mayor. He soon withdrew it, however, amid speculation that an agreement with Fields had been reached. A little more than a year later Ester Saverson died, and on May 22, 1968, Calvert was appointed to fill the vacancy.

After that point, Calvert's ambitions to become mayor were obvious. He pushed hard for patronage to Black committeemen, and became their chief public spokesman. In the school board elections in the spring of 1970, he organized an effort to defeat Charles Merritts's bid for reelection as school board president. Merritts was Calvert's chief challenger for leadership in East St. Louis, and a school board victory constituted an important base for maintaining and consolidating support. Calvert's candidate lost by 121 votes. Merritts accused Calvert, both before and after the election, of turning the school board race into an early contest for mayor. After the election, the Paramount Democratic Club expelled six precinct committeemen for supporting Merritts. On November 22, 1970, Calvert announced his candidacy for mayor of East St. Louis. Mayor Fields affirmed Calvert's right to run for mayor, but said that he was personally still undecided. He realized, however, that he could not postpone a decision for very long. Months before, Commissioner Dan Foley had indicated his desire to quit and had agreed to stay on to the end of his term only at the mayor's insistence. Foley was seventy-two, Commissioner Russell Beebe was sixty-seven, and Fields himself was sixty-eight. No candidates on the machine slate stepped forth, waiting, of course, until Fields made up his mind. On December 3, Fields announced that he would not run, for health reasons. One day later Charles Merritts, the president of the school board, announced his candidacy. Only two days before he had stated firmly that he had no intention of becoming a candidate, even though he was opposed to Calvert. With Merritts's entry the mayoralty race appeared to be settling down to a choice between two arch antagonists for support from the Black community. On December 11, however, James E. Williams, executive director of the St. Clair County Legal Aid Society, also announced his candidacy.

Williams had not previously been highly visible in East St. Louis politics and was, in several ways, a classic reform candidate. He had never run for political office nor held any patronage positions. He did not need the machine, either for employment or for upward mobility. His position as executive director of the St. Clair County Legal Aid Society made him independent of local politics. And yet his twenty years' residency in East St. Louis had given him a solid base among reform-type residents and those who felt victimized by the heavy-handed methods employed at times by the machine. In addition, years of exposés and bad publicity concerning politics had taken their toll. Williams made the machine and city hall leadership his campaign issues. "The time is past when Fields can call the boys in and say 'here's your man.' The time is past when the precinct committeeman can put $5 in your hand and say 'pull that lever.'" [35] Among other reform measures, Williams advocated extension of civil service to all city hall jobs. Calvert was easily labeled the machine candidate. Williams's opposition to Merritts centered on an alleged lack of leadership in school affairs. On this point, Merritts was extremely vulnerable.

Charles Merritts, Sr., a long-time political enemy of Virgil Calvert, was intensively involved in East St. Louis politics. Merritts had become wealthy through twenty-eight years of owning numerous businesses in East St. Louis and had been a Republican precinct committeeman for several years. Though he and Calvert were enemies, Merritts was close to many individuals in the Black machine, and seemed to be trusted more than Calvert by many influential White politicians. From this base, he was elected to the East St. Louis school board in 1967, and in 1968 was chosen school board president. He was periodically accused of treating the schools as his own fiefdom, and in 1969 all but one member of the school board were indicted on charges of letting noncompetitive contracts. The charges were dropped early in January, 1971, by the St. Clair County prosecuting attorney. On another occasion, the hiring of a school board member's wife as an attendance officer received intensive

[35] *Ibid.*, January 19, 1971.

newspaper coverage.[36] Reports of job payoffs, junketing to conventions by school board members, and discrepancies in insurance coverage were carried by the *Metro-East Journal*.[37] The school district was on probationary status with the state because of problems of curriculum, use of substandard rooms, and high teacher-student ratios. In addition, the beginning of each year saw an acrimonious school strike by the militant teachers' union.

Despite these events, Merritts appeared to have great political strength. But in the fall of 1970 a long and exceedingly bitter strike took place. At the height of the stalemate between the school board and the teachers, Merritts left for a tour of Europe, on doctor's orders he said, to settle his nerves. Three weeks later, on October 29, when he returned, the strike was still on. His vacation dealt a crippling blow to his chances for the mayorship, becoming a focus of attack during the primary elections from both Calvert and Williams.

It had long been assumed in East St. Louis that the fight for mayor would be largely limited to Calvert and Merritts. But when the returns came in from the February 9, 1971, primary, Williams beat Merritts by 75 votes. Calvert and Williams, the two run-off candidates for the April election, received 5,193 and 3,898 votes respectively. A White candidate who had run a "law and order and retention of white businesses" campaign received 2,895 ballots.[38] Williams's surprise showing seemed attributable to strong opposition to Merritts's behavior during the school strike as well as to the rapidly changing political scene in East St. Louis.

Williams had been able to mobilize a large following of volunteers who were fed up with machine politics—and, in their eyes, this included Merritts. In a rare East St. Louis election, precinct committeemen and election judges appointed by the election commissioners were closely watched at the polling places by nonmachine poll watchers. The day before the election, members of the Belleville League of Women Voters, the East St.

---

[36] *Ibid.*, November 14, 1969.

[37] *Ibid.*, *Metro-East Journal*, June 18, 1969, March 3, 1970, April 21, 1970, June 26, 1970, July 10, 1970, and November 14, 1969.

[38] A fifth candidate, a young Black who had attempted to "rescue" his friends at the police station a few days earlier, received 74 votes.

Louis United Front, and Citizens for an Aldermanic Government emphasized their intention to closely watch voting and to contest the results in the federal courts if there were irregularities. Even the board of election commissioners felt pressed to warn against irregularities. Their attorney promised to bypass the prosecuting attorney, if necessary, and to take evidence directly to the grand jury. No violations had been prosecuted by the state's attorney in the past ten years, he correctly observed.

The unusual nature of this election was illustrated in other ways, too. On January 26, the four major mayoral candidates engaged in a question-and-answer and debate session before an audience of more than 1,000 people. Such an event would have been scarcely conceivable in previous campaigns. And most of the candidates verbally supported aldermanic government, including Calvert. Despite many irregularities which were reported in the election—voting machines tampered with, prompting of voters, and refusing to allow watchers to look at a voting machine—the election, by East St. Louis standards, was apparently conducted with relative honesty.

Following a vote canvass confirming Merritts's loss to Williams, Merritts publicly gave his support to Williams "to keep out the Calverts." Williams's own view of himself, however, blocked him from seeking Merritts's support. Continuing to attack the machine and politicians generally, he spurned Merritts. He made no rapprochement and lost potential support from machine elements who were opposed to Calvert. In fact, several committeemen who supported Merritts approached Williams after the primary and were met with a standard response—no deals or favors, support me if you wish. Merritts, who reportedly controlled eleven precinct committeemen and who received Mayor Fields's tacit approval, expressed frustration at Williams's attitude as a pure reformer: "In spite of Williams, I have to be for Williams."[39] After the primary, Merritts told the newspapers, he waited in vain for a call from Williams: "I had to call him myself. I'm asking everybody I know to support the man. I don't know how much good it's doing considering his attitude, but [I] won't be guilty of imposing Calvert on East St. Louis

[39] *Metro-East Journal*, March 14, 1971.

regardless of how Williams acts. Anybody's got to be able to deal, to negotiate, to trade favors if they are ever going to get anything done."[40]

Many East St. Louisians predicted that Williams's idealism would cost him the election. Williams's critical failures, according to their analysis, were that he refused to court Merritts and his supporters, and that he ignored James Sinovich, the White candidate who ran fourth in the primary. Sinovich's support would have been vital because of his appeal to the White community, which comprised more than half of the registered voters. Instead, on March 4 Sinovich came out strongly for Calvert, because "Virgil Calvert and his committeemen have pledged their support of me in any election I decide to run in the future."[41] Sinovich's other reason for support was that he and Calvert were both Democrats. It was predicted that Calvert would make inroads into the White vote, retain his massive support in the Black community, and possibly reach some agreement with Mayor Fields.[42] Thus Williams would lose because of his unwillingness to bargain and seek politicans' support: "Williams had the run-off election sewed up the day after the primary last month if he had played his cards right. But the man is stubborn and inexperienced. He thinks he can get elected because God is on his side. Well, God may be on his side—but if he wants to get elected, he also needs political help."[43]

Williams denied disliking politicians, and in early March he issued a statement asking for their support. One group of precinct committeemen endorsed him—the East St. Louis Republican city central committee. In addition, he received other Republican aid. It was rumored that powerful Republicans helped finance his campaign, and it was acknowledged that he received assistance from several young reform-type Republican politicians who were recent victors in countywide elections. On the weekend before the election, Governor Richard Ogilvie, a Republican, promised through one of his appointees to build a state office building in East St. Louis only if Williams were

[40] Ibid.
[41] Ibid., March 4, 1971.
[42] St. Louis Globe Democrat, March 8, 1971.
[43] Ibid.

elected. A traditionally Republican newspaper in St. Louis endorsed Williams in an April 2, 1971, editorial and cast him clearly in the reformer role. A choice was presented to the voters on April 6, who would "be deciding whether East St. Louis makes a clean break with the patronage politics of the past and moves forward or remains mired in its political spoils system which has long impeded progress."[44]

Williams continually emphasized his basic commitment to stay clear of pledges and promises, vowing that he wanted to be free of encumbrances if elected mayor. He invited politicians' support if they accepted his principles. "However," he said, "I cannot betray the people of East St. Louis who have experienced corruption for 20 years. . . ."[45] White politicians' dislike and distrust of Calvert made Williams their natural choice. A deep split in the Black machine also held great promise. But Williams's refusal to "buy in," even minimally, violated all the norms of East St. Louis politics.

While the election results were a symbolic victory for reform in East St. Louis, it is doubtful that they will soon transform East St. Louis into a different community. More spending in the "public interest" will no doubt follow, although by the time Williams took office at least $70-million per year in federal and state aid was coming into the city.[46] Infusions of federal funds and programs have more readily been translated into increased professional activity and fattened agency budgets than into changes in the political and social conditions of East St. Louis.

A review of East St. Louis's political history indicates that it will be extremely difficult for Mayor Williams to maintain his preelection goals of reform and efficiency in local government. Already the mayor has found himself embroiled in conflict not only with diverse groups seeking power and access to resources but also with other members of the five-man city council. To win office is one thing; to enforce decisions is another, espe-

---

[44] *Ibid.*, April 2, 1971.

[45] *Ibid.*

[46] This estimate is based on a summation of all federal and state programs operating in East St. Louis during 1971. An East St. Louis administrator compiled a total which was considerably higher since it was based on multi-year computations.

cially in East St. Louis where reform policies run counter to a political environment which, despite its liabilities, has traditionally provided upward mobility and tangible rewards for people denied entry into usual political structures.

Institutional Stakes
in Renewal Planning

2

Introduction

Urban renewal has been described as an "enterprise . . . in which, formally independent organizations participate, none of which exerts authority crucial for the participation of the others. . . . The relationship is not flagrantly coercive at any link in the chain binding central to state, state to local government, or local government to local corporate authority (LPA)."[1] The process involves the cooperation and coordination of a multitude of public and private agencies and individuals within and outside of the locality. Each of these agencies has peculiar goals, values, and maintenance needs which are normally more important in practice than stated renewal objectives.[2]

Results of urban renewal policy have been determined not primarily by the federal legislation but by the relationships

[1] George S. Duggar, "The Federal Concept in Urban Renewal: The Local Renewal Enterprise," *Community Development in the Western Hemisphere* (San Diego, Calif.: Public Affairs Research Institute of San Diego College, 1961), p. 41.

[2] Martin Meyerson and Edward C. Banfield use the maintenance needs of large organizations as a central focus in studying housing politics in Chicago. See Martin Meyerson and Edward C. Banfield, *Politics, Planning and the Public Interest* (Glencoe, Ill.: Free Press, 1955).

among local political actors.[3] Values that have been most successfully implemented in renewal projects have usually been those held by powerful political and economic interests. Review of urban renewal and planning literature points up the sacrifice of housing for low-income groups, the creation of high-speed highways to the suburbs in redevelopment areas, and a renewal emphasis on protecting downtown financial interests.

Basic federal housing and renewal policies were established with the 1937 Housing Act. It was designed to stimulate new housing starts (through mortgage loans) and to construct low-income public housing. Appropriations, however, did not match the rhetorical goals of alleviating "present and recurring unemployment . . . to remedy the unsafe and unsanitary housing conditions and the acute shortage of decent, safe, and sanitary dwellings for families of low income."[4] This program became one of clearance without a simultaneous large-scale building program, leaving slum dwellers worse off than before.

Principally through the operations of the private construction and mortgage market, the 1949 Housing Act was ostensibly designed to improve the lot of the slum dweller. Public housing was seen as a mechanism for dealing with both the housing shortage and the economic cycle. In response to criticism charging lack of comprehensiveness, the 1949 Act was amended in 1954. President Eisenhower's committee on housing had urged that cities face up to the urban decay on a broader scale and develop a more comprehensive approach to prevent the growth of slums. "Urban renewal" programs were suggested by the committee.[5] An approach to urban renewal which extended beyond redevelopment of deteriorated neighborhoods and construction of public housing was provided in the 1954 Housing Act. Existing housing stock was to be conserved, deteriorating housing was to be rehabilitated, and comprehensive renewal planning stimulated.

[3] Scott Greer, *Urban Renewal and American Cities, the Dilemma of Democratic Intervention* (Indianapolis: Bobbs-Merrill, 1967), p. 35.

[4] Jewel Bellush and Murray Hausknecht, "Urban Renewal: An Historical Overview," in *Urban Renewal: People, Politics, and Planning*, eds. Jewel Bellush and Murray Hausknecht (Garden City, N.Y.: Anchor Books, Doubleday, 1967), p. 35.

[5] *Ibid.*, pp. 13–15.

Although the program attempted to define a comprehensive approach, renewal planning in most cities continued on a project-by-project basis. In 1959 the federal government introduced the Community Renewal Program (CRP), clearly a response to the felt need for long-range programming of renewal activity closely tied to capital financing. In 1965, the GNRP, which originated in the Housing Act of 1956, was expanded to permit inclusion in planning activities of those areas not eligible for renewal projects but containing related problems.

A further effort to achieve comprehensive planning of renewal areas in depressed cities was made in the 1968 Housing and Urban Development Act with the newly titled Neighborhood Development Program (NDP). Designed to stimulate an ongoing process of improvement on a communitywide basis, NDP was aimed at eliminating the conventional project-by-project approach.[6] Because funding by the Department of Housing and Urban Development (HUD) and the local share was to be provided on an annual basis, a city could theoretically undertake as much renewal as it was capable of each year. There was no limitation as to the size of the overall NDP area which could be redeveloped over a period of many years. Flexibility was stressed with periodic changes permitted in the size of the urban renewal areas.

To initiate an NDP the Local Public Agency (LPA), that agency in the city empowered to carry out urban renewal with federal assistance, must prepare an application for loan and grant which includes an overall general renewal plan, a budget, a financing plan, and a program of work activities to be carried out in the first year. After submission of these materials, a master contract between HUD and the LPA is drawn up along with an annual funding agreement which specifies the exact grant for the first year. HUD then advances funds to the LPA for the first-year activities and establishes a grant reservation for the second year.

As described in detail later, East St. Louis, Illinois, chose to participate in the NDP because it appeared to be an improve-

---

[6] Carl G. Lindbloom and Morton Farrah, *The Citizen's Guide to Urban Renewal* (West Trenton, N.J.: Chandler-Davis, 1968), p. 173.

ment over the usual methods employed in federally sponsored urban renewal programs. For a city unable to generate federal allocations for much-needed physical projects, the annual funding of NDP was considered a real innovation. Though a city such as East St. Louis would not be committed to completing the annual plan in its entirety, its contract would be considered fulfilled so long as at least a portion was completed by the year's end. Each year the project would be, in part, planned, executed, and closed out until the area designated was renewed. This meant that planning activities could be phased and paced at the same rate that the city was able to execute renewal activities.

In addition, the NDP allowed for a liberal interpretation of the noncash credit system. (This system permits cities to utilize public expenditures, such as demolition, roads, public buildings, and so forth, in lieu of cash as matching local share for federal grant allocations.) Recognizing that renewal activities take considerable time, the NDP allowed a city to "freeze" credits— that is, any project that was eligible as a noncash credit as of the date of the approval of the application would be eligible throughout the entire period of project execution. It was for this reason that certain geographic areas were included in the East St. Louis NDP. Thus a key element of the program and potentially one of its real benefits was the focusing on programming and timing of activities with the accompanying credits freeze.

As with all other federal renewal programs, the NDP became dependent on the success of the local renewal and planning agency in manipulating the purposes and effects of the federal legislation. Under NDP, the LPA had to be politically adept at coordinating the goals and needs of many local organizations even when they did not correspond to stated federal policies. Though the opportunity to phase renewal and freeze credits was a significant contribution to the usual renewal methods, the NDP did not have the capacity to make radical changes in federal, state, and local bureaucracies responsible for renewal. For planners imbued with an ideology of change and "innovation," NDP was, like other urban renewal efforts, difficult to carry out.

For one thing, NDP failed to recognize the fiscal problems of older cities and the overwhelming difficulties in attracting private investment even when land was cleared and prepared for renewal. NDP was designed to be a staged acquisition and clearance of all project areas, relocation of residents, possibly rehabilitation of sound buildings, and installation of necessary capital improvements. When the land was sold, the loans repaid, and the books audited, the project would be fiscally closed out. At that point, all direct public action would be completed. As in many other urban renewal projects, the LPA had neither assurance that the land could be resold on the private market nor indication as to the kinds of reuse it might be put to based on market conditions. Most realtors have preferred to steer clear of federally sponsored urban renewal due to the red tape and bureaucratic procedures associated with it and the limited prospects of selling the land. This has meant that redevelopment has often been left ultimately to public agencies which are only able to provide public housing or public facilities.

Neither the NDP nor any other of the HUD-sponsored urban renewal programs can solve the difficulty of bridging the clearance and the building stages. In East St. Louis, little that was done during the planning had any effect on the decisions of public and private agencies capable of carrying out rebuilding in the city. A demolition program was the only real commitment that the LPA could make in planning for the NDP. There was still the need for developers to construct houses and create commercial projects. It is not within the power of any LPA to see that plans are translated into brick and mortar even with NDP funding.

Successful implementation of urban renewal programs has been dependent upon the degree to which land that is renewed becomes attractive to developers. The NDP's authority is limited largely to the provision of vacant land and does not extend to the resolution of larger social and economic issues leading to a quality urban environment. It does not recognize, for example, that a physical development program must be supplemented by improved law enforcement, quality schools, a healthy industrial and commercial community, and rising incomes. No percentage of write-down on the cost of the land can compensate for the surrounding neighborhoods in which many urban renewal projects have been located. In East St. Louis when the LPA offers the urban renewal land to private developers the land is placed in competition with land in all parts of the St. Louis metropolitan area, which includes six counties on both sides of the Mississippi River as well as already vacant land within the boundaries of East St. Louis but farther from its most deteriorated neighborhoods.

The NDP is restricted in its ability to respond even to the physical development needs of cities because of its dependence on the noncash credit system for the sharing of costs between the locality and the federal government. Although eligibility requirements in recent years have been significantly liberalized, East St. Louis finds itself in a fiscal crisis which largely eliminates its ability to take advantage of these new funding procedures. Original urban renewal legislation had allowable local contributions limited to streets, utilities, parks, and schools built by the city in the project area. In 1954, allowable credits were extended for public buildings and improvements in the project area, even though they served outside areas. In 1959 and 1961, amendments to the Housing Act permitted certain expenditures by universities, colleges, and hospitals in acquiring land in and near renewal projects and allowed local housing authorities tax exemptions to count toward the local share as noncash payments. Further, the 1961 Housing Act altered the original two-thirds/one-third federal-local matching grant by raising the federal share to three-fourths/one-fourth for certain poorer cities.[7] East St. Louis falls into this category. However, eligible projects are subject to time limitations. In most cases, eligibility is extended to projects begun in the city three years prior to the NDP grant. Even this innovation has not been sufficiently liberal for East St. Louis. The city had only a very few credits and these were already old at the time that NDP project plans were begun. Delay of urban renewal approval has meant that the credits originally planned were no longer eligible. Resubmission of ap-

[7] A clear definition of the noncash credit system can be found in *ibid.*, pp. 179–183.

plications at later dates has been impossible because no future projects that are large enough to support an NDP can be planned by the city without federal and state financing. This type of outside assistance, in addition, is usually ineligible for use as local share.

Federally assisted urban renewal has resulted in little change in the physical and social environment of East St. Louis. The main effect of federal sponsorship through planning advances has been to sustain the employment of planning and renewal specialists who have become a major constituency for redevelopment. As in numerous other older American cities, professionals in poverty programs, social agencies, and at various government levels have provided the impetus and support for renewal and planning. The needs of these professionals to maintain and enhance their positions have had a marked influence in the entire redevelopment process, including the submission of the NDP application. Planning and redevelopment history in East St. Louis illustrates the primacy of these maintenance and enhancement needs.

Urban Renewal Politics in East St. Louis

With the appointment of a city planning director in 1957 a measure of official recognition was granted to planning in East St. Louis. A small office was provided with space for a director and one secretary. His duties were limited to the routine administration of the zoning ordinance, attendance at city council meetings, and direction of the plan commission. Even urban renewal planning was not his concern. Until the mid-1960s, urban renewal was the responsibility of the local housing authority.

An urban renewal project, the Illinois R-11, was begun in 1959 with backing from CPI, a coalition of neighborhood groups assisted by business interests and SIU's Community Development Program. Forty-nine acres of deteriorated housing and commercial facilities were cleared, but left undeveloped. Only approximately 30 percent of the area has been renewed with a new motel, federal building, and expansion of an existing hospital.

Today, the remainder lies vacant. Developers have not been attracted to the site. While the urban renewal land was originally designated primarily for commercial development as an extension of the downtown business district, only a 1970 decision to place more public housing there has made the eventual completion of the project feasible in the next few years.

After five years of unsuccessful marketing of the R-11 land, the city council made a decision to bring the urban renewal function back to the city from the housing authority. As can best be determined, federal demands for land disposition in the R-11 project and downtown pressure to redevelop the business area brought planning and renewal together as a city responsibility. Edwin Denman, a former director of urban renewal in a middle-sized Indiana city, was hired as director of urban renewal and planning in 1964. Without a formal background in planning, Denman was to continue zoning and land-use functions of planning but primarily concern himself with bringing success to the R-11 project and any future renewal projects that East St. Louis might undertake. Preparation of a master plan by a consulting firm in New Jersey had been completed several years prior to Denman's arrival.

Impatient with the results of renewal, the business and banking interests united in 1965 to form East St. Louis CBD Improvement, Inc., the next year renamed PACE (Progress and Action by Citizens Efforts). No longer was their main concern the type of governmental reform which led to the 1963 hiring of George Washnis. They were preoccupied with the economic future of the city and, more particularly, the downtown area. City government had failed to halt the loss in property values, and the bankers and businessmen were feeling the pinch of declining profits and sales. It was apparent that PACE would support the existing government to the extent that the government devoted itself to business district vitality. By 1965 the city was 55 percent Black, a 10 percent increase over the 1960 census, and its per capita income was sliding rapidly. To members of PACE, continuation of these trends was very threatening. Bank loans to the city for temporary financing were becoming indefensible as the city's credit picture became increasingly dismal.

In 1966, PACE contracted with Schwarz and Van Hoefen, a St. Louis architectural firm, and Harland Bartholomew, a nationally known planning firm, to develop a plan for the city with special emphasis on the downtown, including the R-11 project area. Designed for promotional purposes, the final plan was a development scheme which opted for visionary and extravagant proposals. It suggested large-scale clearance of existing residential areas, to be replaced by extensive commercial, recreation, and entertainment areas. A new "future land-use" plan for the entire city was presented. Special attention was focused on the riverfront, the central city which comprised the East St. Louis business district and adjoining sectors, including the R-11 urban renewal area and the southend (or Denverside) residential area. A high-density residential community was projected on the riverfront and commercial usages were proposed for the central city. In the low-income Denverside area the plan suggested a "pilot project" rental development of eighty-six single, two-, three-, and four-bedroom housing units.

When the plan failed to attract developers, PACE reconsidered, revising their hopes downward and amending the Schwarz and Van Hoefen plan. Realizing that there was little future for commercial development on the R-11 urban renewal site, PACE proposed housing; this also brought no response. At the same time the city's department of urban renewal hired a local realtor to market the land. No sales were made. The unproductiveness of PACE's efforts apparently discouraged further activity in downtown renewal. From 1966 to the end of the decade the downtown financial and business interests figured less and less in attempts to revitalize the East St. Louis physical and political environment.

To PACE, urban renewal of the blighted inner-city residential area—the areas that, in 1969, were designated as the NDP areas—was low on the priority list. However, it was PACE which made the first formal proposal for those areas. At a PACE meeting, entitled "Hands Across the River," in January, 1966, a five-

phase urban renewal proposal was revealed to Mayors Alvin G.
Fields and Alfonso Cervantes of East St. Louis and St. Louis.
Since there were no serious proposals for implementation of the
plan there was no difficulty in getting general approval of it at
the meeting.

A few months later Fred Teer, a local schoolteacher, applied
for funds to carry out a 221 (d) (3) housing program in the
NDP area. Federal Housing Authority (FHA) and HUD officials together suggested to the mayor that the city apply for
funds to "seriously" plan urban renewal in the whole of the
Denverside area surrounding Teer's project. These officials felt
they would be unable to insure Teer's project if it were isolated
in a rapidly declining area. Both PACE and Teer's newly organized Denverside Improvement Association expressed enthusiasm for this suggestion. In 1966 Planning Director Denman,
with aid from the Public Administration and Metropolitan Affairs Program of SIU, prepared an application for the 200-acre
R-104 project. With the approval of the urban renewal project
came approval for Teer's project from FHA. Pressure for renewal activity subsided once approval of the application was
obtained. With the exception of hiring a relocation officer,
Charles Means, federal funds were not forthcoming for other
R-104 activities.

By 1967, the year East St. Louis submitted an application for
funds under the newly authorized federal Model Cities program, extremely strained relationships had developed between
Washnis and Denman over the speed of renewal and who had
the final authority for redevelopment. Denman felt he should
report directly to the mayor and council while Washnis, by virtue of his position and salary, felt otherwise. Denman was skeptical about the city's capacity to undertake renewal because of
the shortage of fiscal resources and felt that Washnis's attempts
to bring in outside professionals to push renewal and planning
constituted interference with his job. Washnis, on the other
hand, saw Denman as uncommunicative and an obstruction to
redevelopment. Encouragement for PACE by Washnis, and the
signing of a contract between the Public Administration and
Metropolitan Affairs Program of SIU and the city for planning

and renewal services were perceived by Denman as outright intervention in his responsibilities. He, not the PACE consultants or SIU staff, was the city planner.

There was much unpleasantness and continual confrontation over planning and renewal during that period. Denman's suspicion of PACE and SIU proved to be accurate. In February, 1966, PACE passed a resolution requesting the mayor to fire Denman, but no action was taken. About six months later, SIU made a proposal to sharply curtail Denman's authority.[8] Presented to the mayor and council, the reorganization proposal argued for better integration of the city's renewal and development activities and more clearly defined responsibility and accountability for planning activities. Three separate divisions were to be created for planning, urban renewal, and development regulations enforcement, with George Washnis designated as coordinator for redevelopment activities over all three units. Technical aspects of the university report included functional responsibilities for each of the divisions and specific staff arrangements.

Washnis gained greater control over redevelopment activities toward the end of 1967 when the city's Model City proposal was approved by the federal government. After an attempt by Denman to make himself the local city official responsible for the Model City program, Washnis, with the mayor's support, was assigned that role. HUD officials also intervened in the controversy at that time. While Denman had close ties and respect from key bureaucrats in HUD's urban renewal department at the regional level, several of the new federal officials assigned to administer the Model City program in Chicago were considerably less enthusiastic about him. They agreed with Washnis that he presented an obstacle to planning and recommended to the mayor that the city hire a professional to handle planning and that Denman be assigned solely to urban renewal activities. Their feelings were endorsed by an assistant secretary of HUD who called Mayor Fields from California to advise him that the

[8] Seymour Mann, ed., unpublished study for the mayor of East St. Louis on the reorganization of the East St. Louis urban renewal and planning departments, October 12, 1966.

Model Cities program and other increased federal assistance would create an added demand for expertise in planning activities. He indicated that East St. Louis might receive preferential treatment from HUD if a new planner were hired.

In response to the SIU paper and the encouragement of George Washnis and federal officials, the city council hired Jamie Cannon as director of the planning department in March, 1968. In his early forties, Cannon had been a practicing architect for about ten years. Washnis sought out Cannon, who accepted the position on a six-month trial basis. Cannon was well aware of the problems facing him since he had not only been project director for the architectural firm which prepared the PACE plan, but also had worked many evenings and weekends on a voluntary basis as an advocate planner for a neighborhood organization seeking zoning changes in the city. Though interested in East St. Louis and committed to its change, Cannon's qualifications did not match those outlined by the reorganization proposal. He had neither the master's degree in planning nor the four years of "increasingly responsible city planning experience." But for Washnis, it was a clear-cut victory in that both he and Cannon shared common goals. They both wanted action and felt that, with encouragement, development could be brought to the city. Their concerns were not the technical aspects of planning or strict adherence to federal program requirements, for people could be hired to perform these functions. Their mission was to catalyze renewal.

Washnis's strategy was to hire Cannon and gradually move Denman out. Cannon was to be planner with control over $400,000 in planning monies from the federally assisted GNRP and CRP. Denman was forced to work on programs with very little money for staff—an antiquated urban renewal project adjoining the CBD and a new project whose funding could not be expected immediately. Washnis's strategy was successful. He now had supervision over the Model City program and all redevelopment planning in the city. A few months later, Denman left to take a position as public works director of a Chicago suburb.

When Denman left, Charles Means, the relocation officer on

the R-104 project, assumed the supervision of urban renewal functions. Means, like Cannon, was inexperienced. He was twenty-five years old and, at the time, held a bachelor's degree in political science and was working toward a master's degree. His experience was limited to administration of a Job Corps Center and community organization work. However, both he and Cannon were energetic, outgoing, and impatient with depressed conditions in East St. Louis. Raised in East St. Louis, Means was part of an emerging group of Black professionals who had assumed leadership roles in redevelopment programs. Initially, Means was not chosen as the director to replace Denman, but feeling that his qualifications were equal to those of Cannon's for his job, he pushed for separation of the planning and urban renewal functions. Based on the SIU recommendations, two separate departments were created with Means the new director of urban renewal.

Prior to Denman's departure, plans had been made to relocate the two departments into newly remodeled but entirely separate office spaces. At Denman's insistence, even the door which adjoined the two offices had been covered with wallboard, making physical contact difficult. Further, he had ordered construction of a soundproof office so that negotiations with developers and HUD officials could be conducted privately. Denman never occupied the facilities but his demands for isolation contributed to strained working relationships between the planning and urban renewal departments at a later date. During the tenure of Cannon and Means the wallboard was never taken down to open the passage between the departments.

Though it is not uncommon for urban renewal and planning functions to be located in separate departments, the SIU reorganization study and the ultimate departmental split were influenced by Washnis's opinions of Denman and their inability to get along. Washnis was unable to obtain the results he wanted in urban renewal and planning; yet he could not influence the mayor and council to remove Denman. Fracturing redevelopment helped to solve the problem.

Both Washnis and SIU staff believed that Denman had influence with the mayor which came from his control over receipt of information about federal programs. He was the conduit through which federal bureaucrats were responding about ongoing and possible East St. Louis projects. When the mayor assumed the position of conciliator between Denman and Washnis, he not only minimized the deep cleavage but forced Washnis to take an alternative route. Cannon understood his role at the time, but he felt then and insists even now that the departments should have stayed together. Once division was established, his belief was that it should have taken a different form. Denman should have been given the planning department with control over zoning administration and execution of the $100,000 CRP —essentially a series of consultant contracts. Sharing Washnis's views of Denman, Cannon believed that urban renewal needed revitalization and that whoever would have been hired as urban renewal director should also have been given responsibility to execute the GNRP. Though the GNRP was originally intended for physical planning for the Model City area, its funding was an advance on the R-104 urban renewal project. Cannon reasoned that an energized urban renewal department would have been a logical place for the GNRP since the findings of this planning program were to constitute the logical basis for renewal decisions.[9]

When Means was appointed director of urban renewal after a brief tenure in an acting capacity, he focused much of his attention on the R-104 project. Viewed from his perspective, preoccupation with the ten-year-old R-11 program would neither enhance the image of urban renewal in East St. Louis nor his own professional reputation. Whatever work was necessary on R-11 could be conducted in conjunction with the staff's other activities, especially since successful completion of the project was far from assured. At the time of his appointment to the director's post, there were simply no commercial developers for the land, and Means had no resources to insure implementation of the R-11 project.

In reviewing R-104, Means found that in nine months since approval of the survey and planning (S and P) application, Denman had not drawn any planning money. Denman's re-

[9] Jamie Cannon, interview, St. Louis, Missouri, April 30 and May 26, 1971.

luctance to use the funds was based on his contention that the GNRP had to be completed prior to drawing on the project funds.[10] Means immediately disproved this claim and began to hire staff, using portions of the $301,000 set aside for R-104 planning. Those HUD officials who helped devise the GNRP recognized that the program regulations were meant to be interpreted liberally in the East St. Louis case. Much of the city needed renewal; HUD wanted to use available funds to bolster the Model City planning budget and to supply the city with professional competence.

Means believed, however, that he could not go into the execution phase of conventional urban renewal programs until Cannon completed the planning required in the GNRP. Funds for the GNRP had come from the S and P of the R-104 which had been approved for $4-million (later raised to $6-million). According to Means, he could not receive approval of parts I and II of R-104 until HUD approved the GNRP. When Means became director, he attempted to change the GNRP by excluding the R-104 area from its geographic boundaries. He believed then, and today, that there was no reason to include the R-104 in the much larger GNRP area. He argued that the urban renewal manual stated that if the program of urban renewal would be hampered by a GNRP, then a GNRP should not be submitted. His efforts to alter the original GNRP study design were unsuccessful.[11]

Cannon saw the GNRP in a different light and until the time of his resignation in April, 1970, had not completed the work included in the GNRP. He felt that the GNRP had little to do with blocking implementation of urban renewal and that completion of the GNRP would mean losing a highly skilled staff. Means argued that a substantial number of the planning staff could be picked up on the R-104 planning budget and the remainder on advances from other urban renewal projects. There was no limit on the number of S and P applications the city could have submitted for other urban renewal areas.[12]

[10] *Ibid.*
[11] Charles Means, East St. Louis Urban Renewal Director, interview, East St. Louis, Illinois, May 28, 1971.
[12] *Ibid.*

As the staffs of the two departments were hired and their operations grew, a rivalry developed between them. Both Means and Cannon were trying to define the objectives of their departments and to understand what urban renewal and planning were supposed to encompass. It must be noted that both Cannon and Means feel that this case study overemphasizes their differences. Cannon contends that their competition pushed the two agencies together and that whatever schism existed between the two directors was small compared to poor relationships he discovered between urban renewal and planning directors in other cities. Means's position is that their disagreements were of a professional nature and never affected the cordiality and friendship of the two men.[13]

Both Cannon and Means sought out experienced technicians for their staffs. Cannon hired planners, designers, architects, and professionals equipped to collect and use data. Means, on the other hand, employed practitioners who had been involved in the implementation of urban renewal in St. Louis, a real estate dealer to handle relocation, and several young administrators. The contrast between the two staffs was marked with the planning department mostly White, innovation-conscious physical and social planners who lived outside the city; the urban renewal department Black, bureaucratically oriented technicians, many of whom resided in the East St. Louis area and had strong local ties. Means's hiring practices did not reflect a need for planners to plan the R-104 project. He felt that to hire more planners with R-104 funds would have been a duplication and his highest priority was to acquire an experienced urban renewal staff.

Though the composition of the two departments was decidedly different and this led, at times, to conflict, there were also areas of consensus and instances of a unity based on personal relationships and professional commitments. Most of the staff had not experienced the split and had fewer problems with interdepartmental communications than their directors. There were cases when they ran interference for the department directors and did considerable amounts of work until eventually the directors were better able to work together.

[13] Jamie Cannon, interview; and Charles Means, interview.

Newly formed, the urban renewal department felt the need to strengthen its role by the initiation of additional functions. Neither of their existing projects offered the promise of more funds in the near future. The R-11 project had been in execution for many years and, being zoned commercial, offered little possibility for development, while the planning for R-104 had not even been started. When it was suggested by the HUD field representative, Kenneth Burrows, that there might be money in the new NDP and that it might have more immediate benefits for East St. Louis, Means decided to process the NDP application. NDP was definitely perceived as a way of hastening clearance and redevelopment.

Means, however, needed assistance from Cannon's staff, which was larger and more technically oriented to graphic production and to data collection—both requirements of federal grant processing. Cannon reluctantly agreed to prepare the application. Even at that early date in 1969 it was apparent that the split had created two agencies with different sets of maintenance needs. The urban renewal department needed the NDP to justify the hiring of additional staff and, by extending its activities, guarantee the agency's future. NDP also promised immediate visibility through demolition and could become the vehicle to contrast the new, energized urban renewal department with the city's past renewal efforts. Processing the NDP was, additionally, a way to show results to HUD and carry out federal desires to obtain NDP applications.

On the other hand, the planning department at the time of the initiation of the NDP processing was funded by a $300,000 GNRP grant for staff and supplies. The completion date was set for several years in the future. This program was designed by HUD representatives, Washnis, and SIU staff as a means of providing the city with planners, architects, and sociologists to serve as professional technicians in the Model Cities and other expected federal programs. By 1969, most of these professionals had been hired and Cannon felt approval of the NDP was likely to discontinue the GNRP, restricting both departments to operations allowed in the small NDP planning budget. In addition he was receiving technical assistance requests from such agencies as the local housing authority, Model Cities, and neighborhood groups, and he wanted staff to supply them. While the NDP promised to extend the functions of the urban renewal department and hasten the input of operating funds for redevelopment, it was likely that it would limit the activities of the planning department.

Further, Cannon was skeptical of the federal capacity to act on renewal and saw no evidence that actual funds would be forthcoming. In recent comments he has expressed the feeling that the NDP, at the federal level, was a device to uncommit large sums of urban renewal money for already approved projects. In East St. Louis, this meant taking the committed $6-million R-104 project and changing it to an NDP at a much lower annual allocation.[14]

Cannon had other complaints about switching to NDP. One was that the local noncash credits for the R-104 project would run out and that HUD officials were aware of this. Another was that Means had enough to do if he could clean up the R-11 project and move the R-104 into execution. Cannon was concerned about the dissipation of effort. He believed that R-11 should have had the highest priority and that an intensive marketing effort should have been made. His department had prepared a housing plan for the R-11, and early disposition of the R-11 had been cited as a goal in the PACE plan. He also argued that the credibility of the new urban renewal department should have been established by correcting past failures and that it was counterproductive to use energies on projects which, to him, had little chance of being funded. His third complaint centered on the interoffice rivalry. If the urban renewal department wanted NDP they should have processed the application themselves and not involved his staff in what he considered a "cruelty perpetrated by the feds."[15] This position can be questioned since HUD planning funds are not supposed to be diverted for application processing. In practice, however, few cities heed this urban renewal regulation.

Cannon's perception of what NDP was likely to do to his de-

---

[14] Jamie Cannon, interview, April 30, 1971.
[15] Ibid.

partment led to conflicting goals and strategies pursued by the two departments throughout the application process. When participation of the staff of the planning department in the NDP became an issue with the city council, Cannon finally assigned his staff to the NDP. Not enthusiastic or supportive of the decision, the application was not processed quickly. Thwarting the urban renewal department, the planning department took months to mobilize its staff for the NDP. Several project directors were assigned, but other activities were given higher priority. Lower level staff assigned to the project were given little authority or direction and often they were occupied in playing the intermediary role between the two departments. That the planning department staff pursued the NDP at all was due almost entirely to the individual commitment of staff members rather than to department policy. In the meantime the urban renewal department proceeded in hot pursuit of NDP funds.

Frustration and resentment arose between Cannon and Means, HUD officials, and staff members of each department. Though poles apart, the two arguments were logically defensible. Means wanted a renewal project quickly and there was little doubt that the city needed it. He saw NDP as a mechanism to expedite action. Cannon felt that the regional office of HUD had not given correct guidance to East St. Louis by suggesting in January, 1969, that HUD would look askance at East St. Louis if the city did not apply for an NDP. Based on his discussions in Washington at that time, Cannon predicted that it was highly unlikely that East St. Louis would be allocated any new urban renewal money. He resented the encouragement of what he perceived as false hopes by the regional office. Too many of its past suggestions had led nowhere. He did not feel that he should encourage his staff to get involved in the tedious application process, which if by some accident were approved, might eliminate their jobs.

Through the spring and summer of 1969 little progress was made on the NDP. Work on the application was divided. The urban renewal department prepared reports on relocation acquisition, citizen participation, and land marketability, and the planning department was responsible for the descriptions, justifications, and plans for the three areas, including the detailed ones for two action years and the more general plans for the subsequent two reservation years. But delay followed delay within the two departments. An example of this was the selection of the actual geographic area to be designated for NDP. Although the earliest NDP activity was in January, by July no area had yet been designated as the NDP project area. Planners felt that in choosing the area their computerized information system should be utilized and a choice based upon existing building conditions. Because the East St. Louis Model Cities program had not only included urban renewal in its plan, but also had allocated part of its resources as well as credits for NDP, Means felt that the boundaries ought to be within the Model Cities area. Between January and July the boundaries were amended many times. With each amendment work already completed, according to old boundaries, had to be redone. Not until July did the whole staff meet with the directors to discuss it and together decide the boundaries—a decision logically appropriate at the initiation of the project.

By late summer, 1969, the planning department, under pressure from the HUD regional representative and Means, finally gave high priority to NDP submission. Other projects such as the GNRP and CRP were set aside and most members of the planning staff were engaged in urban renewal planning. Means and federal officials argued that immediate preparation of the NDP application was necessary to avoid the expiration of noncash credits. Their arguments were compelling to Cannon, who not only reached a detente with Means but also assumed active supervision of his staff in the NDP work. Cannon decided to participate in the NDP submission after a meeting with Means, the HUD representative, and the mayor. Called at HUD's request, the mayor did not take a strong position on this seemingly technical matter—a typical response for Mayor Fields. To avoid further confrontations and unpleasantness, however, Cannon reversed his previous stand.[16]

After this decision, both the urban renewal and planning departments contributed $3,000 each to hire a consultant selected

[16] *Ibid.*

by the planning department to advise them on urban renewal and planning. That was the articulated purpose. Actually, the intention was not only technical assistance and the assignment of specific tasks for the application processing but also "coordination" of the two departments. By the time the consultant was hired, the rift between the departments had deepened considerably. Once hired, he was consulted only occasionally and this was in response to interdepartmental tensions. His presence was actually needed to facilitate discussion of the innumerable technical issues and questions that arose in fulfilling HUD requirements. His role was also weakened by the merely "advisory" status of his suggestions. Further, it was never clear to what extent the consultant himself was familiar with the city of East St. Louis, the NDP guidelines, or the personalities he was supposed to coordinate. By calling attention to poor relations between the departments, the hiring of the consultant diverted attention from the need for technical aid and his presence cost many hours of valuable staff time in discussion. This exercise more often than not involved either the urban renewal department or the planning department, rarely together, and focused attention on the rupture rather than healing it.

In any urban renewal project, it is crucial both for efficient processing of the application and for successful program implementation to establish an arrangement of clearly defined responsibilities and linkages between the LPA and the regional office of HUD.[17] In East St. Louis this was the basic responsibility of the HUD field representative. In addition to providing direct urban renewal assistance, he was supposed to provide contact with other local, state, and federal agencies. In 1969 the Chicago regional office was overly burdened with HUD-sponsored programs in their region; the NDP was one of many. Within one year the office received approximately 130 applications for NDP funds from within its ten-state area. Lack of adequate staff and time for reviewing applications and insufficient funding of the NDP ultimately permitted approval of only a few projects from the Chicago regional office.

Delays in processing the East St. Louis application made both

17 Greer, *Urban Renewal and American Cities*, p. 106.

the urban renewal and planning staffs impatient with the regional office. When expiration in January, 1970, of one of the major noncash grant-in-aid credits was recognized, both East St. Louis and regional HUD officials realized that the application had to be submitted by early September, 1969, to insure adequate time for processing in Chicago. Review of the application in Chicago was to take approximately three months. Despite the pressing need for sustained technical discussion during the preparation of the application, local staff working on the NDP received only infrequent visits and phone calls from regional representatives. On these occasions little substantive aid was provided. Throughout the process the regional office was unable to provide the necessary technical assistance to assure quick application preparation, processing, and funding for East St. Louis.

HUD's regional office moved slowly; it was holding its options open in order to maintain its position with its Washington office while retaining some credibility with the LPA. Knowing well that its programs were dependent on budgetary decisions over which it had no control, responses to the planning and urban renewal departments were often vague and evasive, yet through the spring and summer of 1969 East St. Louis was encouraged to pursue NDP funds. This encouragement was given by the field representative, even though the extent of federal allocation to the NDP was unknown. East St. Louis urban renewal officials misinterpreted HUD's informal request for an NDP application as a promise that funds would be forthcoming. In reality the regional office's commitment was contingent on decisions made in Washington.

Early in 1969 it quickly became apparent that the Nixon administration would make changes in federal urban programs. Upon assuming office, HUD Secretary George Romney called a thirty-day suspension of all departmental activity for the purpose of reviewing all programs and activities. Major policy changes resulted, although their implementation was sometimes delayed. At the local level, throughout June, July, and August, 1969, the regional representative continued to encourage the LPA to complete the application. By that time, the total staffs of both LPA departments had been assigned to the project and virtually all other activities had been suspended. By mid-July the directives from Chicago began to change somewhat in tone. A preliminary review team visited East St. Louis and informed the city that NDP funds were running short—that the office, in fact, had approved only four NDP applications in the ten-state region. On August 28, 1969, Charles Means was told that there were no funds remaining for NDP. Even so, East St. Louis later submitted an NDP application on November 14, 1969.

The HUD regional representative's directives reflected the peculiar political squeeze he found himself in. It appeared to members of the planning department that he and other staff members in the regional office were expected to justify all policy decisions that Washington handed down, no matter how contradictory. To protect its position, the regional office seemed forced to maintain that there was a logical, sequential basis for these HUD policies when in fact the chaos of federal redevelopment planning and programming was obvious.

Preparation of the East St. Louis NDP application illustrates the bureaucratic complexities typical of federal grant-in-aid programs. Guidelines for urban renewal are contained in the urban renewal manual as amended by the NDP manual. To adequately interpret and respond to these guidelines requires planning and urban renewal staffs with a wide range of skills. Although the manual provided a straightforward guide for LPA staffing, it proved to be considerably more ambiguous when the East St. Louis staff attempted to plan and budget the NDP. Both the urban renewal and planning departments were initially unfamiliar with the application process, as could be expected. It did not take long for staff members to discover the flexibility of what at first appeared to be rigid requirements. Ultimately the NDP was viewed in the same way as previous federal projects— as a useful avenue for hiring and maintaining staff for planning and urban renewal activities. Engaged in NDP activity in the planning department under Director Jamie Cannon were two architects, two draftsmen, two planners, six resident assistants, and two secretaries being paid out of the GNRP and CRP. In the urban renewal department, the following staff was utilized expressly for the NDP: two housing inspectors, one relocation specialist, one rehabilitation specialist, one community organizer, and one secretary, who were being paid out of federal funds for other renewal projects.

Writing the project improvement reports highlighted the problems encountered in the application process. These reports were designed to show estimates of the cost of each improvement, local design standards, and evidence that improvements were eligible as noncash credits. First, there was the question of defining into which category various capital improvements might logically fit. At issue in one case was the definition of the eligibility of an improvement to the local hospital—depending upon the category, different restrictions could be applied. The manual was too vague to be helpful and the regional coordinator from Chicago did not provide a definite answer. Finally, eligibility was established but there was difficulty in calculating the degree of benefit from that facility. Full cost of any project is eligible only if the renewal area receives more than 80 percent of the total benefit from that facility, according to the urban renewal manual, as follows: "If the project receives from 10% to 80% inclusive of the direct benefit from the facility, the portion of the total cost of the facility which may be credited as non-cash local grant-in-aid is based on the percentage of benefit to the project."[18]

To use this section, a clear measurement device has to be formulated by the LPA to establish to what degree each project is eligible. Although this is a fairly technical procedure, the urban renewal manual does not provide clear regulations that uniformly apply to all projects or to all cities. In their absence, the LPA must develop its own yardsticks. If they are not acceptable to the regional office, which seems to have its own unique criteria, the financing of the whole project can be seriously endangered. Ambiguity of the manual leaves an LPA defenseless, subject to arbitrary judgments from the regional office.

[18] U.S. Department of Housing and Urban Development, *Urban Renewal Handbook*. A HUD Handbook, RHM 7215.1 (Washington, D.C.: Government Printing Office, 1968), ch. 5, sec. 2.

Growth of the original one-volume manual to its present three volumes is evidence of HUD's determination to make policy-making more mechanistic and less judgmental. Its attempt to standardize decisionmaking by including all possible technicalities has been, of course, only partially successful. Technical problems of varying magnitude left unanswered by the manual theoretically still have to be solved by the field representative. Often field representatives have not liked and actually have had no authority to make important judgments and decisions.

In East St. Louis, for example, the feasibility survey as outlined in the manual provided a means of exploring local potential for renewal without actually risking a renewal application. It was designed to show whether successful planning and implementation of the contemplated urban renewal project could be expected by examining such things as adequacy of existing legal powers, feasibility of necessary relocation, and land marketability. Again the manual was ambiguous, particularly concerning the funding of the feasibility survey. It was unclear whether feasibility-survey financing was to be in the form of an outright grant or a loan. Further, the feasibility survey can be construed as a means of avoiding important decisions. In East St. Louis the field representative recommended that a survey be contracted to an outside consultant firm. This firm would take responsibility for analysis and, to that extent, for decisionmaking. Issues involving housing design, relocation of area residents, and extent of rehabilitation would be treated only as technical considerations, ignoring their value-laden, political aspects. In this way the LPA and the regional office would be relieved of troublesome choices, even though they might be better equipped to make these decisions.

Applying for urban renewal has tired and confused many professionals since the initial passage of the legislation. In East St. Louis, over 4,000 man-hours were necessary to produce the NDP application. The commitment to the citizen participation components of the NDP generated additional demands on the city's staff.

Since 1954 citizen participation has been a formal requirement in project planning for urban renewal. What was intended by citizen participation was not clarified by the NDP manual and advice from the regional office was equally ambiguous. While HUD's rhetoric stressed citizen participation, many of those involved in the project application believed that the time constraints imposed by the federal government precluded extensive resident involvement. They interpreted the actions of HUD officials in desiring an application quickly to mean that the community's eligibility would not be based on citizen participation. NDP guidelines suggested neither procedural nor evaluative methods of participation, and it was apparently left up to the LPA to implement participation according to local political circumstances.

When Means and Cannon, particularly the latter, became unusually forceful and decided to pursue the citizens and seek allies in the community by "gathering inputs" for the NDP plans, it came as a surprise to their staffs. Unless the two directors viewed citizen participation as a method for building a supporting constituency, mobilization of citizens seemed a misdirected use of staff time, particularly assuming the need for efficient and speedy completion of the application as requested by HUD. Staff members believed that citizen participation requirements could have been satisfied by a short narrative included in the application.

Means and Cannon explained their actions in different ways. Means claimed that HUD guidelines were explicit that citizen participation was supposed to be a major component for the planning of the NDP. Prior to submission of the plan and HUD approval, a project area committee had to be set up to advise on the planning and programming. Cannon's reasons were more pragmatic. He had just witnessed the rejection of a 5,000-unit housing project because it was improperly presented for the community. At all costs he wanted to avoid the label of planning for, instead of with, the community.[19] Whatever the explanation, this emphasis on citizen participation conflicted with the application deadline.

During August, 1969, the LPA conducted two citizen meetings in each of the two major sections of the NDP project area.

[19] Jamie Cannon, interview.

In these meetings, the concept of NDP was explained and color slides were shown of existing neighborhood conditions. At the first of the two meetings, residents were requested to state their suggestions as to what types of housing and community facilities they would like to see in the neighborhood. At the second meeting, a tentative plan was presented and approval was requested. Attendance at the meetings was modest despite extensive publicity by the LPA. Six resident assistants from the planning department spent a minimum of one full workday each prior to the meetings distributing literature. A community organizer hired by the urban renewal department devoted full time in preparation for these meetings. Resident understanding and commitment to the NDP nevertheless was quite limited, and graphics and photographs dealt with the subject matter superficially, doing little to illuminate the relevant issues.

By asking residents to define needs and desires, the LPA was attempting to share the responsibility for planning and policymaking and thus make itself less vulnerable to criticism from the neighborhood. Due to the internal composition of the LPA, however, citizen participation was not a realistic strategy to pursue. Neither the planning nor the urban renewal department was designed to be a community organization. These departments were official agents of city government and were staffed by technicians and bureaucrats. When their staffs appeared in the community, residents tended to view them as representatives of city hall, even when individual staff members were themselves local residents. As ill-equipped as the LPA was to communicate with citizens, so too were the citizens unprepared to participate in the planning process.

Participation in government policy has, in the past, been severely limited in ghetto communities. Prior experience with public action for most people in East St. Louis consisted of asking personal favors from politicians. Rarely had they been in a situation in which public officials came into the neighborhood to ask them to initiate action. To the citizens of NDP areas this reversed normal operating procedure. And they felt, justifiably, that "planning" was liable to mean public housing. In one NDP area, where rehabilitation of existing structures was planned, residents' approval was attained. In another where large-scale demolition was proposed, the fear of public housing was expressed and the plan was not approved by the residents.

If building local support for urban renewal was considered essential for NDP funding, then going to the neighborhoods was a poor strategy. Opening up communication with citizens was not likely to build a strong resident constituency for the LPA. While the project in one area was easily vetoed by a handful of unorganized citizens, even a large and well organized group could scarcely have constituted enough collective power to get the project approved by HUD. Only those controlling formal political and financial power would have been able to exert sufficient pressure to bring urban renewal funds to East St. Louis; hence there was little potential benefit to the LPA from citizen involvement.

Even considering the efforts of the planning and urban renewal staffs and their relatively strong collective belief in resident involvement, it was impossible for them to make an intensive commitment to citizen participation. Although residents' suggestions were agreeably accepted, very few of their ideas were incorporated into the final plan. Citizens were asked to react to work that had already been completed. According to Cannon, residents were never given the impression that "they were calling the shots," and Means described the process as one in which "the citizens gave much more input than the planners were able to incorporate into the plan."[20] In addition, heavy investment of staff time and money in already completed plans preceded serious consideration of citizen opposition. Since the basic commitment was to submit an NDP application quickly, it would have been contradictory to make extensive content changes after the residents were consulted.

Although NDP guidelines require citizen participation, a serious attempt at urban renewal almost automatically must deemphasize this requirement. Even supposing citizen support had been successfully mobilized in East St. Louis, it would have been an unstable foundation on which to build a program. Obtaining urban renewal funds and carrying out a program of

[20] *Ibid.*; and Charles Means, interview.

clearance and new investment requires powerful allies to guarantee either political or technical assistance, and residents are rarely able to supply these two key commodities. They have no control over the release of monies or mortgage insurance by HUD and they have nothing to say about the inducements necessary to interest developers in re-use of the cleared land. In most instances, it is not even logical to expect residents of an area designated for urban renewal to support redevelopment. They are dependent on depressed conditions for a supply of cheap housing. Physical disruption is threatening because traditionally those displaced by governmental action have had few economic options in the acquisition of housing and have suffered severe dislocations in their social patterns. Further, by an early announcement of urban renewal in East St. Louis, the LPA promised the hope of better futures to the residents and was unable to save face when, as has happened in many cities, the project was never funded.[21]

Lack of agreement between Cannon and Means focused HUD's attention on the general isolation and autonomy between the two agencies whose cooperation was needed to insure success of urban renewal projects. According to reliable sources, the pervasive atmosphere of discord gave the regional office rationale for the rejection of the NDP application and supplied a bureaucratic logic which would not have been available had lack of resources been the only reason for HUD's refusal to fund the program. HUD was able to argue that if NDP were funded, the regional staff would be in the middle of an unreasonable amount of political infighting.

Other explanations for HUD's refusal to fund the East St. Louis NDP can also be found. One was the lack of coordination between the local agencies which would be needed to participate in the implementation of the NDP plan. HUD, in its grant programs, traditionally stresses "coordination." Every urban renewal project is supposed to reflect cooperation from those

---

[21] Harold Kaplan, "NHA: The Strategy of Slum Clearance," in *People, Politics and Planning*, eds. Jewel Bellush and Murray Hausknecht (Garden City, N.Y.: Anchor Books, Doubleday, 1967), pp. 239–255. Kaplan describes the process by which the Newark Housing Authority made its clearance decisions from 1949 to 1959 and the strategies it used to implement policies.

groups involved in the construction of streets, sewers, schools, utilities, housing, and other supportive facilities. No concerted attempt was made by the East St. Louis LPA to acquire promises of cooperation from these agencies. Neither was there a history of cooperative efforts between these agencies and the LPA. HUD was in a position to reason that without established relationships with public bodies at all levels of government, the LPA could have no voice in the allocation of fiscal resources for capital improvements. It was hinted that the absence of a strong local constituency was at least partially responsible for not securing an NDP commitment from Chicago. But ultimately, the lack of federal funds seems to have been the most compelling reason for the NDP failure.

Conclusion

Planning activities in East St. Louis shifted as the percentage of disadvantaged families increased. Concern for enhancement of the downtown business district was transferred to physical and social programs in residential areas. Professionals were hired to seek these funds, and when the funds came, to administer the programs. But the advent of professionalism and increased federal participation often failed to insure problem solutions. This inability to change conditions was increased when professionals failed to realize the extent and limitations of their power. The only real constituency for new programs was the professionals themselves. And the federal government often created more problems than it solved by funding projects which were too little/too late or incapable of reaching stated goals.

With regard to citizen participation, professionals in both departments assumed a willing resident involvement and interest despite the fact that previous renewal attempts in the city had displaced large numbers of people and visibly failed to achieve program objectives. The R-11 project sharply reduced the available supply of low-income housing in the downtown area. Those that were removed found that relocation in standard dwellings, either on the original site or anywhere in the metropolitan area, was very difficult. Nevertheless, the LPA continued to attempt to rally the community around the rhetoric of the program. Although reference was made by professionals to the problems of program approval and problems to be expected during implementation, the real costs and benefits to individuals were not carefully appraised by the LPA. What might have been a long-range, collective good was certain to bring hardships upon individuals who could ill afford the extra burden. This insight did not escape the local residents. Bureaucratic considerations dictated that in the submission of the NDP both departments act expediently and frankly concede the secondary importance of residents' immediate needs and attitudes. Given the nature of the NDP program and the planners' own needs, the staff could hardly afford to allocate large amounts of time and resources in assessing resident opinion. If there was validity at all to the value of NDP as a redevelopment tool, then the LPA miscalculated its strategy in going to the community.

Private financial and political support was never urged for urban renewal. While bankers and businessmen, as late as 1966, did represent a possible constituency for urban renewal activity, by 1969 their support had fallen away considerably. Rapid population changes, declining profits, illness of the mayor, and departure of his administrative assistant all led to declining interest by what were once supposedly committed business and banking interests. Today, many of the financial and business leaders are primarily concerned with leaving East St. Louis, and it is unlikely that their support could have been rallied at all for renewal, primarily in Black residential areas. This type of renewal proposed by the NDP did not appeal directly to their interest in expanding profits and rebuilding the tax base. Without private financial support and the availability of developers for renewal projects, the LPA had few implementation powers.

Essential to the success of urban renewal in East St. Louis was the support of city government, and especially that of the Democratic organization. Probability of eliciting such support was low. Establishing a constituency in city hall would have required a total restructuring of the politicians' overall outlook. There was no recognition that political interests might be championed by planning and renewal; hence the political system of East St. Louis was largely indifferent to planning efforts. Politicians were primarily concerned with using the city's limited resources to support the workings of the political organization.

Federal funding for urban projects has often been described as inadequate, contradictory, confusing, and even destructive. In East St. Louis, however, federal funds are too important to be objectively evaluated in a qualitative sense. They constitute a major generator of economic activity through welfare payments, employment in such programs as education, urban renewal, and recreation, and a series of manpower and training projects. For Means and Cannon, they were "the only game" in town. Without federal funds, both professionals and their staffs would have been eliminated. Uncertainty over federal funding and undependable local constituencies heightened their anxieties about which strategy to pursue for redevelopment. When each director moved in a different direction, their struggle over NDP intensified and the maintenance and enhancement needs of their departments assumed highest priority.

Riverfront Development:
The Politics of Master Planning

3

Schemes for Riverfront Development: A History

"Since the 1930s, when the Jefferson National Expansion was first proposed for the St. Louis Riverfront, there has been periodic concern for the appearance and future of the East St. Louis Riverfront. Beautification, industrial development, and improvement committees have come and gone with regularity."[1]

Most of the 400 acres which comprise the East St. Louis waterfront on the Mississippi River are owned by the railroads. Title to the largest portion of this land between the Veterans and MacArthur Bridges is held by the Terminal Railroad Association. East St. Louis neither owns nor controls the land within its corporate limits which borders the Mississippi River. For the past sixty years attempts to change this condition have been successfully blocked by the Terminal Railroad Association and its wholly owned subsidiary, the Wiggins Ferry Company. The Terminal Railroad Association claim to the riverfront originates from an 1832 purchase of 900 acres and a charter granted by the state of Illinois to Samuel Wiggins in 1819. Essentially, the charter gave Wiggins a monopoly on traffic in the Mississippi

[1] *Metro East Journal,* January 20, 1963.

River between St. Louis and East St. Louis (then Illinoistown).[2] Because of this inability to gain access to the river, past attempts to construct water transport and port facilities on the eastern shore have been unsuccessful. East St. Louis, with its heavy volume of railroad traffic, could have become a logical adjunct to the river transportation industry which developed on the Missouri side.

Various lawsuits have been filed against the Terminal Railroad Association. In 1910, the only way that a levee, to prevent flooding, could be built along the riverfront was to acquire land by condemnation at a cost of $300,000. At that time, the newly established East Side Levee and Sanitary District was forced to use its power of eminent domain. Commenting on the need for legal action, a *Metro-East Journal* article dated May 5, 1946, claimed that "so far as can be determined no other government body has resorted to this method of gaining control of riverfront property."

Another 1910 struggle to wrest control of the riverfront from the Terminal Railroad Association was considerably less successful. The Commercial Club of East St. Louis (later called the Chamber of Commerce) and a local riverfront committee tried to mobilize community support to open the port in East St. Louis to waterborne traffic and commercial ventures other than the railroads. A report was published citing Chicago and Mobile as examples of successful waterfront developments which East St. Louis should try to duplicate. Shortly thereafter, the efforts of the group died when necessary court action failed to materialize.

Twenty-seven years later in 1937, State's Attorney Louis P. Zerweck questioned the authority of the Terminal Railroad to withhold the riverfront from public use. Zerweck took legal action, contending that the justification for his suit was: If East St. Louis had access to the riverfront, the city would grow rapidly to 200,000 in population. . . . Congress has declared the Mississippi a navigable stream and has held that private owner-

---

[2] U.S. Department of Interior, National Park Service, *The East St. Louis, Illinois, Waterfront: Historical Background*, by John W. Bond (Washington, D.C.: Government Printing Office, 1969), pp. 11–12.

ship can extend only to the high water mark adjacent to a navigable stream. . . . The State of Illinois has no right, the Supreme Court has ruled, to barter or sell public rights."[3] Terminal Railroad claimed that previous Supreme Court decisions had clearly established their right of ownership to the middle of the main channel of the Mississippi River, nearly 500 feet west of the Illinois shore. Zerweck also failed, for after intensive activity the case was dismissed when the circuit court adjourned for the summer in 1939.

Though the railroads have proved to be a durable adversary in legal conflicts, there have been other reasons why the city of East St. Louis has not pushed them more vigorously. Railroads were a major employer of local residents and collectively were the city's largest revenue source. When railroad representatives appeared at an East St. Louis city council meeting in May, 1966, to find out why they had been excluded from riverfront planning, former Mayor Alvin Fields agreed that "the railroads are our largest taxpayers and we must work with them."

Local government officials have also realized that it required thirty years for the city of St. Louis to remove the railroads from its riverfront with, in the end, only partial success. Railroad attitudes toward relocation from East St. Louis have softened, but the railroads obviously will not leave until it is in their best interests to do so or until some way can be found to replace existing facilities with better ones. At a February 6, 1969, meeting of the mayor's riverfront task force, the president of the Terminal Railroad Association again made clear that the railroads must be involved in riverfront planning.

Since the Terminal Railroad Association has played a significant role not only on the riverfront, but also in the total metropolitan area, its compliance with riverfront policy is critical. Under its 150-year-old franchise, the Terminal Railroad Association switches trains, compiles shipments, transports railroad cars across the river on the Terminal's Eads Bridge, maintains large railroad yards, and owns St. Louis's largest passenger terminal.

At one time the railroads were a vibrant industry on the

[3] Bill Boyne, article in the *Metro-East Journal*, May 5, 1946.

riverfront. Industrial, commercial, and residential land uses were shaped to meet rail demands. They employed 1,500 people and their less-than-carload freight traffic was thriving. Today the riverfront displays little of the past vibrancy. Employment is only a fraction of what it was twenty-five years ago; several freight depots have burned to the ground and not been rebuilt, and tall weeds cover tracks that were previously in use. Most trains are too long for the switching yards, and some make as many as ten passes to prepare complete shipments of freight.

Post World War II was a period of accelerated land-use obsolescence in East St. Louis. Many of the reasons were the same as those for other older American cities. Trucks replaced railroads as prominent freight transporters; one-story industrial complexes were constructed in outlying areas, resulting in the abandonment of inefficient loft buildings; increased auto ownership and highway construction took people and industry to the suburbs; and FHA, VA, and conventional financing were not readily available in older central city neighborhoods.

Very early in their histories, many major American river cities allocated prime frontage for industrial and transportation purposes. Within the past twenty-five years, most of these original uses have ceased to function efficiently, and the productivity of riverfront land has declined rapidly. Because many riverfronts are located near the concentrated office and retail functions of downtown business districts, their re-use potential is great. They lend themselves to the placement of housing, parks, and office buildings. In the case of East St. Louis, this riverfront tract is situated in the heart of the metropolitan area directly across a major river from and easily accessible to the core city of the region.

Changed technology and railroad mergers have diminished the use of riverfront land. Reflecting this lack of industrial activity, East St. Louis railroad assessments have declined steadily over the past fifteen years. Assessed valuation of Terminal Railroad Association properties in St. Clair County, most of which are in East St. Louis, dropped from $12,849,225 in 1950 to $10,877,356 in 1960. The total valuation of railroads in East St.

Louis Township alone decreased from $13,622,613 in 1967 to $13,424,285 one year later.[4]

Clearly the railroads have dominated the riverfront. They have controlled the use of land and have successfully impeded attempts to fully redevelop the present combination of wasteland and railroad trackage. Conditions affecting the riverfront have changed, however, over the last two decades. Not only has there been an increased demand from St. Louis business and financial interests to clean up the "backyard" of their downtown and riverfront renewal, but railroad needs for the riverfront have also declined considerably. Most of the railroads are no longer functionally dependent on being located on the East St. Louis riverfront.

The amount of vacant riverfront land has been steadily increasing. As far back as 1963 over 30 percent of the acreage was completely unused, another 30 percent was actual railroad right-of-way, and much of the remainder was used for expressways and roads.[5] Electric transmission lines, an interstate highway system of interchanges, and four bridges occupy portions of this potentially valuable land. Other industrial facilities occupying a small part of the riverfront are the loading docks of Peabody Coal and the Continental Grain Company elevators.

With large sections abandoned and debris-strewn, the riverfront is not an attractive site from either ground level or from 630 feet above ground in the Gateway Arch. Since the land provides little in the way of jobs, housing, usable open space, cultural facilities, or tax revenues, it is underutilized and contrasts sharply with the redevelopment on the Missouri side of the river. A study completed in February, 1970, by a Chicago-based management firm for the Terminal Railroad Association clearly established the physical and economic feasibility of moving Terminal facilities to a modern yard away from the riverfront.

In St. Louis in less than a decade, approximately $400 million has been spent in new construction on the riverfront and ad-

[4] Railroad assessment rates are fixed by the State Revenue Department; *Metro-East Journal*, January 27, 1963, and April 16, 1969.

[5] *Illinoistown*, Report to the Port Authority of Southwestern Illinois, July, 1964 (St. Louis: Fruco and Associates, 1964).

joining areas. Catalyzed by the Jefferson National Expansion Memorial of the U.S. Department of the Interior and principally by the famous Gateway Arch, the new projects include a 55,000-seat stadium, the Spanish Pavilion from the 1964 to 1965 New York World's Fair, a residential and commercial complex consisting of three twenty-eight–story apartment buildings, riverfront motels, downtown office buildings, and new riverboats and museums.

Construction of the Arch concluded many years of planning which without federal assistance would still be only on paper. At the end of 1966, after forty years, nearly $37 million had been expended on the eighty-acre Jefferson National Expansion Memorial. Approximately $13 million was spent on the Gateway Arch alone. Another $8 million is still needed to build theaters and museums in the base of the Arch and a massive grand stairway from the base to the river's edge. The local share of $2 million has already been raised through passage of a bond issue, but the federal government has not appropriated the balance.

Tourist activity has shown a marked rise since the construction of the Arch, and the image of the riverfront and downtown St. Louis has appreciably changed. Even a downward trend in assessed valuations in St. Louis was finally reversed in 1968, and construction of the Arch is certainly partially responsible.

St. Louis development has meant little to East St. Louis except that the view of the St. Louis skyline has become magnificent from the Illinois side of the river. East St. Louis has also received more plans for its riverfront—no operating programs, but plenty of discussion and meetings. New proposals and riverfront improvement committees have kindled temporary fires of excitement, and planners and development consultants have come and gone. Nothing has happened. While the St. Louis riverfront acquired a $37-million memorial and a spin-off in additional development, the East St. Louis riverfront became the home of a writhing, spaghetti-shaped, interstate highway system which displaced hundreds of families and which became a high-speed raceway through desirable riverfront property and through the city as a whole.

East St. Louis, however, was not totally disregarded. On

several occasions during construction of the Arch, the director of the Jefferson National Expansion Memorial made public statements calling for complementary efforts on the east and west banks of the Mississippi River.[6] Eero Saarinen, designer of the Gateway Arch, also expressed the feeling that the East St. Louis riverfront should have extensive plantings and a parklike environment. Funds, however, for landscaping described in a 1962 National Park Service plan were impossible to obtain, and the railroads would not agree to voluntary relocation.

East St. Louis has been unable to take advantage of its location in the metropolitan area partly because it does not have the local resources to redevelop its riverfront. Redevelopment is necessary for the long-range solution of many of the city's current financial problems. It can provide additional property tax revenues for the deficit-ridden city and school district, create employment opportunities where few presently exist, and reduce the economic and functional obsolescence of the physical facilities in the city.

Over the past twenty years (1950 to 1970), there have been numerous plans and ideas for the East St. Louis riverfront, but none have ever entered the action phase. Considerable attention and thought have been given to traffic circulation systems. Three types of roads have been considered—internal street patterns, local sightseeing roads, and connections with the Great River Road. Planners and developers alike have viewed access as a critical element in riverfront redevelopment. A former manager of the East St. Louis Chamber of Commerce gave accessibility prime importance and said that "nothing will happen unless we open the riverfront area with a convenient complex of roads and highways."[7]

Riverfront renewal plans prepared by public and private agencies have given high priority to the installation of a circulation system with an easy flow of traffic from all directions. These plans considered improved accessibility necessary to insure success of tourist attractions.[8] East-west traffic from Missouri

---

[6] Curt Mathews, article in the *Metro-East Journal*, January 20, 1963.

[7] *Ibid.*, February 17, 1963.

[8] For further details see *Illinoistown*, and *The "PACE" Plan for East St. Louis* (St. Louis: Schwarz and Van Hoefen, Architects, 1966).

needed improvement, and there were no direct ties to the Illinois cities of Granite City and Alton to the north or Cahokia and Columbia to the south.

Only three thoroughfares lead onto Front Street, a narrow, curbless road running north and south parallel to the river behind a levee which prevents periodic riverfront flooding. Front Street serves several functions. It is a connector between Terminal Railroad Association yards at the extremities of the riverfront, and it carries traffic to Continental Grain Company, which is also located on the riverfront. Two of the three streets perpendicular to Front Street are poorly maintained; the third is an extension of the Eads Bridge and is in much better condition (Eads is the only bridge with a direct route to the riverfront).

Inaccessibility and poor internal circulation have placed severe limitations on riverfront development. Perhaps these drawbacks were not as severe as the inability to purchase the land and prepare it for re-use, but they were, nevertheless, obstacles that had to be overcome. Even creation of an interstate highway with numerous interchanges on the riverfront has done nothing to improve accessibility. It merely speeds motorists through the area more quickly.

In the past decade, a series of actions has been initiated to carry out various road proposals. A June, 1963, report to the East St. Louis plan commission by the city's consultant engineer advocated creation of a highway 6.5 miles in length from Venice to Cahokia along the East St. Louis waterfront. That thoroughfare was to provide truck entry to the railroad yards adjoining Front Street, serve as a north-south vehicular route bypassing traffic in the urban centers on the Illinois side of the river, and become a sightseeing road to view the urban vista of the Mississippi against the new St. Louis skyline.[9]

Since no single road could achieve all of the purposes described in the plan, separate roadways were recommended for trucks and automobiles—the latter to be placed on the river side of the seaway. Front Street was to be reached from an arterial road rather than from city streets. Estimated cost of the project was between $18 and $25 million and the project received only

[9] *Metro-East Journal*, June 19, 1969.

limited encouragement from the state of Illinois. While the riverfront road concept was endorsed by the state traffic consultant and included in his twenty-year highway recommendations to the state, it was given low priority and not seriously considered in the state's allocation of resources.

Repeated requests for state assistance were made by the local daily newspaper. Open letters were printed from the editor of the *Metro-East Journal* to the director of the Illinois Department of Public Works and Buildings of which the Division of Highways is a part. State officials promised cooperation but their vows were never matched by money. Informed sources in East St. Louis claim that definite assurances to create the riverfront road were given publicly in 1963 by the state director of Public Works at the dedication of an interstate highway overpass in the city. Failure to get endorsement for the scenic parkway from the Illinois Division of Highways prompted an editorial in February, 1966, requesting the Governor to introduce special legislation: "Governor Otto Kerner has pledged to the Metro-East area, on appearances here, that such a road would be built. However, it is not included in the 10 years expectations of the highway district offices."[10]

It was anticipated that Mayor Alvin Fields would use his power as head of the Democratic party in St. Clair and Madison Counties to obtain state approval of the riverfront road. As state central committeeman, he and his bicounty machine have delivered three-, four-, and five-to-one majorities for their candidates with amazing regularity. Many East St. Louisans claim that Fields's strength in the Illinois Democratic party was, a few years ago, second only to that of Mayor Daley of Chicago. On March 4, 1966, Fields went to Springfield to see fellow Democrat, Governor Otto Kerner, and to try to obtain a commitment for a one-mile scenic parkway across the river from the Gateway Arch. Local officials had decided to push for a shorter road than the 6.5-mile highway originally proposed. Approximately one mile in length, this new thoroughfare was to be designed with parking spaces to take advantage of the beauty of the St. Louis riverfront and, eventually, to tie into the Great River Road sys-

[10] *Ibid.*, February 9, 1966.

tem planned to parallel the Mississippi River from Minnesota to Louisiana.

After the meeting between Fields and Kerner in March, 1966, there was supposed agreement that the city of East St. Louis would prepare plans for the scenic roadway and that the Governor would endorse them. Fields told the city council that specific dollar amounts were not promised, but that there was an initial promise for a river road. Supposedly this commitment was made independent of the Illinois legislature's obtaining additional revenues to pay for the road or granting an increase in the motor fuel tax rebate to cities. Backers of riverfront development were optimistic in the spring of 1966. Everything was falling into place. Plans had been prepared and presented to the Illinois Division of Highways. They were endorsed by the Governor, but nothing happened.[11]

Later discussions with state highway officials indicate that Kerner's support was far from unconditional. They claim that it was contingent upon additional funds from the legislature, and none were ever made available. Since the road did not fit into the traffic generation criteria of the Division of Highways, it was given a low rating and considered to have primarily recreational value.[12]

In the past decade, circulation planning for the East St. Louis riverfront has been predicated on the desire of a tie-in with the Great River Road system. To do so would have made the riverfront accessible to automobile traffic moving parallel to the Mississippi River. This system which seemed so desirable to potential developers of riverfront museums, hotels, and other tourist facilities had the following rationale and purpose:

> The Great River Road was conceived originally by the Mississippi River Parkway Planning Commission . . . as a national parkway to be developed in the pattern of the Blue Ridge Parkway . . . and the Natchez Trace Parkway. . . .

[11] *Ibid.*, March 3 and March 7, 1966.
[12] Illinois State Division of Highways, interview with Robert Kronst, District Engineer, and Edwin R. Ailes, Assistant District Engineer, Belleville, Illinois, June 2, 1969.

The Blue Ridge and Natchez Trace Parkways are examples of the rural type of national parkway and are essentially elongated parks. The lands necessary are acquired by the respective states and given to the United States which, through the National Park Service, then constructs, maintains, and administers the roadways and other facilities for public use. . . . Since national parkways are essentially recreational developments, all commercial traffic is excluded.

The Congress of the United States in the act of August 24, 1949 (Public Law 262 81st Congress) instructed the Bureau of Public Roads, U.S. Department of Commerce; and the National Park Service, U.S. Department of the Interior; to survey and study the possibility of developing a national parkway generally following the course of the Mississippi River.[13]

When the study that was authorized by the 1949 enabling legislation was published in November, 1951, it recommended against the establishment of a new federal highway in favor of the creation of a state-by-state system. Reasons for this were prohibitive costs, duplication of existing routes, utilization of scenic locations, and difficulties of federal administration. Whenever possible, existing highways would be used in each state. Roads would be upgraded to provide scenic vistas and, if necessary, new sections would be constructed under federal-state highway funding ratios. No special funds were provided by Congress except for two commitments—of $250,000 each—for planning, coordination, and advisory services to states participating in the Great River Road system.

The roadway was to become a scenic corridor with access control, wide rights-of-way, and scenic easements without formal federal regulation. Selection of the highways included in the system was left entirely up to the states. Today, the road varies in quality, in width, and in designation. (Some portions are marked temporary and others permanent.) Construction of

---

[13] Wallace A. Johnson and J. L. Obenschain, *Great River Road, Illinois— Recommendations for Land Acquisition, Scenic Easement and Control of Access for a Portion of the Great River Road in the State of Illinois—Part II, East Hannibal to Kentucky Border* (Washington, D.C.: U.S. Department of Commerce, Bureau of Public Roads, 1966), pp. 1–4.

new portions is based largely on traffic service needs as defined by individual states under the 50-50 federal-state funding ratio. Since previously built roads are used in the system, it is common to be unable to view the river and, in some cases, to be as far as five miles away from it.

East St. Louis planning dreams were for a 6.5-mile waterfront highway from Venice to Cahokia which would be a part of the Great River Road system. Financial aid from the state was obviously needed and state efforts at Alton, Illinois (twenty miles north), were cited as a precedent for this support. It was at Alton, and for a distance of fourteen miles north to Grafton, that a magnificent highway and an exciting visual experience were created as part of the Great River Road system. Flanked on one side by the Mississippi River and on the other by steep bluffs, the first portion of the highway was constructed during the Depression as a federally assisted work project to create employment. State fiscal limitations necessitated completion of the remainder over a phased period with successive extensions made in 1958, 1963, and 1965.[14]

As the St. Louis waterfront was developed and the view from East St. Louis improved, the idea for a shortened version of the Alton road became very enticing. However, East St. Louis had no funds to finance either the Venice-to-Cahokia highway or the one-mile scenic road along the riverfront, so it turned to the state for help, and the state never responded. Though inclusion of the Venice-to-Cahokia highway as part of the Great River Road system was endorsed by the state's highway consultant in 1964, it was never put on the state highway plan. Unless roads are part of this plan, they cannot be constructed with state and federal funds. Except for the interstate system, no state or federal route along the East St. Louis riverfront has ever received official approval.

Local proponents of the roadway believed that riverfront development was contingent upon accessibility and circulation. They wanted the 6.5-mile road, or at the very minimum, a one-mile scenic roadway. This project had been endorsed by local government officials and financial leaders, the state consultant,

[14] Illinois State Division of Highways, interview.

the National Park Service, and the Bureau of Public Roads. However, the state assigned the road a low rating in relation to its overall needs and limited funds. State highway officials estimated that the longer road would cost $30 million—a figure four times greater than the annual budget for new construction and road modernization in the eleven-county area included in District 8 of the Illinois Division of Highways.

Future state funding seems doubtful. Repeated attempts to get support from the state have all been unsuccessful. At a meeting to discuss the riverfront in East St. Louis on February 7, 1969, Robert Kronst, district highway engineer, was pessimistic about the road being constructed within ten years. He had no idea where the money would come from.

The National Museum of Transport

Periods of optimism and pessimism have characterized East St. Louis riverfront history. One of the high periods came in 1962 and lasted for over three years. At that time, the National Museum of Transport in Kirkwood, Missouri, wanted to relocate on the riverfront.[15]

Founded in 1944 when the Missouri Pacific Railroad abandoned acreage near Barrett Station Road, the museum's leader and curator from its inception has been Dr. John Payne Roberts. In 1946 he played a major part in the incorporation of the museum's operating agency, the St. Louis Railway Historical Society. He was also the driving force in building attendance to 65,000 in 1969, in expanding the original site from five to forty acres, and in accumulating the largest and most comprehensive public collection of historic railroad equipment in the country. With support from bankers, railroad executives, industrialists, and labor officials, this nonprofit enterprise grew from one horsecar to over 300 exhibits. Much of the credit belongs to Dr. Roberts, whose home adjoins the museum grounds and who, as an army physician from 1946 to 1948, commuted weekly from a base 200 miles away to supervise and direct the museum.

[15] Kirkwood was one of St. Louis's early suburbs incorporated in 1865. Though approximately fifteen miles west of downtown St. Louis, it was originally connected by commuter rail service.

As the number of exhibits increased, plans were made to expand museum facilities. In 1960 a proposal was made to build eight buildings on the present site at a cost of $5-million. Structures were to be used not only for historic equipment but also for a library and classrooms. Leaders of the museum wanted to create a repository for transportation research in addition to their tourist exhibits. One year later, plans were changed and it was decided to seek a more accessible site than the one in Kirkwood, which was on a barren wooded area served only by a narrow road with no public transportation. A tract of land was selected adjacent to the Jefferson National Expansion Memorial. It was north of the Eads Bridge on the St. Louis side of the Mississippi River. This site seemed particularly appropriate when the National Park Service of the Department of the Interior announced in 1961 that two planned transportation museums within the memorial might be eliminated due to lack of funds.[16]

At the same time, the city of St. Louis was considering a bond issue referendum for a series of public improvement projects. About fifty St. Louis civic leaders petitioned the project screening committee to include in the bond issue funds to purchase a riverfront site for the museum. Dr. Roberts pushed for the move to the St. Louis riverfront, claiming that the downtown site would draw 1,000,000 people annually. He saw the move as essential if the museum were to stay in St. Louis—especially since other cities were showing considerable interest in helping the museum relocate.[17] His position was endorsed by the largest local newspaper, the *St. Louis Post-Dispatch*.

When Mayor Raymond Tucker submitted recommendations to the citizens' bond issue committee for study and review, one of the items was $1 million to buy land for the museum and erect at least one building in the area between Eads Bridge and Carr Street, Wharf to Third—a redevelopment area known as Laclede's Landing. The citizen committee affirmed the mayor's action; ultimately the board of estimate and apportionment, which consists of the mayor, the president of the board of aldermen, and the city comptroller, decided to include the museum

[16] *St. Louis Post-Dispatch*, May 7, 1961.
[17] *Ibid.*, January 8, 1961, and editorial July 28, 1961.

as one of eleven proposals in a January 23, 1962, referendum. However, when the total bond issue package of $26,566,000 was completed, the original $1 million for the museum was reduced to $100,000. This new figure was to be used as an initial investment for seed money, development cost, and partial moving expense. It was expected that a much larger private and public investment program would be needed at a later date.

Only one item was approved in the bond issue election; the museum finished fourth from last, obtaining a 60 percent positive vote (two-thirds was needed for passage). Resubmission of items to the voters a few months later again resulted in rejection for the museum, although approval increased 5 percentage points. Only a few items were defeated. After the election, museum directors still felt that their institution should be located near the Gateway Arch due to the historical ties between transportation and the Jefferson National Expansion Memorial. Far from being discouraged, they interpreted the 65 percent approbation as somewhat of an endorsement of the project by the people of St. Louis, even though no funds were forthcoming.

Encouraged by the interest generated in the museum, not only in St. Louis, but also on a metropolitan basis, and convinced of the desirability of a location near the Gateway Arch, the museum directors were drawn to the other side of the river with its large amounts of vacant and underutilized land. In addition there was a governmental vehicle available in East St. Louis ready to assist the museum in relocation. This state-empowered body, the Southwest Regional Port District, was created on August 9, 1961, to promote industrial, commercial, transportation, and recreation activities and facilities in Canteen, Centreville, East St. Louis, Stites, and Sugar Loaf Townships of St. Clair County.[18]

Under its enabling legislation, the board of the Port District was appointed by the governor and made politically independent. It was given the power of eminent domain, the capacity to issue tax-free revenue bonds, and even the ability to issue general obligation bonds to be repaid through assessments lev-

[18] *Illinois, Revised Statutes, State Bar Association Edition* (1967), I, Ch. 19, Sec. 453, p. 495.

ied on real property with approval of the electorate.[19] If asked for, however, approval would be extremely unlikely because the residents of the area included in the Port District have extremely low incomes and are not likely to tax themselves voluntarily.

The Southwest Regional Port District appeared to be an ideal vehicle for the National Museum of Transport. It had the power to condemn land, except in the case of railroad property where prior approval from the Illinois Commerce Commission was needed. Through revenue bond funding, the district could purchase and develop tracts of land and construct buildings for lease to the museum. Once financial feasibility of the revenue bonds was established, a leasehold between the district and the museum could be used as the basis for bond amortization. Lease payments would come from admissions. Donations, grants, and other available museum resources would then be available to purchase or renovate equipment. As the redevelopment agency for the museum, the district had the responsibility for getting control of the riverfront from the railroads by seeking permission of the Illinois Commerce Commission and then using its power of eminent domain for condemnation.

Daily newspapers on both sides of the river endorsed the National Museum of Transport move to East St. Louis. It was viewed by the *Metro-East Journal* as an "incentive for a much-needed sprucing up of the East St. Louis riverfront"[20] and as the initial step toward the development of a tourist center. Placement of the museum was seen as a real opportunity to change the community image and improve the local economy. At a later date George McCue, design critic of the *St. Louis Post-Dispatch*, extolled the advantages of the Illinois site: "It would be hard to imagine a location more admirably suited to the display of industrial conveyances and communications than the one now about to be developed, nor one that could offer a more viable staging. The riverfront tract is bounded by the Mississippi River, first transportation route to this region, by international highways, a railroad line and four bridges. All of these contribute to

---

[19] Power to issue revenue bonds for a museum was granted to the Port District by the Illinois legislature in August, 1963.

[20] Curt Mathews, *Metro-East Journal*, June 3, 1962.

the spectacle of transportation-in-being to the scene, the Today, as against the museum's recapitulations of Yesterday."[21]

In August, 1965, the East St. Louis Chamber of Commerce launched a campaign to raise $25,000 for a museum office in East St. Louis. Eventually, a major portion of the money was obtained and a fulltime director was hired—a past mayor of Dupo, Illinois, and a board member of the Southwest Regional Port District. The city, too, prepared for the coming of the transportation exhibits. In the beginning of 1966 rezoning of the riverfront was approved by the city council as an amendment to the zoning ordinance. By this action, museums, libraries, and community centers were allowed in heavy and medium manufacturing and industrial zones, the zoning classification of the riverfront.

It was obvious in 1965 that the railroads had no intention of voluntarily relinquishing land for such noneconomic uses as an educational institution, even though changing transportation techniques had made the riverfront yards inefficient and obsolete. Initial museum requirements were for approximately twenty acres with five times as much acreage planned for the future. Battlelines were drawn to wrest riverfront lands from the railroads, which had proved to be a tough foe. Initial strategy was for the Southwest Regional Port District to acquire twenty-two acres located on an axis with the Gateway Arch. This land was owned by the Illinois Central Railroad and was directly east of Continental Grain's elevators.[22] After acquisition and site preparation, the Port District was to construct facilities and lease them back to the National Museum of Transport.

To obtain the acreage without railroad agreement required condemnation by the Port District with prior approval of the Illinois Commerce Commission. Illinois Central Railroad opposed this action, claiming that it wanted to place industry there which would increase rail revenues. Even with reduced

[21] George McCue, St. Louis Post-Dispatch, February 13, 1966.

[22] Urban designers such as Joseph Passonneau have expressed opinions that Continental Grain Company elevators and Peabody Coal Company loading docks now on the riverfront could be compatible with future development. They felt that the structures were interesting and historically related to American industry and rail and river transportation systems.

rail activity and the functional obsolescence of the riverfront, railroad attorneys contended that there were still industrial inquiries for the land. A *St. Louis Post-Dispatch* editorial dated September 11, 1965, attacked the railroad position, pointing out that although the Illinois Central had owned the land since 1907 it had never attempted development. In fact, the land had been used as a city dump until it was closed due to numerous complaints.

While the Illinois Commerce Commission hearings were underway, four of the twenty-two acres desired by the Port District were sold by the Illinois Central Railroad to Continental Grain Company. In testimony before the commission on September 24, 1965, Port District attorneys conceded that there was still ample space to start the museum.[23] At the same time, the *Metro-East Journal* implored the railroad to recognize the changing importance of the riverfront which had become "the front yard of a great national park" and which was no longer suitable for industrial development.[24]

Optimistic about the outcome of the hearings, the Port District began negotiations to acquire other riverfront land from the Gulf, Mobile and Ohio Railroad and the Terminal Railroad Association. Reactions from these two railroads were favorable, and riverfront development seemed imminent.

After two hearings before the Commerce Commission, the Illinois Central still refused to concede rights to the land. A request from the Jefferson National Expansion Memorial Association (an influential St. Louis group which sponsored creation of the Gateway Arch) to release the land was rejected. Two months after the second hearing in January, 1966, the Illinois Commerce Commission granted permission to the Southwest Regional Port District to acquire approximately eighteen acres from the Illinois Central Railroad with the authorization extending for a two-year period.

With commission approval, the Port District was able to avoid litigation. Instead of condemnation, a contract was negotiated

---

[23] *Metro-East Journal*, September 26, 1965; *St. Louis Post-Dispatch*, October 17, 1965.
[24] *Metro-East Journal*, editorial, November 14, 1965.

within a few months to transfer the land for approximately $11,000 per acre. Both parties ultimately signed the two-year option agreement in March, 1967. Based on the pact with Illinois Central and a positive response from the Gulf, Mobile and Ohio to the Port District's offer to buy additional tracts, the renewal process seemed to be definitely in motion. A nationally known architectural firm was selected by the museum to prepare a design concept for the first eighteen acres and a total development approach for the larger area of surrounding riverfront land. The East St. Louis city council budgeted $100,000 from anticipated motor fuel tax rebates from the state for improved accessibility to the museum site.

Adversity struck in mid-1966 when Dr. Roberts and several other board members began to express grave misgivings about moving the National Museum of Transport to East St. Louis. Roberts was in favor of leaving Kirkwood, but he wanted to stay on the Missouri side of the river, claiming that: (1) the East St. Louis riverfront had poor accessibility which had not been improved by the building of an interstate highway through the area, (2) the unattractive neighborhoods surrounding the museum would remain for many years and deter prospective patrons, and (3) funding through revenue bond issues would be inadequate for the museum needs.[25]

With Roberts's encouragement, oppposition to the East St. Louis move grew. He argued that if the museum were built, it would be an unsupported institution standing alone on the 400-acre riverfront. Total renewal of the area seemed too far in the future, and creation of an extension to the Jefferson National Expansion Memorial only a wish and an unsupported promise. Without an upgrading of the entire riverfront and adjoining neighborhoods, the museum's failure would be assured. Rather than improving East St. Louis, the museum would itself be pulled down by the hopeless blight. Furthermore, faced with isolation from other attractions, opponents of East St. Louis saw few prospects for aid if revenues did not meet expenses. Funds could not be raised locally or in surrounding Illinois areas, and Missourians were not responsive to an east side project. It was

[25] *St. Louis Post-Dispatch*, July 1 and July 10, 1966.

also contended that revenue bonds were a poor substitute for taxes and grants in financing educational institutions, and that the character of the museum would be changed by an emphasis on admissions.[26] Strong arguments had been advanced to fight the move to East St. Louis.

One issue in the controversy which erupted over the proposed move from Kirkwood was a report prepared by Port District consultants to substantiate the economic feasibility of revenue bonds as a means of museum support. Results of the study predicted first-year attendance of 450,000 at the East St. Louis site with net revenues of $155,000, thus providing economic justification for the issuance of $1 million in revenue bonds. East St. Louis proponents on the museum board hailed the findings as validating their actions, while Dr. Roberts and his supporters felt that $1 million was woefully inadequate. At least double that amount was necessary for land purchase, site preparation, fencing, utilities, relocation of displays, and initial construction. Roberts maintained that more than $600,000 would be needed just to fill the site, which was ten feet below surrounding grade at some points.[27]

On July 19, 1966, the museum board affirmed the decision to relocate to East St. Louis by a 10 to 2 majority—Roberts and another member dissenting. Roberts offered to resign but the board refused his resignation. Newspaper accounts gave the impression that, after the vote, consensus had been reached and that the entire board accepted the majority decision and was prepared to implement it. Six weeks later, however, Roberts called for a return of equipment stored in East St. Louis railroad yards, citing excessive vandalism as his reason. At the same time, ten members of the National Museum of Transport filed suit against the officers and directors of the museum.[28] Legally the suit was designed to compel an election of directors. It was alleged that the board was illegal because the time period since

[26] "Position Paper on the Move of the National Museum of Transport to East St. Louis," unpublished pamphlet.

[27] St. Louis Post-Dispatch, July 17, 1966.

[28] There were twenty-six directors and approximately 300 members of the museum in 1966.

the last election had been excessive. Its purpose in reality was to block the move to East St. Louis.

Rival factions split into two boards of directors—each meeting separately. One group, headed by a prominent St. Louis attorney, Malcolm Martin, filed a petition in court to affirm its election and to facilitate the move to East St. Louis. At the meeting of the group led by Dr. Roberts, it was voted to confiscate the museum's bank account, disavow the debts of the other board, move sixteen exhibits from East St. Louis, and fire the accountants who were paying the salary of the director in his East St. Louis office. After suits and countersuits were filed by the two groups, a court ruling in April, 1967, affirmed the Martin faction as the board of directors but said there could be no further relocation until the articles of incorporation ceased to show the museum as located in Kirkwood.[29]

In the fall of 1967, the quarrel broke out again. This time it concerned the slate of directors sent to members for an October 6, 1967, election of the board. Roberts claimed that a promise of equal representation on the slate had been broken. He maintained that his group was not being permitted to participate adequately and sent a letter to all museum members urging them to vote against thirteen of the sixteen candidates. When the ballots were compiled, only Roberts and his two supporters had received the majority of votes necessary for election. The other thirteen from the original slate had been rejected. Negotiations between the two groups became necessary, but Roberts was clearly in control when a new board was formed.

First order of business for the new board was to cancel the move to East St. Louis and file legal action to remove sixteen pieces of equipment from the Alton and Southern Yards located there. Subsequent legal rulings strengthened control by the Roberts board and effectively eliminated any possibility of having the National Museum of Transport on the East St. Louis riverfront.

Three years later the museum is still located in Kirkwood. Attendance has increased by about 6,000 patrons over the 1968

[29] *St. Louis Post-Dispatch*, April, 1967.

figure of 59,095; permanent display housing has been constructed; low ground has been filled; and parking areas have
been paved. Nothing has changed on the East St. Louis riverfront except the addition of another set of high voltage towers
and completion of portions of the interstate highway. There has
been no building, no urban renewal, and no extension of the
Jefferson National Expansion Memorial.

No title to land ownership has as yet been transferred as a
result of museum events, except for the few acres used for the
expansion of Continental Grain Company. A two-year option
granted by Illinois Central Railroad to the Southwest Regional
Port District expired and was renewed for three additional years.
There has been talk of a science and industry museum on the
riverfront, and the Port District has been working with a group
of St. Louis businessmen and financiers, headed by Malcolm
Martin. (Some of these men were board members of the defeated Transport Museum faction.) According to Port District
officials, negotiations are still underway with the Gulf, Mobile,
and Ohio for an additional ten acres, and assurances of first call
have been granted on New York Central riverfront properties.[30]

The National Museum of Transport would have been a valuable asset to the East St. Louis riverfront, but it could not stand
alone there. It had to be part of an overall renewal program that
included facilities for housing, employment, education, and recreation. To date it has been impossible to implement any such
plans—large or small.

Other Redevelopment Planning

In 1963, when there was optimism about East St. Louis redevelopment, two subsidiary enterprises of one of the largest and
oldest construction companies in St. Louis (Fruin-Colnon Contracting Company) became interested in promoting riverfront
renewal. Encouraged by officials of the Southwest Regional
Port District, Fruco Realty Company (the investment part of
the construction firm) assessed the feasibility of a riverfront

[30] James Reed, interview, General Manager, East St. Louis Chamber of
Commerce, June 17, 1969.

motel. Their accountants estimated potential profits; Fruco and Associates (another subsidiary) prepared preliminary design and engineering plans; and Fruin-Colnon (the parent company) figured project costs.[31]

Results were a design plan called "Gateway Marina City" which advocated placing a 288-room hotel and marina directly on the riverfront. It was to be located just south of the historic Eads Bridge between the levee wall and the riverfront. Access to the hotel was provided through spans of the bridge. Special features of the plan included the following:

> Located directly on the riverbank, Gateway Marina City returns to the historical river for its charm. A pleasure boat pier will be a part of the first phase of the development. Eventually, a complete marina basin to accommodate several hundred boats will be built.... In addition to the privately owned boats, which will be berthed at Gateway Marina City, charter boats will afford the visitor with a leisurely water tour of the bustling city complex. A passenger ferry boat will shuttle visitors across to the grand stair of the "Gateway to the West" Arch.[32]

Maximum advantage was to be derived from scenic vistas of the river and of the St. Louis skyline. Construction was to be over the river, which meant negotiation of a lease with the Terminal Railroad Association.

Included in "Gateway Marina City" were sketches of the proposed development and an economic study which projected profitability at a 65 percent occupancy level. Preliminary endorsement of the project was given by the United States Corps of Engineers and by the Southwest Regional Port District, which has development control over the riverfront and is empowered to see that projects do not detract from transportation and promotional uses of the river.[33]

According to the completed report and to plan sponsors, the

[31] Bernard H. Poelker, interview, Fruco and Associates, Inc., St. Louis, July 2, 1969.
[32] *Gateway Marina City, East St. Louis, Illinois* (St. Louis: Fruco Realty Co., 1963).
[33] Enabling legislation for the Southwest Regional Port District is found in *Illinois, Revised Statutes, State Bar Association Edition* (1963), 1, Ch. 19, Sec. 451–488.

feasibility of the hotel and marina was dependent on good accessibility from all directions. Success of the project was particularly related to construction of the 6.5-mile thoroughfare as part of the Great River Road system. Without the new road, tourist accessibility to the riverfront would be inadequate.[34] Acting as project promoter, Fruco Realty encountered reluctance from large financial investors to loan money or to take an equity position in the project, especially when the seeming impossibility of an extension of the Great River Road through the riverfront became apparent. Fruco had no desire to have the only development on the East St. Louis riverfront, wanting instead to be part of a larger comprehensive scheme for the area.[35] This same fear of being isolated from other attractions was voiced by opponents of the National Museum of Transport move. When it became obvious that there would be no state-sponsored riverfront highway and when financing sources dried up because investors shied away from the East St. Louis riverfront and because of a tight money market, the dream of "Gateway Marina City" died.

During the period when the hotel and marina idea was still very much alive, Fruco and Associates, designers and engineers, also became attracted to the riverfront. They expanded the limited design concept of "Gateway Marina City" into a development plan for the entire riverfront and called it "Illinoistown." Like Fruco Realty, Fruco and Associates foresaw large profits in riverfront development in 1963 to 1964. Neither company was ever hired by the Southwest Regional Port District, though both were encouraged by Port District officials. Money expended on riverfront planning ($50,000) was promotional. It was anticipated that profits from real estate development and construction as well as from site preparation studies would far exceed original planning costs.[36]

Concepts underlying "Illinoistown" were broader than and different from those of "Gateway Marina City." In fact, different groups of planners and designers worked on the two schemes.

[34] George Washnis, interview, and James Reed, interview, July 1, 1969.
[35] Bernard H. Poelker, interview.
[36] Ibid.

Education and recreation were the dominant themes of "Illinois-town." Such activities as "the National Museum of Transport, aquarium, golf course, art museum, residential town houses, river museum, educational complex, museum of science and industry, riverfront activities, industrial display areas, and a commercial-recreational development of theatres, restaurants, bars and active physical sports" were projected for the area.[37]

"Illinoistown" traced the historical significance of the East St. Louis area, pointing out the possibilities of attracting tourists on both short trips and two-week vacations. Content of the plan was generalized, and sketches displayed land-use relationships for a wide range of activities, including lagoons, vocational and junior colleges, hotels, and marinas. Another section of the report described the development procedures necessary to implement "Illinoistown." Procedures to implement the plan were suggestive rather than definitive, and based on land acquisition with federal assistance.

Both "Gateway Marina City" and "Illinoistown" were presented to city officials, who received them enthusiastically. These plans were intended to bring about public and private resource allocations. Five years later, it is difficult to find even one copy of either plan. When no funds came, nothing happened. Planning without predetermined resources is a common phenomenon in East St. Louis and so is the uniform failure of such plans.

Shortly thereafter, in June, 1965, a federal grant from the Area Redevelopment Administration, now called the Economic Development Administration, was made to Checchi and Company to examine the tourism potential of the East St. Louis riverfront.[38] That Washington, D.C., consulting firm received $13,750 to produce a feasibility study and a development concept for three riverfront projects—a museum, a civic-convention center, and a motor hotel. According to the study, labeled "The Future of Tourism in East St. Louis," the riverfront's potential was somewhere in between the single project of the National Museum of Transport and the broad approach of "Illinoistown." Checchi's report was intended to justify the economic feasibility

[37] *Illinoistown.*
[38] *Metro-East Journal,* June 20 and June 21, 1965.

of the three tourism projects and to suggest the Southwest Regional Port District as the redevelopment agency.[39] It did both, and it also placed the Port District in a position to issue revenue bonds through the feasibility determination. Checchi proposed combining the National Museum of Transport, a 3,000-seat, 40,000-square foot convention center, and a luxury 300-room motor hotel into one riverfront project. This action would permit anticipated profits of the hotel and museum to cover expected convention center losses and create a large enough impact on the riverfront to catalyze additional construction.

Checchi and Company examined the existing tourist industry in the St. Louis region and concluded that East St. Louis could derive a share of tourism through these three projects. Acreage requirements and preliminary site drawings were included in the study, along with illustrations of how the development would look on an eighty-acre site. Projections of revenue and expenditures for the motel, museum, and convention center were the basis of Checchi's recommendations that financing could come from a combination of revenue bonds and equity capital. The Port District was to issue $9,385,000 in revenue bonds, and an equity position of $3,615,000 was to be raised from private individuals, industry, and grants from public agencies such as the Department of Housing and Urban Development and the state of Illinois. Of the $13-million total cost, $9.4 million was direct project cost, $2 million in public area development, and $1.6 million in land cost.[40]

Though the Checchi report named the Port District as the logical agency to control and manage the entire project, it discussed briefly the alternative possibility of a nonprofit corporation to "amalgamate the interests of public and quasi-public agencies, private organizations and individuals in expediting common desires for maximum economic and social benefits from the riverfront."[41] The purpose of the nonprofit corporation was to coordinate the activities of many diverse groups and handle the input of funds from public and private sources. This type of

[39] *The Future of Tourism in East St. Louis* (*Including Three Feasibility Studies*) (Washington, D.C.: Checchi and Co., August, 1966), p. 22.
[40] *Ibid.*, p. 138.
[41] *Ibid.*, pp. 139–140.

body was created in 1969. Like all other riverfront organizations, it has been unable to mobilize sufficient resources to redevelop the area.

While the three projects recommended for the riverfront were nontaxable, they were intended to generate additional development which would in turn enhance the tax base of the city and its related special districts. To insure compatibility of all waterfront redevelopment, Checchi recommended that a master plan be prepared for the entire area that would include appropriate land-use control and would reflect community consensus. Within six months after the release of Checchi's study, the master plan was produced by another nongovernmental riverfront planning group. Yet in 1966, when the museum and the river road became impossible dreams, they were joined by the proposals found in "The Future of Tourism in East St. Louis." Today, few remember the purpose of the Checchi study or who authorized the expenditure of funds for this planning.

In October, 1965, a short time after the Checchi report was commissioned, a group of East St. Louis financiers, businessmen, and governmental leaders organized, pooled some money, and hired a consultant, Arthur Klein, whose purpose was to prepare and carry out a master plan for the downtown and riverfront areas. In a letter to one of the originators of the group, the consultant described his function as follows: "To simply express the scope of services and capacity of the Consultant, one should view him as the one who creates the Overall Master Plan which best achieves the objectives of the sponsor. Once approved by the sponsor the plan fragmentizes, criterions become established, and the Consultant's responsibility is to coagulate, expedite, analyze and control this plan in the best interests of the sponsor until concretized and these critiques are translated into reality."[42]

Eager for physical change and an enhanced tax base, the East St. Louis interests retained the consultant at $2,000 per month. Other positions in the St. Louis area held by Klein at that time included being fulltime director of a trade-union–sponsored

<hr />

[42] "PACE File," papers and letters from the East St. Louis Planning Commission, 1965–69, September 15, 1965.

housing project for the elderly and fee consultant to nonprofit and profit developmental groups involved in building federally assisted residential and medical facilities. He was hired to break through the federal red tape and expedite programs, to create a community consensus for renewal, and to program major land-use changes in the central business district and riverfront. One of his first actions was to change the name of his sponsoring group from the East St. Louis Central Business District Improvement, Inc., to PACE (Progress and Action by Citizens Efforts). Membership on the general board of the organization was expanded to fifty people, with a cross section of bankers, businessmen, residents, labor leaders, ministers, and educators. Though 20 percent were Black, the board was establishment-oriented and the controlling elite, the executive board, was completely dominated by business and financial interests.

PACE's executive board was composed of those with sizable financial investments in East St. Louis, whose intent was to revitalize a dying retail center and utilize the riverfront to create added commercial sales, a tourist business, and a solvent local government. Very quickly, however, the emphasis of PACE was expanded into a ten-year development program which included the elimination of all East St. Louis slums.[43] This pronouncement was made at the "Hands Across the River" meeting, and called for over 300 governmental and civic leaders from both sides of the Mississippi. It was held in East St. Louis in early 1966 to promote bistate cooperation and to announce PACE's role in changing the future of East St. Louis.

Included in the ten-year project was "utilization of dormant urban renewal land" within six months by creating 750 housing units and commercial facilities on the long-vacant thirty acres. Over 5,000 new housing units were to be created in neighborhoods adjoining the CBD. Along with new housing, there was to be a new downtown and riverfront.[44] These immodest goals were to be achieved through the use of all available federal, local, and state resources.

[43] St. Louis Post-Dispatch, January 14, 1966.
[44] Ibid.

Widespread acclaim followed the January, 1966, meeting. Mayors of both East St. Louis and St. Louis endorsed the idea. Genuine enthusiasm and optimism were indicated in a *Metro-East Journal* quote from the president of the East St. Louis Chamber of Commerce: "It's a realistic plan. For the first time in my memory, it seems that East St. Louis is really beginning to move forward. I think we have quit marking time. For too long we have been talking, without results. This time, we'll see the ball rolling within 180 days."[45] In the newspaper additional comments were attributed to the head of Community Progress, Incorporated (CPI), organization of East St. Louis neighborhood associations: "It is a very impressive development. I would like to commend the Chamber of Commerce and private enterprise for undertaking such a major and much needed project. I'm sure the community is ready to offer its support in any way possible."[46]

Soon after the meeting, PACE hired two professional firms to work under the supervision of the consultant. Both of the firms were well known, one in urban planning and the other in architecture. Their $10,000 contract called for preparation of a plan which would point out East St. Louis renewal opportunities to developers, citizens, federal officials, and state agencies. The principal partner in the architectural firm had traveled this route before and had been instrumental in the rebirth of the St. Louis waterfront, both as a designer of riverfront projects and as an active leader of the St. Louis plan commission. He had seen how the massive input of federal and local resources had combined with planning and design to build the Arch and stadium and bring several hundred million dollars in construction to the Missouri side of the Mississippi River.

East St. Louis wanted to duplicate this success. PACE would become a counterpart to St. Louis's Civic Progress, Incorporated —a group of "shakers and movers" from the business and industrial community who pushed and supported St. Louis riverfront rebirth. Through the technical efforts of the development

---

[45] *Metro-East Journal,* January 23, 1966.
[46] *Ibid.*

consultant, the architects, and the planners, an inspiration was
to be produced which would emulate the success of Edward
Logue in New Haven or the Golden Triangle in Pittsburgh.

A planning committee was formed to provide physical, social,
and economic data. This group included the PACE consultant,
architect, and planner, the city planner, the administrative assistant to the mayor, the city engineer, and the director of a
Southern Illinois University program which was under contract with the city for planning and renewal services. Approximately six meetings were held; at each, research and opinions
were provided to PACE's technicians by city and university
staff. While technical efforts were proceeding, the PACE organization was concerned with how to dispose of urban renewal
land bordering on the CBD and how to build hotels and commercial facilities within the district. Discussions were held with
officials of the railroads and the National Museum of Transport
to coordinate activities, and several thousand dollars were spent
to advertise that PACE was "on the move."

During 1966 PACE met often. They sponsored a training
course in sales management and advanced approximately $1,000
to pay for title searches to Fred Teer's nonprofit, sixty-unit housing project federally assisted under the 221 (d) (3) program
(a federal low-cost housing program under 1968 legislation).
Urban renewal and FHA officials spoke before PACE, and the
group discussed issues and policies of local government to find
methods of expediting development. No physical change in the
community took place—no new houses were started, no new
jobs were created, and the blight spiral was not arrested, but a
plan was produced. In the process of its preparation, discussions
were held with leaders in the political, economic, religious, and
social worlds of East St. Louis. Though ideas from these groups
were incorporated into the plan, the underlying concepts for the
riverfront were decided upon by the PACE planners and architects. It was a design-oriented plan aimed at cleaning up the
backyard of St. Louis and improving the view from the Gateway
Arch; at changing the image of East St. Louis as a low-income,
vice-ridden, politically corrupt, and labor-plagued community;

and at enhancing the property tax base of the city and school district.

On December 1, 1966, the plan was presented to the PACE general and executive board members and two weeks later to approximately 200 East St. Louis area business, governmental, and citizen representatives. Format for the physical proposals was a series of drawings, schematic land-use maps, and renderings superimposed on aerial photographs. Similar procedures had been used to generate interest in the St. Louis riverfront several decades before. Graphics were placed on matted boards of varying sizes that could easily be displayed in prominent places. They were also reduced in size to 8 1/2 x 11-inch black and white reproductions and, along with press releases, bound together as the formal PACE plan. Reproductions and press releases were only to serve as an interim report, with a more detailed document to be prepared later. When no further funds were allocated by PACE, however, the interim report became the final product.

The PACE plan was called an "imagineering study" by its creators and focused on about 60 percent of East St. Louis— specifically the riverfront, the CBD, the central city, and the south end.[47] Included were proposed new land uses for the entire city based on changed road and rail circulation patterns and extensive use of green belts. A new city within a city of 30,000 people was envisioned for the riverfront, with as many as 10,000 dwellings of various types and choices. Housing units ranged from twenty-story high-rise buildings to two- and three-story garden-type units. Financing mechanisms were to include conventional methods, federally assisted FHA programs, and condominiums. No public housing was slated for the riverfront. Planning was predicated on moderate-to-higher income families and individuals moving into the area. In particular, prospective residents were sought who would place minimum demands on the tax base and bring purchasing power to the community.

Other facilities were also to be located on the riverfront. Commercial construction was to serve not only the residents but also

[47] The central city and south end are residential neighborhoods with extensive blight. Both are now part of the Model City area.

a projected tourist trade. Tourists were expected to stay at two large motor hotels, to travel over a scenic river road, and to visit both the National Museum of Transport and the eastern extension of the Jefferson National Expansion Memorial—all planned by PACE for the riverfront.

PACE's recommended roadway was to become a part of the Great River Road system. Forty-five acres were allocated to the east side extension of the Jefferson National Expansion Memorial, twenty-five of them for an "overlook park." On an axis with the Gateway Arch the park was to provide cultural displays and scenic vistas of the river and the St. Louis skyline. At the eastern portion of the "overlook park" and on the same axis was to be the fifty-acre National Museum of Transport. Two hundred riverfront acres were to be devoted to a balanced in-town residential community with churches, schools, and the type of shopping and open-space amenities found in cosmopolitan urban areas. PACE press releases estimated that the residential construction would total over $200 million and that "several redevelopers of national reputation have expressed interest and are awaiting release of the plans."[48]

Again the plaudits came to PACE and its consultants, not only for their creativity on the riverfront, but also for their planned change of the entire community. New land uses were recommended for East St. Louis—educational complexes, a retail automotive distribution center, and an industrial research park. Residential neighborhoods were to be rebuilt and extensive green belts used to separate incompatible activities. Inadequate schools, substandard housing, and obsolete land uses, such as the railroads, were eliminated in the PACE plans for a reborn East St. Louis.

St. Louis newspapers praised the city-within-a-city concept of the riverfront. It was called "breathtaking" by the *Globe-Democrat*, and the *Post-Dispatch* felt that the billion-dollar plan for East St. Louis was "great." PACE designers named the riverfront "the central living room of the metropolitan area," and this notion was enthusiastically embraced by businessmen, financiers, and politicians on both sides of the Mississippi. Daniel

[48] The "PACE" Plan for East St. Louis, Illinois.

Burnham's famous statement about making no small plans was quoted in reference to the PACE plan. By the beginning of 1967, development of the riverfront seemed only a hairbreadth away. Even without specific commitment of public or private funds, it was assumed that there could be little difficulty in mobilizing federal, state, and private support to carry out plan proposals.

A new vision had been designed for the riverfront—no more railroads, no more Continental Grain Company, and no more city dumps. In their place would be a moderate-to-upper income community with a racial, social, and educational balance. Hundreds of thousands would flock to the tourist attractions and the luxury hotels. The feasibility of this plan went unquestioned. Supposedly the railroads would move, developers were waiting in the wings, and outside financial assistance was readily available. Supposedly also, the disadvantaged residents whose homes would be eliminated would melt away.

Residents were far less enthusiastic than the financial interests and their planners. Three open meetings advertised as discussions of the PACE plan drew a total of less than 100 residents. Scheduled by the plan commission as public hearings prior to city council adoption of the plan, the three meetings were held in different sections of the city. Soon after the meetings, the council approved the PACE plan by resolution, incorporating it as the city's guide for future growth.

Optimistically, the PACE development consultant continued his efforts. In his year-end report for 1967, he offered the following hope for the future:

In less than two years, PACE has rooted out the problems of which there have been many. Before we could have "brick and mortar," the past had to be reorganized . . . the "Establishment" had to know we meant business . . . all the people had to recognize our purpose was in their cause . . . and most of all the word hope had to be put back into the language of East St. Louis. This much has now been accomplished by PACE. For in our own eyes and . . . in those of the public . . . the city administration . . . the federal government, a welded concerted effort is in evidence for the first time with purpose . . . understanding . . . and determination of "let's get the job done." Beginning in 1968, we will start with action programs to systematically eliminate in part those problems that face the community and help to rebuild our City socially, financially and physically.

As we face the problems head on and recognize how deep and well entrenched they are, we come to realize that there is no single solution as a panacea for our urban ills . . . but rather that it lies with those influential citizens coming to their own rescue as well as that of the City. Dependence on public agencies exclusively cannot and will not get the job done. What is needed and what PACE has is the perpetual vigorous pursuit of solutions by the morally-social citizen fibers . . . in a continuing force for progress. It will be under the courageous leadership of men of vision, tolerance, optimism, self-confidence . . . and by all means, through the participation of men who act rather than merely talk that the necessary forward thrusts are to be achieved The task before us is now less difficult for our understanding is greater and that task will be accomplished . . . because it has to be accomplished . . . if we are to survive not only as this City but as the Nation.[49]

Nothing happened in 1968 or 1969, but for three and one-half years, the development consultant remained on PACE's payroll. Virtually none of the PACE proposals have been implemented. People do not talk much about the PACE plan anymore —not even those who still recall its basic elements. Letters of commendation from federal and state agencies have not brought renewal funds to East St. Louis; nor have the railroads vacated the area, though they are still in the process of studying relocation feasibility. In an early 1970 television interview, Jamie Cannon, the East St. Louis city planner at that time, mentioned that lack of local funds and unavailability of outside resources have made the riverfront into a long-range abstraction which occupies little of his staff's time.

Implementation Failure

Though the East St. Louis waterfront has often been regarded as a unique opportunity to create a new environment on the

[49] "P.A.C.E. Progress and Action by Citizen Efforts for the Year Ending 1967," East St. Louis, Illinois, pp. 1–2 (mimeographed).

Mississippi River, there is a growing recognition that successful redevelopment is, at the very minimum, difficult and elusive, Until recently, the railroads vehemently opposed renewal proposals and adamantly refused to give up riverfront land. Severe financial reverses and the unsuitability of the riverfront for rail needs have tempered their position. However, funds have not been available to purchase the land from the railroads and to subsidize their move to improved facilities. Municipal fiscal crisis in East St. Louis has not permitted assistance for acquisition, site improvement, and, where necessary, land write-down. In case after case, the city has turned to the federal and state governments to provide these funds and has consistently been rejected.

A typical example of the immobility caused by local resource shortages was the failure to build the river road in East St. Louis. Access was considered essential by planners and prospective developers, yet there was no way to finance either the 6.5-mile or the shortened version of this thoroughfare. Frequent requests to the state had no effect. State officials considered it a luxury which could not be justified by their traffic projections. In referring to the lack of funds for construction and maintenance of higher priority roads, the district engineer of the Illinois Division of Highways claimed that "I think it (the river road) would be a very beneficial project, but . . . you don't get dessert when you've got nothing else to eat." [50]

For the past four years, an attempt has been made to obtain a federal commitment from the National Park Service of the Department of the Interior for either an urban park or an extension of the Jefferson National Expansion Memorial. Planning funds have been allocated and four alternative plans have been prepared by the Park Service, but these plans have not yet induced resources for capital improvements. As of February, 1971, a final decision had not been reached by this federal agency as to which plan will be recommended. This planning succeeds previous planning by the National Park Service which analyzed the riverfront's historical significance. Further planning will be necessary to assess the costs and benefits of riverfront involve-

[50] *Metro-East Journal,* November 19, 1967.

ment, and whatever project is selected will need a National Park Service priority rating. This rating will determine whether a fund request is made to Congress. Various East St. Louis planners have viewed the National Park Service as the catalyst to create other federal and state participation in riverfront projects. On the basis of past experience it is difficult to be optimistic about Department of the Interior involvement in the immediate future. (Creation of St. Louis's Gateway Arch was a forty-year project.)

To insure riverfront redevelopment, public funds, acting as a substitute for private investment, will also be required for the creation of jobs and the subsidization of housing. Many East St. Louis plans discussed the importance of increased employment, but there was no way to bring these commercial and institutional activities to the riverfront. There were visions of such facilities as a state office building which the city has made repeated attempts to obtain. This structure, with a potential for 250 jobs, was designated for a community near East St. Louis several years ago. Plans were changed, however, when the present governor was elected in 1968. Placement in the neighboring community was canceled soon after the gubernatorial vote. Several days prior to the election of Mayor Williams, the issue of the state office building arose again. Speaking through an aide, the governor told the electorate of East St. Louis that he would try to bring the building to the city but only if Williams were elected. If redeveloped the riverfront could have been a suitable location for it and for the state-sponsored community college now renting space in a high-rise structure built early in this century in downtown East St. Louis.

Besides bringing jobs to the riverfronts, it will be necessary to have a sizable housing subsidy to accommodate the 30,000 people planned by PACE for the East St. Louis riverfront. Much of the housing slated for the riverfront has been for a moderate income population, and to create dwelling units for this clientele requires rental and/or purchase payment assistance. This means a subsidy from either the FHA or in Illinois, from a newly formed development agency. To date, neither source has demonstrated an ability to influence the construction of a sizable number of residential units. According to one federal housing official, there were only 1,500 units of Section 236 (moderate-income rental housing) available in 1969 for all Illinois cities outside Chicago. This meant 100 to 200 units for East St. Louis— hardly enough to consider for extensive residential planning.

If the riverfront held such great promise, as described in various plans, why has the planning never been translated into "brick and mortar" programs? For one obvious reason, the constituency for change has been historically powerless. Newspaper editors, professional city administrators, planners, and university staff have had no control over the allocation of resources and have been incapable of bringing either private or public funds to the riverfronts.

Often those with power were noticeably detached from the renewal process. *Metro-East Journal* editorials over the past decade criticized East St. Louis political leaders for their non-involvement, especially when Democratic administrations were in Springfield and Washington. Elected local officials rarely spearheaded the fight for federal and state aid programs, such as the junior college district, Model Cities, and antipoverty effort, leaving the leadership instead to professionals and a limited number of resident committees.

Several reasons can be given why there was not greater support for riverfront renewal in East St. Louis. The goals of political machines have been traditionally short range—to create situations where rewards accrue to organization leaders. Despite the East St. Louis economic crisis and community disadvantage, the machine has functioned well for those at the top and, to a lesser extent, still does today. Its existence was maintained because enough was distributed to insure victory at election time. However, in the long run there was little overlap between the objectives of the machine and redevelopment of the community. Many politicians, far from interested in renewal, were opposed to it because it might bring new residents to the area who were neither dependent nor easily manipulatable.

In addition, the seriousness of the East St. Louis area economic interests can be questioned in devising riverfront programs. It seems that PACE could have pumped more into the community than paying the consultant's fee for three and one-half years and making a few minor contributions. Within a few years after preparation of the PACE plan, several of the financial institutions which had paid for it were making efforts to leave the city. Most of the large industrial firms never really became involved in the community and consequently were not interested in the riverfront. They were not desirous of attracting, through redevelopment, residents who might object to their tax-sheltered communities just outside the city limits, their pollution of East St. Louis air, and their use of city streets without paying for their support.

Time after time planners described the feasibility of riverfront development and pointed out the fiscal and aesthetic benefits which could accrue to East St. Louis. Yet, it must be concluded that planning became a substitute for action. Public funds for planning were certainly easier to obtain than funds for operational programs, and local professionals were too desperate to reject planning money. There was always the hope that more funds would be forthcoming later. Often the planning process seemed like a game of simulated resource allocation which was played by local planners and federal and state bureaucrats, all groups afraid to admit that it was not the real thing.

Today, it is even more difficult to be optimistic about riverfront development since it will require a level of outside funding far above anything previously received by East St. Louis. Federal urban renewal funds are very scarce throughout the country, and future increases for inner city redevelopment are not likely.

In East St. Louis some plans and studies of questionable local value were undertaken only because planning money was available. One in particular was prepared when a federal official thought it would be a good idea. A consultant who performed the study, at considerable cost, was a former federal bureaucrat. The final report added little to the body of knowledge about East St. Louis, and implementation of its recommendations was, once again, dependent on massive federal and state aid.

While technical planning has supported riverfront redevelopment and described the fiscal and aesthetic payoffs which would accrue to East St. Louis, it has not seemed to materially improve the prospects for redevelopment. Planning for the riverfront has persisted without a public or private commitment of resources, and the myth has endured that somehow, some-where, money would be forthcoming if the proposals were sufficiently innovative and creative. Implementation of the plans was outside the capacity of the local government. There was always the assumption that the state would put large sums of money into riverfront roads; that the federal government would supply urban renewal funds; and that private developers would eagerly want riverfront land. Never were plans predicated on prior commitment of resources. As a result, they became pro-motional devices to induce resource allocations which never materialized. In many instances, the sources of implementation money were unknown at the time of planning. In other cases, plans were aimed at unpredictable federal and state assistance programs.

Development of the riverfront was not an accomplished fact, yet planners and other professionals deluded themselves into believing that physical projects automatically followed the pro-duction of plans. There were illusions of power, fictions which were dispelled when attempts were made to change plan recom-mendations into tangible accomplishments. Never was a public agency backed by the legal powers and resources of all levels of government to manage the renewal of the East St. Louis river-fronts. For these reasons, the riverfront was never a real oppor-tunity. It was a trap which continually lured those concerned with change but rarely attracted those with power to carry out the change.

Most of those involved in riverfront planning did not see their activities as political in nature nor did they perceive them-selves as actors in a political scenario. Planners for PACE, Fruco, Checchi, the National Park Service, and the National Museum of Transport almost unanimously believed in the logic of river-front development. To them the riverfront was a highly desirable tract of land centrally located in a highly populated region. It was reasonable, then, to conclude that if the plan were creative enough, it would attract developers and eventually a complete renaissance. Even today much of the riverfront planning is based on this premise.

Instead of being concerned with the preparation of dramatic and physically oriented plans, riverfront planners might have examined the self-interests of those groups which were crucial to the success of redevelopment and outlined ways to make these self-interests coincided with projects on the riverfront. In the case of the railroads, the best conceived ideas and the most beautifully prepared graphics were no substitute for knowing the amount of money needed by the railroads to move and then negotiating with potential sources of funds and the railroads to carry out relocation. Assuming that the railroads would want more efficient yards without subsidization was a naive basis for planning. Yet the possibilities were there. The railroads had considered relocation. At a cost of $110,000 a study was completed for the Terminal Railroad Association in February, 1970, which not only established relocation cost but also capitalized rail savings possible in newer yards.

Because planning has endured without a concentration on project costs and fund availability, it has not been directly associated with action. Adequate resources have never been available to those involved in East St. Louis redevelopment. As a result planning and implementation have become alienated. Yet in spite of the apparent futility, planning has continued. Over 125 studies relating to community problems have been produced between 1960 to 1968, but there is so little redevelopment activity that one city official commented, "I would like to see one plan implemented—even a bad one." The frustration of many residents and professionals is described in an editorial in the February 6, 1969, edition of the *East St. Louis Monitor*:

> The city has been studied enough, dissected enough, drawn upon enough, cut up enough (through gerrymandering and highway building). It is time ACTION is taken to arrest the downslide of the community. And such ACTION will not be prompted by continued study and analysis. This community (East St. Louis) may very well be the most studied in the country. Was Watts studied as much? Was Harlem? Was Fill-

more District? Was Southside Chicago? No. But most of these communities have aid that is allowing them to move along self-help lines. Why cannot East St. Louis get similar help (not handouts) instead of remaining a guinea pig for rich white school boys and the professoriate?

Blacks in East St. Louis have recently demanded a greater role in all planning, including that for the riverfront. There will be no more riverfront committees dominated and controlled by White business leaders. In 1963, Mayor Fields appointed a seventeen-man committee to study riverfront development. It included the editor of the local newspaper, bankers, railroad executives, and only one Black—the city's salaried human relations director who is also the editor of a weekly newspaper sympathetic to the local government. Five years later, another task force was formed and again there was only one Black, a representative from the regional office of HUD. Among the remaining members were the PACE consultant, the district engineer of the Illinois Division of Highways, the mayor's administrative assistant, and the executive director of the regional planning council.

Soon after its formation in 1968, this second task force became dormant. About one year later, in February, 1969, when a meeting was called to review "progress" on the riverfront, representatives from Black Unity appeared. Formed in the winter of 1968, Black Unity was a coalition of organizations and individuals who wanted a voice in all matters concerning Blacks in East St. Louis. After hearing reports at the meeting from the railroads, the Division of Highways, and Congressman Melvin Price, a spokesman for Black Unity asked to be recognized. He said that his group felt that Blacks should have at least 51 percent of the membership on the task force and voiced the complaint that "once again you're planning our city for us. How many of you live in East St. Louis?"

There has been extensive political change in East St. Louis over the past five years. Black gains from the civil rights demonstration and antipoverty programs were extended. Both candidates for mayor in the April, 1971, election were Black—the winner having genuine reform support. Power in East St. Louis has never been exchanged gracefully and the shift from White to Black leadership has been no exception. At one stage confrontations were so frequent and violent at city council meetings that one commissioner confided that "he didn't want to come to City Hall on the day of council meetings." One argument broke up a council meeting. When the crowd had disbursed, a group of defiant young men broke chairs and urinated on the chamber floor.

The style of planning changed too. Black involvement and participation in all East St. Louis programs was the one fundamental principle that characterized planning in East St. Louis in 1967 to 1969. Such East St. Louis functions as Model Cities, city planning, urban renewal, building inspections, antipoverty, the school district, the community college, and a state nonprofit housing corporation are now directed by Blacks. Blacks are receiving both the high-ranking positions and most of the jobs in newly created federal and state programs and East St. Louis has its first Black mayor.

Planning for the riverfront has also reflected greater Black involvement. In the spring of 1969, a White builder of high-rise commercial and residential structures on the St. Louis riverfront became interested in the east side of the Mississippi. To avoid the problems and confrontations which erupted over other renewal ideas, a representative group was formed to act as a liaison between developers and the community.[51]

According to one of its founders, Dr. Jefferson Ware, this organization, later named Metro-Progress, Incorporated, was designed as a vehicle to obtain citizen endorsement for a variety of redevelopment projects. It had a steering committee of about twenty-five members, the majority of whom were Black. Ware contended that it was neither a showcase nor a legitimizing group and that activists were included because no group can come into East St. Louis now without support from the militant establishment. Membership in Metro-Progress, Incorporated, cut across the entire community, including youth, businessmen, and public agency officials.[52]

[51] Ibid., April 30, 1969.
[52] Jefferson Ware, interview, East St. Louis, Illinois, June 17, 1969.

Though originally intended to serve as a citizen participation mechanism for one particular developer, the group continued in existence when the developer lost interest in East St. Louis. Metro-Progress wanted to become a catalyst for socio-economic and physical renewal through its own participation and by encouraging others to become involved. Soon after formation, the shortage of local redevelopment funds was immediately recognized and outside help was requested. In a letter to the Ford Foundation, critical resource shortages were cited, and East St. Louis was described as a city in unparalleled need of external funding requiring "an early heavy commitment of resources by the State of Illinois, the Federal Government, semi-private funds and private investors."[53]

Metro-Progress, Incorporated, focused its planning on the riverfront, aware that redevelopment there could potentially turn the city around. The riverfront was a large enough tract of land to double the city's assessed valuation and completely alter the community image. Members of the group wanted new housing and employment opportunities on the riverfront, and they felt that eventually the railroads would relocate, citing the relocation study of the Terminal Railroad Association as indication of serious intent. Metro-Progress goals were to speed up development in East St. Louis, and it was recognized that this is not usually accomplished by being hostile to developers, even White ones. Businessmen on the steering committee also wanted to encourage Black entrepreneurship in redevelopment activities.

Creation of Metro-Progress, Incorporated, represented an orderly shift in power from the White financial-labor-government bloc which had previously dominated riverfront planning to a group with a majority of Black representation. Included in the membership were Black professionals, White financiers, Black and White politicians, Southern Illinois University staff, young activists, and public agency directors. Whether this body will continue to function depends on its capacity to generate projects and on a steady and large amount of outside funding assistance. It may follow the trail of PACE into oblivion (lately

---

[53] Letter to Ford Foundation from Metro-Progress, Inc., requesting planning assistance, March 15, 1969.

the activities of the group have been extremely limited). At the time of this writing, there is no serious riverfront developer and the leadership for riverfront development has switched to such organizations as the East St. Louis's economic development and plan commission—both with extensive Black leadership.

Until the recent changes in community leadership, the constituency for riverfront planning was primarily the financial interests. These interests wanted elaborate proposals and planners were enthusiastic in encouraging them. Yet even the more recent promoters of riverfront development have not discouraged the creation of speculative designs. In March, 1971, world famous R. Buckminster Fuller introduced his concept of how the East St. Louis riverfront should be redeveloped. Titled "Old Man River," it is candidly divorced from the issues of financing. Fuller proposed a transparent version of his geodesic dome, one-half mile in diameter and 918 feet high, to house 30,000 to 40,000 people. Pollution-free with climate controls, the structure is projected to contain four levels of housing, schools, churches, and shopping—almost every land use found in a city of that size except roads.[54] Whether this or any other riverfront plan ever gets built is a supposition. It is likely, however, that more time and money will be spent on further planning, whether it is done by consultants or the staffs of public agencies. But until such time as planners are sure of the power of their constituencies and recognize the political difficulties of their proposals, they will likely continue to pursue their own interests and will certainly be unable to translate the abstract nature of their plans into reality.

During the final revisions of this case study, the funding of a new riverfront planning study was announced. According to the September 14, 1971, edition of the *Metro-East Journal*, the East-West Gateway Coordinating Council (the regional council of governments) was to receive $465,000 to examine the feasibility of relocating railroad tracks and facilities. Three agencies were financing the two-year study, with $400,000 coming from the federal Department of Transportation, $30,000 from the Department of Housing and Urban Development, and $35,000

---

[54] Newsletter, East St. Louis Chamber of Commerce, April, 1971.

from the state of Illinois. Consultants were to be used to carry out this planning. Both the large appropriation for planning and the apparent redundancy of past efforts caught the attention of Mayor Williams and several other commissioners, especially since they did not even have a copy of the proposal submitted to the federal and state agencies for funding. This was not implementation, new construction, or an enhancement of the city's renewal capacity. Key city officials asked: Wouldn't this duplicate the Terminal Railroad study, the PACE plan, the $40,000 sewer study financed by the Economic Development Administration, the findings of the National Park Service, and many other riverfront plans? Convinced of the merits of this position, the mayor wanted power to direct the focus of the study, to maximize the city's interests in the riverfront, and to use this funding for operational purposes.[55] Not only was this a challenge to the notion of comprehensive planning but also to professionalism as well. For now it was obvious that planning and renewal are political; that the finest and most sincere technical efforts do not insure redevelopment nor do the poorest and most self-serving negate it. Proliferating planning expenditures alone were not the answer. Williams recognized this by stating, "We've had studies on top of studies on top of studies. This time, we want implementation."[56]

[55] *Metro-East Journal*, September 20, 1971.
[56] *Ibid.*

Model Cities Planning:
The Clash of Two Doctrines

4

Early Involvement in Model Cities

Seymour Mann, the director of the Public Administration and Metropolitan Affairs Program at Southern Illinois University (SIU), Edwardsville, can be credited with showing the first interest in a possible Model Cities program for East St. Louis.[1] In March, 1966, shortly after the introduction of the Demonstration Cities Act into Congress, Mann brought the subject up in informal conversations with his staff. Though Mann's program had been supplying consulting services in planning and renewal to East St. Louis for several years, an official contract had been signed only one month earlier. From 1962 to 1970 the SIU program had published several detailed studies of East St. Louis. Mann's early interest, however, was more than academic. A 1960 report on reorganization of the city government by SIU resulted in the recruitment of George Washnis as administrative assistant to the mayor. Further, the university had loaned help for an antipoverty application in 1964. Data collected through his program's research had regularly been used to support fund-

---

[1] This program at Southern Illinois University has since been renamed Regional and Urban Development Studies and Services.

ing applications or to support reform attempts. An activist role by the SIU staff in promoting a major urban program like Model Cities was not unexpected.

Mann and Robert Mendelson, a research associate on the program staff, followed the progress of the Model Cities legislation. During the summer of 1966 they talked to Washnis about the possibility of East St. Louis applying for Model Cities funds, assuming the legislation passed. Mendelson was assigned the task of seeing how the Model Cities program might relate to East St. Louis.

On October 20, 1966, the Demonstration Cities Act was sent to President Johnson for his signature. Mann and Mendelson immediately contacted Washnis and strongly encouraged an effort to get Model Cities funds. Mendelson promised his full-time help in writing an application, and assumed the task of writing a needs study to show the adverse social and physical conditions in East St. Louis. Washnis agreed to contact local government officials, agency representatives, businessmen, and a limited number of residents in an attempt to coordinate local efforts. In October, Washnis called the first meeting of the demonstration cities technical committee. Approximately twenty-five people attended. Washnis asked those present if they would be willing to volunteer help in working on an application for Model Cities funds. Enthusiastic endorsement was given, especially by representatives from PACE. Arthur Klein, the consultant to PACE who had recently drawn up the ambitious PACE plan for redevelopment in East St. Louis, was selected as the group's chairman. Mendelson was asked to contact HUD officials to get information on how to apply for the Model Cities funds.

On November 3, 1966, the day the president signed the Model Cities legislation, Mendelson called George Williams at the Washington HUD offices and asked several questions about the application process: "Should the entire city of East St. Louis be included as a Demonstration City?" "No. It is the purpose of the Act to include an area of about 10 percent of a city's population. The term 'Demonstration City' is a misnomer—the intent of the act is to refer to a 'Model Neighborhood.'" "Why should the

target area be that small?" "The target area must be of such size
that there will be a marked change, physically and socially,
within a five year period. The size must also be small enough to
be meaningfully related to the resources available in the community." Williams encouraged East St. Louis to begin a "micro-
scopic analysis" of the selected target neighborhood in such areas
as unemployment, health, housing, and education. He indicated
that the HUD guidelines would probably be distributed by the
end of November.[2]

During November and December, Mendelson contacted the
St. Louis Model Cities agency, and discussions were held concerning the possibility of a joint application by the two cities.
The technical committee held meetings in mid-November and
mid-December, though at this point Washnis and Mendelson
were doing most of the exploratory work. It was difficult to know
exactly how the application should be put together, since HUD
officials were themselves still unsure. For example, Washnis
talked to H. Ralph Taylor, HUD Assistant Secretary for Dem-
onstrations and Inter-governmental Relations, on December 27,
and the next day sent a memorandum to the technical committee
announcing that the scheduled January 5 meeting of the group
would explore the possibility of a regional program, to include
St. Louis, East St. Louis, and surrounding communities. When
HUD guidelines came out a month later, it was evident that a
regional approach had never been considered at the federal
level.

At a meeting of the technical committee in December, 1966,
ten task force committee chairman were designated to write
research papers in the areas of antipoverty, employment, utilities, education, recreation and culture, housing, economic development, health and community services, transportation, and
civil rights. In early January, 1967, two more committee chairmen were assigned research on community involvement and
crime and delinquency. At this point, twenty-nine people were
on the technical committee. Each of them was assigned to one

[2] Memorandum from Robert Mendelson to East St. Louis Demonstration
Cities Technical Committee, November 7, 1966.

of the task force subcommittees, though in practice the reports were prepared, if at all, by the committee chairmen.

The technical committee was composed almost entirely of representatives from city departments, local governmental agencies, Southern Illinois University, and downtown financial interests. Arthur Klein, the PACE consultant, served as the formal chairman from November to January 12, 1967. After that point, he dropped active participation in the group. Washnis did much of the legwork in contacting HUD and in sending meeting notices and memorandums to technical committee members. After mid-January he assumed the chairmanship. Mendelson and Paula Parks, a staff member on loan from the St. Clair County Economic Opportunity Commission (EOC, the local community action agency) did most of the editing and revising on the proposal that was submitted to HUD (as will be noted later, the task force chairmen did little of this work). Chairmen of the task force subcommittees represented several agencies and groups: St. Clair EOC, the Illinois State Employment Service, the Board of Education, East-West Gateway Coordinating Council, East St. Louis Housing Authority, St. Clair County Health and Welfare Council, the Chamber of Commerce, and a representative of the mayor. Copies of memoranda and meeting notices were distributed to the city council, the PACE executive committee (a businessmen's organization), the chairman of the citizen's advisory committee on the workable program, the chairman of the plan commission, a member of the County Board of Supervisors, the director of the St. Louis Model Cities agency, and a partner in a consulting firm working on a plan for the riverfront and downtown area of East St. Louis.

Subcommittee chairmen were appointed in mid-December, and asked to deliver preliminary reports at a January 12 technical committee meeting. By that meeting, only three paper reports were completed, and these were exceedingly sketchy. Arthur Klein, the chairman, expressed great dissatisfaction about the lack of progress, and insisted that East St. Louis simply did not have the ability to independently prepare an application. He strongly suggested the hiring of a consulting firm that he was familiar with. Following extensive discussion, in which Washnis and Mendelson insisted that the application be prepared locally, Klein agreed to "wait two weeks to see what progress can be made."[3] Klein never again took an active part in the group, and Washnis assumed the chairmanship.

Weekly meetings were held during the month of January. Although total membership increased somewhat, from twenty-nine to forty-three, attendance varied from ten to fifteen members. Seven of those who regularly attended represented either the city of East St. Louis or SIU; two others came from the EOC. Three or four members could have been classified as "grass-rooters" without professional or agency ties.

At a meeting on February 1, the city council passed a resolution requesting federal assistance for a Demonstration Cities program. The resolution was supported by a document entitled "Why East St. Louis Needs to Be a Demonstration City," completed by Mendelson and Paula Parks in early January. That report consisted primarily of an edited compendium of papers published by SIU documenting the depressed social and physical conditions in East St. Louis. In addition to the report, the city council sent HUD a copy of the PACE plan. Following submission of these materials, Washnis and Mendelson kept in frequent contact with HUD officials. Representative Melvin Price, a longtime House Democrat from East St. Louis, also pushed the city's interest with HUD.

Meanwhile, steps had been taken to expand the size of the technical committee to include a contingent of nonprofessionals from the Model City neighborhoods. At the February 1 session of the city council, the Demonstration Cities agency (or Model Cities agency, MCA, as it was also known) was officially created and sixty-seven members were named to it. Twenty of the people lived in the target area—though most were professionals in some capacity. One day later, when the Model Cities agency met, a Black minister delivered a report criticizing the absence of "grassroots" involvement on the agency. Washnis responded

[3] Model City technical committee of East St. Louis, Illinois, minutes of the meeting, January 12, 1967.

by suggesting that the target area be broken down into its "logical neighborhoods" so that representatives could be chosen for an MCA advisory committee. There was no follow-up to Washnis's suggestion.

Although the city council had requested federal help and had sent in Mendelson's report describing the city's social and physical problems, the city had not yet satisfied HUD's guidelines for a formal application for Model Cities funds. A comprehensive application had to contain budget details for MCA staffing and program planning, a detailed summary of social and physical conditions, a set of strategies for changing conditions, and a summary of local resources that could be used in program implementation. Washnis finally received HUD guidelines on January 26, two months after the expected date.

By the February 2 meeting of the technical committee all of the task force reports had been completed. In general, the reports were so sketchy as to be useless for inclusion into the Model Cities application. Paula Parks, Robert Mendelson, and David Ranney of the SIU staff and Ed O'Boyle of the Illinois State Employment Service relied heavily on data that had previously been collected by the SIU Metropolitan Affairs Program to prepare the application. By April 6, 1967, the completed 400-page application was ready for submission to HUD.

On April 15 an eleven-member East St. Louis delegation including three Blacks junketed to Washington to present the city's Model City application to HUD officials. The meeting had been arranged by Representative Price. The composition of the group told much about whose support of the program was considered important. Mayor Fields led the delegation. Washnis and Mendelson also attended. Others who made the trip were Fred L. Teer, Chairman of the Denverside Improvement Association (a nonprofit housing sponsor), Paula Parks, Edwin Denman (city planner), the chairman of the board of directors of the First National Bank of East St. Louis, the executive director of the St. Clair County EOC, the vice-president and secretary of the Southern Illinois Building Trades Council, and a politically strong local Black attorney. Mayor Fields and Repre-

sentative Price made presentations to Ralph Taylor, assistant
secretary of HUD, and to Walter Farr, administrator of the
Model Cities Program in Washington. They were told that the
review process would take about two months.

The East St. Louis daily newspaper, the *Metro-East Journal*,
and the two weekly Black newspapers, the *Monitor* and the
Crusader, carried large stories on the Model Cities application.
Interest quickly dropped, however. In June, the *Journal* carried
a seven-part series describing the proposal; otherwise attention
by the news media was negligible. Despite the promise of a
sixty-day review, the first announcement of Model Cities grants
did not come until November 16—seven months after East St.
Louis had applied. East St. Louis was among sixty-three first-
round cities selected on November 16, 1967.

Announcement of East St. Louis as a first-round city was
greeted with unrestrained optimism by local officials and by the
newspapers. Although East St. Louis's planning allotment was
only $85,000, less than a third of the $265,410 it had requested,
there was a "feeling among many of the business and civic
leaders that application of the government money will bring a
long-awaited civic renaissance."[4] The newspaper was hardly
exaggerating the mood, and the executive vice-president of the
Chamber of Commerce rated the announcement as one of "the
largest steps for improvement of East St. Louis in 35 years."[5]
Representative Price hailed it as "a magnificent breakthrough
for East St. Louis."[6] Model Cities goals, as stated in the proposal
to HUD, encouraged optimism: objectives included cutting the
unemployment in half by 1970 and reducing the stock of substandard housing by 50 percent in five years. Though the nam-
ing of East St. Louis as a Model City was widely acclaimed, the
program was understood by only a handful of residents and
professionals. Some equated the Model City competition with
the *Look* magazine All-American City awards which East St.
Louis had received in 1958.

[4] *East St. Louis Monitor*, November 19, 1967.
[5] *Metro-East Journal*, November 16, 1967.
[6] *Ibid.*

Control of the Model Cities Program

City officials and community leaders who had participated in the technical committee expected to have a controlling voice in running the program, with the Model Cities agency operating as part of the office of the mayor. Washnis was to remain as chairman of the Model Cities agency and supervise the professional director when he was hired. One of the tasks of the professional staff, as described in the April application, was "to keep citizens informed of its activities, and to encourage participation of citizens in its programs."[7]

On November 17, Washnis announced the strategy for implementation. To cut planning costs, as made necessary by the large cut in the Model Cities grant, Washnis suggested assistance by SIU staff members. He announced that a team of HUD officials from the Chicago regional office would be in town in early December to meet with local officials to revise the Model Cities plans to conform to the reduced grant. A few days later, the expected make-up of the MCA took more specific form. Five professionals—a planner, an economist, a sociologist, an architect, and a housing expert—were to make up the staff. A much larger staff had been planned in the original application. To augment the technical capacities of the MCA the president of PACE offered to lend its consultant at no cost.[8] On November 28, the day after a meeting with a contingent of federal officials, Washnis announced that immediate recruitment would start for the staff. A few days later Washnis placed advertisements in newspapers and professional planning and public administration journals for the position of program director.

Details of staffing and budgeting had been worked out with federal officials who, like the local leaders, expected few changes in the way the East St. Louis program would be run. On November 27, an orientation meeting between city officials and federal representatives was held in East St. Louis. An impressive showing was made by the federal government, with key officials not only from HUD, but representatives from HEW, the De-

[7] *Ibid.*, April 23, 1967.
[8] *Ibid.*, November 26, 1967.

partments of Labor and Justice, and the Office of Economic Opportunity (OEO) as well. One major question in the minds of the HUD representatives concerned the extent of citizen participation in the East St. Louis plans. Washnis was advised that participation would have to be increased and that revisions in the East St. Louis application would have to reflect this. On December 12, Ted Robinson, the East St. Louis lead man, from HUD, and Alan Baxter, an OEO representative, met with Washnis and suggested several alternatives in the plans for citizen participation. As it turned out, federal officials need not have been overly concerned; Black leaders in East St. Louis were already taking steps to modify the structure and operations of the MCA.

Public excitement generated by the announcement of the Model Cities grant was matched by activity of local Black leaders who felt themselves excluded from the original application and from current action in setting up the Model Cities program. Earlier in the year, dissatisfaction had been expressed concerning the lack of citizen participation in preparing the application. In late April, Mendelson had been invited to explain the Model Cities proposal to a meeting of the East St. Louis council of neighborhood units, a conglomeration of several neighborhood organizations. Elmo Bush, who had headed a recently defeated Black slate for mayor and city council, criticized the Model Cities application for its lack of involvement by grassroots citizens and its domination by professionals. Mendelson pointed out, somewhat defensively, that the meetings of the technical committee had been open, that they had been advertised in the local newspapers, and that eighty personal invitations had been sent out announcing each of the technical committee meetings. Many of those at the meeting were not satisfied by this explanation and Mendelson himself was not fully content with it. In a speech prepared more than a year later, he admitted: "The truth is we just could not get the people out to the meetings and we did not have time to really take the meetings out into the neighborhoods where we should have."

Shortly after the announcement of the East St. Louis grant, dissatisfaction was publicly aired by Clyde Jordan, the publisher of the *East St. Louis Monitor*, the larger of the two weekly Black newspapers. At a city council meeting on December 4, Jordan questioned Mayor Fields about the city's intentions regarding hiring for the six positions on the MCA staff. Reacting to Fields's ambiguity on whether or not Blacks would be sought for the positions, Jordan commented:

> There should be grass roots people in the organization. The people in the area covered by the program want to be represented.
> . . . The people in these neighborhoods are beginning to feel strongly about this already. They think this is just another way to get SIU people in, put them in high-paying positions and tell the people in the neighborhood how to live.
>
> The city has got to make a decision to put Negroes in these positions or this will create trouble for the city council.[9]

Fields responded by saying "every effort will be made to include Negroes in the program, but we must first make sure we have the right people."[10] Washnis promised that there would be "excellent coordination with the citizens" in the running of the program.[11]

Jordan was not making unfounded statements. On the evening of Saturday, December 2, representatives from thirty local Black groups and private individuals met to unify Blacks and seek greater involvement in East St. Louis development programs. Called by leaders of the local NAACP, the specific purpose was to discuss strategies for impacting on the Model Cities program. Intensive preparation had preceded the meeting. Numerous private conversations and meetings had been held among Black leaders, including Bush supporters in the previous election, young militants demanding a greater "piece of the action," and residents who had achieved high position in public agencies. At the meeting an NAACP Model Cities committee was established and Fred Teer, a target area resident and local schoolteacher, was proposed for the position of director of the MCA. In a communication to Mayor Fields sent under the letterhead of the NAACP, Teer was recommended on the grounds that "The director should be a local person, involved in the critical poverty area

[9] Ibid., December 4, 1967.
[10] Ibid.
[11] Ibid.

and knowledgeable and experienced in the problems of housing which are basic to the evils of the ghetto and basic to the Model Cities concept."[12] Professional qualifications were only one of two necessary qualifications. On this count, Teer's educational experience was cited—two degrees from the University of Illinois, as well as leadership in a federally funded housing project. He also had the second necessary qualification—he lived in the Model Cities target area.

City officials were noncommittal concerning the letter, though it was generally known that they considered Teer insufficiently qualified. Mayor Fields stated that Teer's application would be reviewed and the commissioners said they would follow the mayor's recommendations.[13] Washnis was noncommittal but tried to discourage lobbying for Teer. He emphasized that the decision to hire a director would be based on merit, not pressure. It was his opinion, stated publicly, that pushing too hard might harm an applicant's chances.

Backing Teer for directorship of the Model Cities agency was only part of the Negro Unity Planners' objectives. They also wanted to insure that Blacks—particularly those from the target area—would be well represented in the MCA membership and staff positions. On December 9 the Negro Unity Planners held another meeting to discuss strategy. Only a few of the fifty people attending the meeting could be regarded as nonprofessional, grassroots citizens. An editorial by the publisher of the *Crusader* caught the feeling of the meeting:

> Last Saturday night at the South End Center, a large group of people met as concerned black people to unite our forces in the struggle for human dignity and justice. This group included religious leaders, professionals, business people, civil rights leaders . . . educators and just about every facet of our community. . . .
>
> Of primary concern is the Model Cities program . . . we must be sure that the people who are going to be affected MUST be included in the planning . . . it CANNOT (work) unless there is community participation.[14]

[12] *Ibid.*, December 5, 1967.
[13] *Ibid.*
[14] *Crusader*, December 14, 1967.

Another meeting of Negro Unity Planners was held on Monday, December 11, specifically to discuss the Model Cities program. It was preceded by a press release revealing an intention to take action.[15] Confrontation between the Black leaders and the MCA leadership was not long in coming.

On Thursday evening, December 14, Washnis called a meeting of the MCA membership to organize efforts to revise the Model Cities application and to go over plans for recruiting a Model Cities staff. Shortly after announcement of the first-round cities on November 16, HUD officials had sent letters to the mayors notifying them of a forty-five-day application revision period. By the end of that period, cities were expected to submit revised applications that would reflect the actual money made available by HUD and that would contain changes in conformance to HUD guidelines in citizen participation and program administration. East St. Louis had until January 12 to submit its application.

Not much interest in the December 14 meeting was shown by the White professionals who had been active before the original application had been submitted in April. A great deal of interest was displayed by Negro Unity Planners, however. About forty people attended the meeting; only about a dozen were not members of Negro Unity Planners. Just after the meeting had been called to order by Washnis and he had discussed the history of Model Cities, one of the Black leaders asked for more participation by target area residents. He was joined by the president of the NAACP, who proceeded to criticize the composition of the MCA. A demand immediately followed for the creation of a steering committee to suggest revisions in MCA structure and membership. Within a few minutes a motion was made, seconded, and overwhelmingly passed to dissolve the MCA and to give the steering committee the duty of making recommendations for the future MCA composition. Cleveland Chandler, a local schoolteacher, was selected chairman of the steering committee, as agreed in an earlier secret meeting.

Reaction to these developments was immediate. After the motion dissolving the old MCA was passed, several White pro-

[15] *East St. Louis Monitor*, December 11, 1967.

fessionals stalked out of the meeting in disgust. At a Monday, December 18, meeting of the city council, Mayor Fields protested that only the city council possessed the authority to dissolve the MCA. "No group is going to tell us what we can and can't do. That kind of stuff burns you up. Why are they objecting to George (Washnis) being head of the agency? The mayor is head of the program," fumed Fields.[16] Mayor Fields pushed harder for representation by political figures on the MCA, asserting that precinct committeemen of both parties should be included. According to him, they truly represented the grass-roots residents, and he apparently saw in Model Cities a potential for federally sponsored jobs and contracts to be distributed by the machine.

Those behind the overthrow intensified their efforts, claiming that there should be no politics in the Model Cities program. Their fear was that those politicians currently in control of the city would extend their influence over the program. And Model Cities represented the only chance to work effectively outside of the machine. This is one reason why so many people who had supported Elmo Bush in the previous election joined and organized the Negro Unity Planners coalition. One of the coalition leaders, a defeated candidate for commissioner on the Bush slate, wrote an open letter in the December 21 edition of the *East St. Louis Monitor* attacking the mayor's position. Calling himself a "Grass-roots Concerned Citizen," he said:

> East St. Louis' Mayor Alvin G. Fields is quoted in the Tuesday, December 19, 1967 issue of the *Metro-East Journal* as saying, "No group is going to tell (me) what I can and can't do. That kind of stuff burns me up." This is indeed a disgraceful and deplorable statement for an elected public official to make to the citizens he represents. It is an erroneous and feeble attempt to intimidate public spirited citizens who are insuring that the Model Cities Program will be set up within the federal guidelines. That is, with full participation of grass roots and area residents. Furthermore, if citizen participation in the affairs of East St. Louis burns the Mayor, let him burn.

16 *Metro-East Journal*, December 19, 1967.

All three East St. Louis newspapers supported the move by the Negro Unity Planners. On December 15 and again on December 24 the *Metro-East Journal* editorialized in favor of the December 14 coup. Endorsement from the *Journal*, by no means assured (the *Journal* tends to be relatively independent), was important not only in gaining support within the Black community but also from White government and business leaders as well. The *Journal* cast the take-over both in terms of citizen participation and community progress, emphasizing that the actions in the coup were consistent with HUD guidelines for Model Cities and that they could lead to a rebuilding of East St. Louis.[17]

Negro Unity Planners immediately began to recruit membership for a restructured MCA. On December 15, the day after the take-over, eleven members of the steering committee met and approved a motion that MCA membership be composed of 80 percent from the target area, 20 percent from outside. By Monday, December 18, surveys of the target area had been organized to recruit membership. Although the canvassing tended to be directed most heavily toward people already known to members of the steering committee, large numbers of people were contacted. On December 27, the *Journal* began running notices inviting people to volunteer for membership on the MCA board. At a January 4 meeting the steering committee considered the names of 105 people who had applied for MCA membership. Will McGaughy, one of the committee members, charged that city hall was trying to get twelve or thirteen precinct committeemen on the new MCA. "We are trying to set up a new image. This is not the place for politicians."[18] One precinct committeeman, a principal at one of the city schools, defended precinct committeemen, saying they had "knowledge of the areas involved" and should not be "stereotyped as politicians."[19] This, of course, substantiated the charges of attempts of political control in the eyes of the steering committee members. On January 10 the steering committee submitted the names

[17] *Ibid.*, December 24, 1967.
[18] *Ibid.*, January 5, 1968.
[19] *Ibid.*

of sixty-seven persons and ten organizations to the city council for approval as the new Model Cities Agency.

Soon after the dissolution of the old MCA and the creation of the steering committee, several city and state agency representatives protested—mostly to one another—that the action of December 14 had been illegal. There was no doubt that the mayor was correct, as the newspapers repeatedly reported, that only the city council could approve a new MCA. Despite this, no overt action was ever taken to dislodge the Negro Unity Planners from control of the MCA. One reason was that those who opposed the coup were faced with a powerful alliance of Black leaders, the newspapers, and even a few agency professionals. Negro Unity Planners included within the ranks probably a majority of the nonparty machine Black leaders in East St. Louis. Names submitted to the city council January 10 were revealing in this regard. The list was heavily loaded with the names of Black professionals or businessmen. Some of them also had political attachments, with five precinct committeemen being recommended. Of a list of sixty-seven, approximately twenty-five were without occupational or leadership status in the Black community.

At the January 10 city council meeting, Cleveland Chandler, chairman of the steering committee, asked for immediate approval of the names. Mayor Fields deferred action, claiming that another week was needed to see if other people wanted to be considered: "We have gotten calls from several people wanting to know how they can get involved in the program. We want to give them a chance to get in on it."[20] Chandler, sensing a possible attempt by the mayor to add political figures, interjected, "We are strictly against having a lot of politicians on the Model Cities Agency."[21] "Who are these people you are going to add?" "I don't know who they are," Fields replied. Chandler fired back, "If you don't know who they are, how do you know they can make the program work? I don't believe the Model City program is that important to you. You just want to sabotage it." After further exchange, Chandler accused Fields of acting in a

[20] *Ibid.*, January 11, 1968.
[21] *East St. Louis Monitor*, January 11, 1968.

"dictatorial manner," and added, "You're trying to put things into the same pattern you've followed all our lives. You're the dictator. We're tired of it."[22] The next day the *Journal*, in an editorial, criticized the mayor for passing by "another opportunity for true statesmanship" by tabling the names submitted by Chandler.[23] What subsequently happened behind the scenes is unknown, but two days later the city council approved the names, officially giving life to the new Model Cities agency.

One of the reasons that the Negro Unity Planners did not meet massive opposition in their successful bid for control of the MCA was that they did not interfere with the work of professionals who were called upon by city officials and HUD to modify the East St. Louis application by the January 12 deadline. In fact, two professionals who had been members of the old MCA were included on the new membership list: a representative of the Illinois State Employment Service and the director of the St. Clair County EOC. Mendelson continued to attend meetings of the steering committee, as did Washnis, who remained acting chairman of the MCA until the official designation of the new membership. He sent memorandums and notices concerning the Model Cities program and played a leadership role through the first half of January when the East St. Louis application was revised to conform to federal guidelines.

HUD had given forty-five days from the time of official designation for cities to submit a revised work program. Originally, the purpose of the December 14 meeting had been to organize a local team that could work on revisions to meet the January 12 deadline. This effort, needless to say, had been delayed. HUD was also slow in gearing up for program revisions. In mid-December, HUD officials informed East St. Louis that a federal team would be in the city in early January to assist local efforts in revising the Model Cities plans. It was agreed to concentrate the work into the first two weeks of January.

On the morning of January 2 federal representatives including an assistant secretary of HUD met with Mayor Fields, the city council, Washnis, Mendelson, and several others to for-

[22] *Metro-East Journal*, January 11, 1968.
[23] *Ibid.*

mally launch the revision work. The mayor and city council were not expected to exert technical leadership, but it was assumed that the mayor might encourage reluctant agency representatives to cooperate with the Model Cities effort. It was emphasized for the council's benefit that Model Cities must be coordinated with other federal, state, and local programs. Federal officials stressed that Model Cities was the central federal program in East St. Louis. With these preliminaries out of the way, the federal representatives held an afternoon meeting with local officials and professionals who would make up the revision team.

On January 3 and 4 day-long workshops involving federal officials and local professionals were held at city hall. According to the federal team, a lengthy list of revisions was needed. By January 5 Mendelson and several others began to write the stipulated changes. Washnis, meanwhile, made contacts with community leaders and agencies, and obtained "commitments" which would "demonstrate" East St. Louis's technical capacity to run a Model Cities program.

A meeting was arranged for January 8 between members of the legally constituted MCA and the steering committee. About seventy people, most of them members of the Negro Unity Planners, attended the meeting. Washnis presided, with the intention of presenting some of the revised plans to the steering committee. Cleveland Chandler, as chairman of the steering committee, asked for endorsement of a new membership list for the MCA and the eighteen members of the MCA who were present quickly approved the list. This move, a preliminary to presenting the names to the city council for official approval as the new MCA, solidified the position of the Negro Unity Planners. Chandler was careful to observe the niceties at the same time that he championed the prerogatives of his group. Immediately after the vote, he criticized the revision of Model Cities plans without including "grassrooters": "These people know what they want and must be consulted in these plans. The city council has the last word but the Model City Agency must call the shots."[24] At Washnis's request, four members of the steering

[24] *Ibid.*, January 9, 1968.

committee were appointed to work with professionals in making final revisions. For three days, January 9, 10, and 11, the four members consulted with professionals while the revisions were being written. On Friday, January 12, the city council approved the revised work program for the first planning year and a new MCA membership proposed by the steering committee. These plans were sent to HUD offices on Saturday, January 13, to arrive by the January 14 deadline (the original January 12 deadline had been moved back two days by HUD officials).

Selection of the Director

On January 14, Washnis announced that the recruitment of staff for positions in the MCA would begin immediately. These positions, as described in the revised plans sent to HUD, included a director at $16,500, a chief planner, two resident planners, and a stenographer-office manager. Washnis indicated that several people had applied for the director position, and that the positions would be filled within several weeks.[25] Subsequent events revealed the process to be far more difficult than predicted by Washnis.

At the first official meeting of the newly constructed MCA held on January 18, Cleveland Chandler, the head of the steering committee, was elected chairman of the MCA, "by acclamation." Chandler immediately appointed a personnel committee and a committee on constitution and bylaws. Though the personnel committee was charged with reviewing applications for the MCA directorship and recommending names for appointment, it was understood that the city council would make the final choice. This procedure was given approval by Washnis, who turned the application material over to the committee.

At the next meeting of the MCA on January 23, Washnis read a letter from the city council requesting that the personnel committee recommend three names for the directorship. Instead, the personnel committee only a few moments later reported two names—Fred L. Teer and Jefferson Ware. Teer was the first choice, and Ware second. A resolution transmitting these pref-

[25] *St. Louis Globe-Democrat*, January 15, 1968.

erences to the city council instructed the council to offer the
position to Teer and to consider Ware only if Teer refused the
position or was physically unable to serve.

Within the personnel committee, there had been division on
the recommendations. Though there were eight applicants for
the directorship most were not given serious consideration, including a local Black schoolteacher supported by a small group
of precinct committeemen, a White real estate operator from
St. Louis, and a White executive director of a redevelopment
authority in an eastern city with extensive experience in renewal
and planning. Only three applicants were even remotely acceptable: Fred Teer, Jefferson Ware, and Walter Robinson. All
three were Black and known, though with varying recognition,
in East St. Louis.

Fred Teer held a bachelor's and master's degree in education,
had spent over twenty-five years in the East St. Louis school
system, and had lived most of his fifty-five years in the heart of
the Model City area. Teer was the candidate consistently characterized as "one of the people," and this was viewed as his
main qualification for the job. To many East St. Louisans he had
become controversial due both to his personal style and his
degree of involvement in public issues. For example, only a few
months earlier, he had been removed as assistant director of
the adult education program of District 189 and transferred to
the position of high school civics instructor—a job he had held
when he started in the system. Prior to his removal, Teer had
tried vigorously to obtain the job of director of adult education
which had been vacated by Elmo Bush when he became assistant principal at Lincoln High School. There were student strikes
and picketing at the Adult Education Building in support of
Teer's unsuccessful effort.

Fred Teer was a public figure though he had never held an
elective office. He could inspire audiences and generate constituencies for projects in which he was interested. In his struggle to build sixty-two units of 221 (d)(3) housing in the inner
area of East St. Louis, he attracted over 1,000 people to a meeting in a neighborhood school. Both Teer and his family had pro-

fessional and personal commitments to East St. Louis and close identification with the Black community.

His campaign for Model City director was based on the premise that people from the neighborhood know best how to solve neighborhood problems. He cited his experience with federal programs through leadership in the nonprofit housing project. Teer was called singleminded by his detractors. They claimed that he could not grasp the inter-relationships in a program as complex as Model Cities and that he did not have the administrative ability to work with public and private agencies. His supporters disagreed, countering with the argument that indigenous Blacks must be given opportunities to learn and grow in executive positions and that Teer's qualifications fit the job requirements very adequately.

Another candidate, Jefferson Ware, had a background in law and a doctorate in education. His retiring and soft-spoken personality projected self-assurance and patience, in contrast to Teer's somewhat explosive style. Born and raised in East St. Louis, Ware spent the first half of his forty-five years in the Model Cities neighborhood. The fact that he was living in a nearby predominately White Illinois community contributed to his image as an "outsider." Ware's credentials included extensive experience in crime and delinquency with an emphasis on correction and rehabilitation. He had been employed by the Center for the Study of Crime and Delinquency of Southern Illinois University and, at the time of the selection of the director, was an Assistant Professor in the School of Social Service at St. Louis University.

A third applicant was Walter Robinson, who, at that time, was director of the Neighborhood Youth Corps, a contracting agency under the local Community Action Agency (CAA). Robinson prided himself in being a public official who could act authoritatively in his own program and who was capable of understanding and implementing public projects like Model Cities. Close associates shared his self-conception, and he was recommended as a sound administrator by the assistant director of the Community Action Agency which had loaned Robinson to the city a few months earlier for the forty-five–day Model City revision. Youngest of the three, he was in his late thirties and had a master's degree in social work.

Considering the constraints imposed on program operations by HUD and by the diverse local interests, all three of the candidates were qualified, and barring overwhelming resistance by militants to Ware and Robinson, any of the three probably could have adequately filled the directorship position. At the time, there was sizable sentiment within the personnel committee of the MCA that Robinson was identified with the city administration. Without a longtime identification with East St. Louis, having come from St. Louis only a few years earlier, and with only a reputation among social and governmental agency professionals, he could not refute these allegations. Ware was also distrusted. Many on the personnel committee felt he was an egghead who could not identify with "the cats on the corner"— even though he had grown up on those very corners.

Negro Unity Planners wanted total control of the MCA— they had, for example, attempted to form a corporation independent of the city to run the MCA, but HUD had said "no." To recommend all three men might lessen the possibility of having Teer appointed—and to a majority of the group, Teer was the only acceptable choice. Most of the seven-member personnel committee favored Teer; and, according to one of the members, selection of criteria for the director's employment was slanted toward Teer. Half of the eight applicants were rejected immediately, including Robinson, who lost in a close vote at a committee meeting on January 20, 1968. Only four names went through the committee's evaluative process—Teer, Ware, the schoolteacher, and the redevelopment professional. Ware and Teer were interviewed by the committee, though the interview had no bearing on the decision. Teer was the first choice. When the personnel committee delivered only two instead of three names to the larger MCA for forwarding to the city council, partiality and bias toward Teer were charged. Heated arguments developed at a January 23 agency meeting over the selection procedure, and there was further resentment when the minutes of the personnel committee were never made public to dispel these charges.[26] The MCA only narrowly approved the recommendation of Teer first and then Ware if Teer could not serve. On January 24, the recommendation was sent to the city council.

Most of the personnel committee would have preferred to recommend only Teer, but they felt that this might engender too much opposition. They were probably correct, for the selection process illuminated divergent views within both the Negro Unity Planners and the MCA. According to one of Teer's supporters, he would not have attracted so much backing if the Black leadership had been more closely tied to city hall and established social agency leadership. Teer reflected their aspirations for greater control over the allocation of jobs and resources within the East St. Louis political arena.[27]

Within the MCA, several individuals were covertly opposed to Teer. After the January 23 MCA meeting, these persons and a few precinct committeemen met the mayor at his plumbing shop to discuss what could be done to block the Teer appointment. Mayor Fields scolded them for allowing themselves to get into that position, then suggested that they get a petition together to present to the city council. Under any circumstances, he said, he would not go against majority sentiment. At the January 31 meeting of the council, the existence of a petition signed by forty persons, some of them MCA members, was revealed. It protested the favoritism of the personnel committee's report. The petition had earlier been presented privately to the mayor and was circulated to force consideration of a third candidate, Walter Robinson. According to the February 3, 1968, edition of the *Metro-East Journal* the petition accused the personnel committee of acting "unfairly and dictatorially by discriminating against certain other applicants who are very highly qualified and deserving. After having interviewed them and, by their own admission, acknowledged his [Robinson's] high qualifications they left his name off the report."

The petition brought immediate and strong protest from

---

[26] Discussions held with several members of the personnel committee of the Model Cities agency in February, 1968.

[27] Negro Unity Planners, interview with a member, February, 1968.

Teer's backers. Teer's proponents knew of the petition before its presentation to the council, since some of the MCA members were themselves involved. At the February 1 MCA meeting, one member suggested including in the MCA bylaws a rule for expulsion of members who took unilateral action against the majority of MCA members. Chandler attacked the petition and said that plans were being made to gather 15,000 signatures to protest any city council decision which deviated from MCA recommendations. Further he promised that the list of signatures would be delivered personally to the Chicago office of HUD.[28] To avert possible opposition and to force the council's hand, the majority of the MCA members wanted a quick decision on the director appointment. At the January 31 council meeting, Chandler and several other members objected to the delay. A special meeting was called for the next night to discuss strategy in reacting to the council's inaction.

Behind Teer was a coalition with powerful resources. Activities of this group carried the implied and explicit threat of disrupting the program if the council failed to make the "proper" choice. It was apparent that the coalition opposition to the Model Cities program could be extremely effective or even fatal to the program, since a large number of Black leaders in the target area were involved. Many of these leaders were careful to point out this possibility. For example, one of Teer's backers called Mendelson the night before the city council's decision and asked him to put pressure on Washnis to support Teer. If Teer was not selected, it was hinted, it would be disastrous and might even destroy the program. No threats had to be made to remind the mayor and others that the city had very narrowly avoided racial violence the previous summer; this program could either partly satisfy or further anger Black militants.

But the opposition to Teer grew, even considering his support. Many factors were cited by the opponents. Some were concerned about his perceived personality traits and background. He was thought by some to be bombastic and unpredictable, in contrast to Ware, who was "sophisticated—he could work well

[28] *Metro-East Journal*, February 2, 1968.

with the bankers."[29] There were also objections to Teer's past politics, including the late August, 1967, controversy over his expected promotion to the directorship of the adult education program. His competence as an administrator was also questioned, though his leadership in attracting federal money for a local housing project was universally praised. Further, many opponents objected to the composition of Negro Unity Planners because of their claim that the group was dominated by dissident, defeated political opportunists and militants.

Phone calls and requests for private meetings deluged the mayor's office in the two weeks prior to the city council's February 7 decision. Washnis was opposed to Teer and said so publicly. He, along with other key city administrators (most of whom were Black), including two administrative assistants to Fields and the heads of about five city departments, met with the mayor and some of them questioned Teer's ability and the motives of the group supporting him. Business and labor leaders called and talked with the mayor individually, while PACE passed a resolution calling for three recommendations for the Model Cities position to be sent to the city council, and appointed a committee of businessmen to meet with the mayor. Representatives of many public agencies in East St. Louis were opposed to Teer on the grounds that he would not be able to relate to professional administrators at the local, state, or federal level. SIU representatives who had been involved in earlier programs with Teer told both Washnis and the mayor that Ware had better professional qualifications and that Teer would be the captive of his supporters. Precinct committeemen and other members of the Fields political machine were opposed, for obvious reasons—the Unity Planners represented a threat to established machine leadership. Even the federal administrators arranged a meeting with the mayor to express their concern about Teer's qualifications. And finally, some of Teer's nominal supporters, including leaders of community organizations, privately expressed opposition.

On February 6, 1968, Teer and Ware were interviewed by the

[29] Interview with a prominent city official, February, 1968.

mayor and the city council. Ware apparently impressed the commissioners, who seemed to be leaning strongly in his favor. At
the city council meeting the next day, the appointment of the
director was not on the agenda. Forty or fifty members of the
Unity Planners were on hand to protest the delay in the appointment, but they were soon upstaged by the council. At the end
of its regular business meeting, the mayor announced that the
council would recess for a short caucus, after which "an important announcement might be made." Ten minutes later the
council returned, and Fields announced: "Since the agency
named Fred Teer as its first choice and since he has worked on
various programs in the area without pay we have selected him.
We hope all citizens will rally behind him and help him do a
good job." Chandler thanked the council and promised "we will
do all we can to help him." [30]

In the face of overwhelming opposition, re-enforced by their
apparent preference for Ware, why did the council make the
choice it did? The lone Black council member, Ester Saverson,
was apparently the key. Saverson, as the Black representative
on the city council, had an informal veto power over matters directly affecting Blacks. On all other matters—and sometimes
on Black issues too—Fields called the shots. Saverson apparently persuaded Mayor Fields that the pressure from the Black
community was such that Teer had to be the choice. The mayor
and other commissioners, though leaning to Ware, deferred to
Saverson because of the importance of this appointment to him.
Whether Saverson made a trade-off with Black leaders is not
known; incentives for a bargain of some kind were clearly
present. In exchange for Teer's appointment, implicit or explicit promises of "cooling it" might have been made.

Two days after his appointment, Teer, in search of Saverson,
crossed paths with him in city hall. Teer thanked him for his
efforts in backing him. Saverson acknowledged the thanks, then
told Teer that he was going to have to work with the agencies
and city hall in his capacity as Model Cities director. This, most
likely, had been the concern of the mayor and other commis-

[30] *Metro-East Journal*, February 7, 1968.

sioners in their conversations with Saverson, and he more or less relayed the message. The meeting ended amicably.

Following the two victories by the coalition of Black leaders —the winning of control of the MCA membership, and the selection of Teer as MCA director—the Model Cities program moved in three separate directions. One direction was to consolidate and maintain the position of Model Cities against possible encroachments from city hall and local public and private agencies and organizations. This was an essential move, for while Black leaders had succeeded in gaining total control of the MCA, the victory was a precarious one. Another direction was the emergence of a more or less constant struggle within the MCA between established Black leaders and younger, more aggressive militants. Still a third political development was dictated by the necessities for meeting HUD's planning requirements and administering the program. Those involved in the program, and especially the director, became progressively more willing to adhere to constraints imposed by the planning process. Politics moved in these three directions throughout the rest of the Model Cities program in East St. Louis. Sometimes one aspect occupied the center of attention to the temporary exclusion of the others; nevertheless, all three elements became permanent features.

Consolidating and Maintaining Control

Immediately after assuming official control of the MCA on January 18, 1968, Black leaders began to consolidate their hold on the MCA. Besides the election of Cleveland Chandler as MCA chairman, two committees were appointed at the January 18 meeting. The personnel committee, as has been seen, took action to insure the selection of Teer for director. Another committee, on constitution and bylaws, was equally zealous in protecting the position of those in control of the MCA through the creation of rules and procedures for MCA membership.

Strengthening control through rules and procedures had begun shortly after the December 14 formation of the steering committee to guide the newly constituted MCA. At the first steering committee meeting on December 15 a proposal was made to require that target area residents comprise 80 percent of the MCA membership and that professionals and other residents of East St. Louis from outside the target area be allotted the remaining 20 percent. Although HUD approval was needed before such a rule could be accepted as official policy, the suggestion received informal agreement immediately. In February, it was inserted into the MCA constitution and bylaws.

Consolidation of control showed up not only in the internal politics of the MCA but also in its relations to city hall. Distrust for city hall politicians was extended as well to the professionals working for the city. Many MCA members were suspicious of and hostile to George Washnis. They saw him as the mayor's representative who had headed the original Model Cities effort and who might attempt to regain control. After the December 14 formation of the steering committee, Washnis continued to act as the chief liaison between the official MCA and the steering committee, and as official MCA chairman until Chandler's selection on January 18. But in early February, Chandler and other Black leaders requested that Clyde Jordan, an assistant to Mayor Fields, become the official liaison between city hall and the MCA. Jordan, the publisher of the *East St. Louis Monitor*, was a member of the Negro Unity Planners. "They apparently feel a trust in him," Washnis said in announcing that Jordan's duties would probably be changed.[31] Washnis never actually gave up his role as Model Cities liaison, probably because Jordan did not want the position. Distrust for Washnis had been registered, however.

Two months later the MCA was publicly at loggerheads with city hall for the first time since the selection of the MCA director. Since their takeover of the Model Cities program, Teer, Chandler, and other black leaders had come under pressure from more militant members of the MCA who wanted to push confrontation with city hall. At an April 16 MCA meeting several militants (as directed by Chandler) pushed for MCA action to oust the police commissioner from office. One week earlier, an MCA member had appeared before the city council demanding the

[31] *Ibid.*, February 13, 1968.

ouster. When he carried his case to the April 16 meeting, a heated discussion broke out. Finally, the MCA voted for the commissioner's removal, although Chandler and several others abstained. "The militants feel we should do it today; but I think we must do it properly if it is to be effective," Chandler told a newspaper reporter.[32] A public meeting was called for Sunday, April 21, to air complaints, and following the meeting, the MCA voted to approve a report of its committee on police relations to ask for the removal of the police commissioner. At its April 22 meeting, the city council received the MCA resolution.

This action attracted little support from Teer or Chandler. In the absence of a real clash of interests between city hall and the MCA, they preferred to avoid confrontation. Their position was supported by HUD. After a meeting with Ted Robinson, HUD's lead man from the regional office, Teer reported to the MCA that "Our agency has been misdirected. We are a planning agency, not an action group."[33] The report was presented as a HUD directive; given their stakes in getting eventual approval for the program, the MCA membership approved it, amid grumbling from militant members.

Teer's and Chandler's willingness to avoid confrontation in the police matter did not mean they avoided confrontation in principle. It was only that the MCA's interests were not directly involved. Several months later they led a clash with city hall that equaled the selection of Teer in intensity and importance.

Two major federal programs accompanied the Model Cities grant to East St. Louis. They were the Concentrated Employment Program (CEP), funded by the Department of Labor, and a General Neighborhood Renewal Plan (GNRP) grant, funded by HUD. Federal officials stated that these programs were given to East St. Louis because of its Model City designation, and MCA leaders had high hopes that the relationship would be more than verbal. Ties between the GNRP and Model Cities were particularly obvious. When HUD allocated only one-third of the East St. Louis request for Model City planning funds ($85,000), mention was made that $100,000 could be made

[32] *Ibid.*, April 18, 1968.
[33] *Ibid.*, May 8, 1968.

available to supplement the Model City grant if both planning projects could be legitimately related. Ted Robinson, Teer, Washnis, and Mendelson decided to propose that the GNRP would become the physical planning input for the Model Cities area and proceeded to prepare an application in conjunction with the city planner, Ed Denman. Prior to completion of the application a few weeks later, Robinson told Teer, Washnis, and Mendelson that HUD could raise the GNRP amount to $300,000 if it could be used partially as a vehicle for citizen participation in the Model Cities area. One of the ways to insure participation, they agreed, was to employ one subprofessional as a resident assistant for each professional that was to be hired in this multi-year project. Six residents were to be selected and were to be trained in the planning process. They were to perform surveys and acquire skills that would permit them to interpret the technical work to other residents. Further, it would enable the resident assistants to learn techniques which they might transfer to other planning projects. An application was submitted in the late spring of 1968 and the $300,000 grant was approved in December of that year.

When Mayor Fields tried to use these six positions for patronage purposes, he initiated a confrontation that endangered the Model Cities program and that set the tone for future relations between the MCA and city hall. Following approval of the GNRP grant, Fields announced that he was recommending six persons for the resident assistant posts (recommendation by the mayor meant automatic city council approval). Four of the six were Democratic precinct committeemen, three of which had recently lost state patronage jobs because of the election of a Republican governor. One, a St. Clair County deputy sheriff, was under indictment for his alleged involvement in a holdup in October, 1967. Another appointee was a party lieutenant in the Fields machine.

The day after Fields's announcement, the regularly scheduled MCA meeting was heavily packed with militants from the MCA area. Teer, Chandler, and McGaughy, however, needed no prodding to confront the city—the jobs in question were, in their judgment, supposed to be filled through MCA appointment. Chandler warned the city that "we ought to get the whole bag or no bag. We're going to run it or wreck it. Politicians are welcome as citizens but they're certainly not going to come in here and run things."[34] McGaughy was equally militant: "We'll bring whatever pressure is necessary to bring about citizens' participation in the program. If we're going to let politicians come into this program, we might as well give up the program. Citizens must take a stand. They are the people who should say who gets the jobs."[35] A motion was loudly passed encouraging MCA members to attend the city council meeting scheduled for December 12. "If you people are really concerned about Model Cities, I want you there," said Chandler. "It burns me up to find them playing the same old game. Are the politicians going to step in to get the gravy?"[36]

About 100 Model Cities members and their supporters attended the city council meeting, filling the mayor's office and spilling out in the reception area and the hallway. Some of the supporters were militant members of youth gangs, mostly from East St. Louis, but a few also from St. Louis. To the right and left of the mayor's desk the other four commissioners were seated. Standing in back of them were about ten Black precinct committeemen. As the crowd pushed into the mayor's office, some of the gang members climbed over furniture and shouted down attempts by city officials to make statements. At one point, a Christmas tree in the room was knocked over. At another, someone threatened that the houses of the precinct committeemen might be burned down and that there might be physical harm. One of the precinct committeemen boldly took a pack of matches out of his pocket and tossed it in the direction of the threatening voice. He then replied "that is the reason we have carpenters" (to rebuild fire-damaged homes). After twenty minutes of shouting and confusion, Chandler led the group out, deciding that little could be accomplished under the circumstances. Six policemen arrived and assisted the stragglers in their departure from the mayor's office.

[34] *Ibid.*, December 11, 1968.
[35] *Ibid.*
[36] *Ibid.*

Following the encounter, the Model Cities group went to the Model Cities office located in a former bank building adjoining city hall. Their meeting was brief and noisy, but little was decided. Simultaneously, several precinct committeemen met in the office of Commissioner Virgil Calvert, the lone Black on the city council. Calvert defended the appointments on the ground that the precinct committeemen were qualified by virtue of their familiarity with the neighborhoods and their work in the party which, he said, closely paralleled the work of resident assistants. The precinct committeemen called the protests sour grapes and accused the Model Cities group of trying to build a power structure.

In its Sunday, December 15, edition, the *Metro-East Journal* attacked Calvert for being a spoils politician: "If the politicians get the appointments, it will be good old Commissioner Calvert who got them their jobs."[37] In fact, Calvert had given the names to Fields, since all but one were Black appointments. With Calvert's encouragement, precinct committeemen staged a counterattack. On December 16, forty committeemen appeared at a city council caucus meeting to defend their rights to hold the jobs. Calvert asserted that the committeemen were already dealing with the kinds of problems that would be involved in the GNRP and Model Cities. He added, "The only reason these fellows made application is they lost their jobs. They're not interested in running it, or they wouldn't have applied for these jobs. All these jobs are low on the totem pole."[38] Complete support for the committeemen's position was promised by the state representative from the area who attended the meeting.[39] When told by Washnis that they should get more involved in Model Cities and other programs, several of the committeemen claimed that they were unwanted in the Model Cities program, and that they had been repeatedly criticized at Model Cities meetings.[40]

[37] *Ibid.*, December 15, 1968.
[38] *Ibid.*
[39] *Ibid.*
[40] The headline of the newspaper article was: "Committeemen Explain They Felt Unwanted in Model City Program." Its subtitle said, "Ready to Do Battle to Be Included."

Mayor Fields, as usual, attempted to play the role of peace-maker and mediator. "I am hoping that we can still sit down and work this thing out . . .," he stated. On Model Cities, he said, "We certainly want to cooperate with Model City and I think we've shown that by approving everything they've done. Fred Teer wouldn't have been appointed without me. I took a lot of heat to get him appointed."[41]

Later the same day, Cleveland Chandler told a reporter that he would recommend to the Model Cities board that the program be scrapped if political interference with the program continued. That evening two strong resolutions were unanimously passed by the Model Cities board. One petitioned HUD to withdraw the Model Cities program from East St. Louis if the mayor's appointments were not rescinded. Another resolved to hire a lawyer to file suit for enjoining operation of the GNRP program until the controversy was resolved. More than 200 people attended the meeting, and noisily approved the board actions. Two militant organizations in St. Louis, the Black Liberators led by Reverend Charles Koen and the Zulu 1,200s, phoned their support to the meeting. Clyde Jordan, administrative assistant to the mayor, arranged a conference in the mayor's office for the following day.

A seventeen-member delegation from the MCA met with the mayor the next day, December 18. Two policemen guarded the door in anticipation of a recurrence of the disruptions that had occurred the previous week. A group of thirty-five supporters waited in another room in city hall, accompanied by four Black Liberators from St. Louis. At the meeting, Fields suggested that a screening committee be formed to process the applications for the resident assistant positions. One day later, another meeting resulted in an agreement to review the personnel ordinance of the city. Every weapon had been used by the Model Cities group and they had influenced the mayor who, as in previous confrontations, stayed neutral to assess the strength of the contending forces. This time the confrontation had been clear-cut, the issue central. Model Cities had won a resounding

41 *Ibid.*

victory. One important outcome was to establish the permanent strength of the Model Cities group. No major confrontations followed.

Building Neighborhood Support

One of the most important political resources of the insurgent Black leaders was their ability to claim the backing of a large segment of the Black community in East St. Louis. Also important, and absolutely essential over the long run, was the claim to legitimate representation of the population of the target area. From the takeover of the MCA in December, 1967, to the autumn of 1968 the politics of building a neighborhood base of support dominated Model Cities activities. Building this support helped to develop a strong resource for bargaining with established local political leaders and agencies and with neighborhood leaders who competed for perquisites and leadership in the Model Cities program.

One of the first actions of the Model Cities leaders had been the forcing of changes in the work program submitted to HUD on January 13, 1968. Of major importance was the revision calling for an expenditure of $20,000, nearly one-fourth of the $85,000 total planning grant, for citizen participation activities. Part of this money was slated for hiring nonprofessional community workers who would assist in building neighborhood participation. A reserve of $10,000 was for use by two subcity organizations. These two organizations, one for each of the noncontiguous parts of the Model Cities target area, were to be set up by residents in the neighborhoods. Later in the year the subcity organizations were incorporated as official organizations apart from the MCA.

At the February 27, 1968, MCA meeting the subcity plan gained membership approval and a group was appointed to recruit members for the subcity organizations. Ten MCA task force committees in substantive areas such as housing, health, recreation, and physical development were also set up to "start working with the various agencies" in East St. Louis. At this time there were only a few active members of the MCA—a total of twenty-three people manned the ten task force committees. With no exceptions, the committees were composed of the insurgent Black leaders in the MCA or the few members who had been recruited from the target area.

The task force committees were slow in getting underway, for two reasons. One was that the MCA provided little or no leadership in instructing the committees on what to do. Throughout March the committees, with only a few active members each, searched for ideas and direction. Second, the vagueness of the mandate given the committees more or less forced a waiting period. It appeared that a committee structure had been created to give the impression of activity and structure when actually there was little. In reality, activity was centered in the hands of a very few of the leaders.

In early April the committees were re-formed to include agency professionals in advisory positions, while committee chairmanships remained with neighborhood residents. Little was accomplished through the spring and summer of 1968. In late August, 1968, a meeting of the committee chairmen was called to explore the relationship between the professionals and residents, but very little was accomplished in meeting that objective. Such was the extent of committee progress.

Staffing the MCA emphasized the stakes of the Black leaders in keeping tight control and underscored their fear that agency professionals might try to take over the MCA. In March a second staff member, in addition to Teer, was added to the MCA. At $6,000 a year Teer selected Will McGaughy as the MCA resident assistant. As resident assistant, McGaughy was assigned the task of developing citizen participation through the subcity organizations. Within a year and a half McGaughy's salary was raised first to $7,500 and then to $12,500 and his position retitled director of citizen participation. Following McGaughy's appointment, five community worker positions were filled. On April 10 the city council approved five persons as community workers; five more were later added. Community workers earned $300 a month and were hired for four months to organize residents in their neighborhoods.

At the same time the first professional was named to the MCA staff. Walter Robinson, one of the original contestants for MCA director, was hired as chief planner. Robinson's appointment was a natural one. He had been favored by a number of people in the MCA for the directorship, and he was known for his work in the Neighborhood Youth Corps. He was considered an acceptable professional.

Robinson's stay was a short one. In early June he handed in his resignation to accept a position at Southern Illinois University. In an effort to save money, the MCA replaced Robinson with a team of White university professionals who were loaned by their respective institutions as consultants. Both the personnel and then the executive committees had recommended the team approach on the premise that "the responsibility for planning in at least 12 (task force) areas is an impossible task for one individual."[42]

Using the team approach was a natural outgrowth of the stress put on voluntary efforts by agencies and organizations. Much of Teer's energy in March and April had been spent in soliciting help from state and local agency representatives. It had long been known that SIU would be willing to contribute personnel to the program. MCA leadership was, at first, too distrustful of agency professionals to initially fill staff positions with them. By June, however, enough commitments from agencies had been solicited by Teer to make any other approach than the use of a loaned professional team illogical. Southern Illinois University, St. Louis University, and several departments of the state of Illinois volunteered personnel.

Administering the Program

Although dominated by insurgent Black leaders the MCA was never totally divorced from established institutions and political actors. Its leaders instinctively knew the value of keeping contact with established leaders and building and maintaining support outside the target area. Black leaders, by virtue of their control of the MCA, had a vested interest in its continued existence and future funding. Because of this they were willing to

[42] *Ibid.*, June 4, 1968.

establish contacts with local and state agencies, seek out technical help for the program, and abide by guidelines set down by
the federal government.

City officials as well as Model Cities leaders, mainly Fred
Teer, made strenuous efforts to elicit commitments from local
and state agencies to the program. In the first week of February,
Mayor Fields and Washnis journeyed to Springfield to meet with
state agency representatives in a meeting presided over by Governor Otto Kerner. Despite the take-over of the MCA by the
insurgent Blacks, city officials, especially Washnis, felt that the
Model Cities program was central to the renewal of East St.
Louis. Tentative commitments were made to East St. Louis,
principally from the Departments of Business and Economic
Development and Public Aid, but mainly it was agreed to hold
further meetings.

Meanwhile, many members of the MCA were sold on the idea
of recruiting professional help on a consulting and loaned basis.
This idea was not new—Washnis had broached it in December
and repeated it several times—and it fit in well with the limited
planning funds and the desire to spend as little as possible for
professional planners. At a February 13 meeting the MCA
membership turned down a proposal that a professional consultant be hired to assist the subcity organizations in planning.
Objection to the proposal was raised on the ground that consulting aid from SIU might be available on a loaned basis.

Partly because several agencies were alienated from the group
that controlled the MCA, Washnis and a couple of city officials
made many of the contacts with local and state agencies for the
MCA. And because Washnis was in a far better position to coordinate local activities than Teer, HUD representatives con-
ferred with him as often as with Teer. On February 21 and 22,
HUD representatives came into East St. Louis and talked
with Washnis, other city officials, and Teer. Their conversation
focused on how East St. Louis intended to prepare for the planning effort. Stress was placed on getting commitments from local
and state agencies. HUD officials also reported on a meeting
held the week before between federal and state agencies in
which the agencies had been encouraged to review their re-

sources and make commitments to the then two Model Cities programs in Illinois—Chicago and East St. Louis.

On February 29 Washnis, Mendelson, and Teer attended a meeting of state officials held in Springfield, the state capital of Illinois. This meeting had been urged by the federal representatives. At the Governor's insistence officials from all of the major state agencies were in attendance. The response from the state agencies to East St. Louis's pleas for help seemed overwhelming. Twenty-six agencies made commitments of personnel and other types of aid to the East St. Louis MCA. It now appeared as if Model Cities would be a larger operation than originally anticipated. "I was impressed with the dedication and sincerity expressed by the heads of the 26 agencies who attended the meeting." Teer later said, "The agencies made available personnel, consulting services, and in some instances, possibilities of financial assistance."[43] Teer optimistically predicted a MCA staff of thirty-five to forty persons. "Now it remains for us at the citizen level and the local city administrative level to come forth with a similar effort and cooperation."[44] Washnis at the same time announced plans for calling regular meetings at the local level to get city departments and local agencies to assist in the program.

Later, in May, extensive publicity preceded a meeting of state officials in East St. Louis "to show the people in East St. Louis that the state is interested, wants to help in the program, and in fact has already assisted the local agency (MCA)."[45] The newly formed state coordinating committee, otherwise labeled the governor's "cabinet," was, according to a governor's aide, meeting in East St. Louis to demonstrate the state's commitment. "So far as I know, nothing like this has ever been done in any of the states, and certainly not in this region," stated the governor's aide. On May 23, directors of eighteen departments and representatives from three others met in East St. Louis with city officials and MCA members. Glowing promises were made at the meeting. In addition to its supplemental fund appropriation,

[43] *Ibid.*, March 1, 1968.
[44] *Ibid.*
[45] *Ibid.*, May 8, 1968. This quote is a statement of Sam Eubanks, administrative aid to then Governor Otto Kerner.

the MCA was promised $500,000 in state and federal funds, and millions in additional money were hinted at. About 150 local people attended the marathon eight-hour session.

Several universities promised technical assistance to Model Cities. Teer had gone to the presidents and chancellors of Southern Illinois University, St. Louis University, and the University of Illinois for help. Personnel were committed by Southern Illinois and St. Louis universities. On July 12, nineteen faculty members from the University of Illinois met with Teer and others in East St. Louis, and agreed to help review the East St. Louis plans.

These and other contacts held great promise, but failed to yield the anticipated commitment. Many state agencies did not come through on promises of personnel and programs. Some additional federal funds were forthcoming. These, however, were not closely connected to Model Cities: they were beyond the control and scope of attention of the Model Cities program, even though they represented important increments of federal funds to East St. Louis.

Though Teer's efforts in recruiting assistance did not all directly succeed, he was able to add to the list of endorsers of the East St. Louis effort. When the federal government later asked for a demonstration of support by local institutions for the East St. Louis Model Cities program, a lengthy list of endorsements could be assembled. For example, in mid-October a meeting between MCA staff and several faculty members from the University of Illinois was scheduled. Ostensibly the purpose was to have the Illinois professors review East St. Louis's first planning document. In reality, of course, the meeting was intended to gain the approval of the Illinois group. As it turned out, the meeting was canceled, but the MCA could still list the University of Illinois as one of its supporting institutions.

Those commitments that materialized from the state agencies and universities were crucial, since no other source for filling the professional planning positions existed. Mendelson from Southern Illinois University was loaned to the MCA staff, and became the chief planner (although he never officially held that title). Arthur Stickgold, of the Center for Urban Programs, St.

Louis University, became an extremely important member of the MCA planning staff. Stickgold came from the St. Louis Model Cities program after a dispute between himself and the director. He was originally contacted by Mendelson, who resisted assuming the responsibility for the planning after Robinson left until guarantees of sufficient technical support were available. When an official of the Illinois Department of Business and Economic Development offered $12,000 to hire a planner and then loan him to the MCA, Stickgold was immediately escorted to Springfield by Teer and Mendelson to interview for the job. Though accepted for the position, Stickgold subsequently went to St. Louis University. Teer shuffled his budget and signed a contract with St. Louis University to obtain Stickgold halftime. Mendelson and Stickgold officially began work in early June, 1968. At the same time, the state OEO provided $3,000 which was used to employ Mary Ellen Ross and Esley Hamilton, graduate students in planning at the University of Wisconsin, for the summer. A public administration specialist from the University of Missouri, provided four days per month after September and an assistant to Washnis, was assigned to coordinate Model Cities with other city programs and to create management controls on the increased funds coming from the federal and state governments.

The offer of $12,000 was eagerly accepted in the fall of 1968. Harvey Henderson, who was a resident of the target area, a student of planning at Southern Illinois University, and a member of Negro Unity Planners when that organization took over control of the MCA, along with another planner formerly with the regional council of governments, were hired by the state and loaned to Model Cities. Henderson, in January, 1968, had been elected second vice-chairman of the MCA.

Other state assistance was also tendered. As early as February, 1968, the Department of Public Aid had contributed an experienced caseworker who became fiscal director for the MCA until he went back to his old job in mid-1969. A physician was loaned fulltime from the Department of Public Health to plan the health component of Model Cities. She not only directed the planning but also spearheaded the implementation of action health care projects. Assistance was provided by the Illinois Youth Commission who sent a technical advisor to East St. Louis to work as a consultant in the crime and delinquency and cultural components.

A very small planning staff was available in the summer of 1968. Mendelson, Stickgold, Ross, and Hamilton spent most of June, July, and August attempting to establish relationships with local professionals who were to provide technical assistance to the task force committees being set up in the neighborhoods. By attending the task force meetings, which were made up of and led by grassrooters, these local professionals were to write and summarize problems and proposals brought up by committee members. Each professional was to submit a paper on behalf of his committee summarizing the problems in that committee's substantive area and setting forth the preferred solutions. Papers were to be forwarded to the MCA staff (Mendelson, Stickgold, and the rest), who had the job of relating them to one another, refining them when necessary to conform to HUD guidelines, and uniting the total planning package.

Task force committees were organized in varying degrees by September. Before then little was accomplished, though some meetings were held. A stable group of local professionals was also slow in getting organized. It was not until the first of a series of three workshops held in the fall and winter of 1968 that the planning process came together.

Groundwork for the workshops was laid at a meeting in the MCA building on September 3. This meeting marked the first time that a combined meeting of the subcity ogranizations had been held with all MCA staff. The meeting, termed "very successful" by Teer, was attended by about 125 people. Teer proposed the workshop idea to "get the planning process going."[46] His rhetoric was close to the mark; the workshop marked the first occasion on which the members of the task force committees got a chance to interact with the professionals in a formal, organized setting.

Because the task force committees had not previously been in effective operation the workshop was important in giving

[46] *Metro-East Journal*, September 5, 1968.

form to the committee structure. It was there that the local professionals had their first sustained contact with target area committee members. Some of these professionals had met with the
committees before—as early as July in one case—but little else
had been accomplished other than the selection of the target
area committee chairmen.

Except for these local professional advisors, the component
committees had virtually no ties to important local institutions.
But the professionals did not speak for their agencies, and were
not really "representatives" in any strict sense. Their activities
were voluntary and largely unknown to their agencies. For example, well after the committees had been organized, Teer attended a meeting of the school board, and got the board to
authorize school personnel to work with the education committee. It was apparent that the board was not aware that Leo
Hicks, director of research for school district 189, was already
working with the committee.

Pressures from the Planning Process

At a November 19 MCA meeting, Teer announced a new, earlier
target date for submission of Phases I and II of the Model Cities
plan to the regional office of HUD. The circumstances requiring
an earlier submission were the election of Richard Nixon to the
Presidency three weeks before. HUD, obviously, wanted as
many cities approved by the date of inauguration as possible,
making it harder for the new President to scuttle the program.
In addition to this, Ted Robinson conveyed another message to
Teer. If the new target date and the stipulated guidelines could
be met, the MCA could qualify for as much as a 175 percent increase in its allotted funds, because of the necessity to spend all
HUD funds prior to the expiration of the "congressional year."
Teer imparted a sense of high urgency to the MCA members:

> It is crucial that you give me the authority to make decisions for
> you now! An effort is being made to get our plans accepted and
> the funds ear marked before the deadline expires. I cannot im-
> press you as to how important this is.

I study the guidelines constantly and I do not intend to deceive you. In the coming weeks important decisions must be made, sometimes on the spur of the moment. I am asking your approval for me to make the necessary decisions in keeping with Agency policy.[47]

Teer went on to ask for permission to bypass a formal submission of the Phase I document, which would require approval of the executive board and review by the task force committees with the possibility of further revisions and conflict. Instead, he said, it would be necessary to make an informal submission, after which Model Cities neighborhood residents could review the document and record their objections. With the prospect of possibly losing funds with a negative decision, the MCA membership gave its approval.

Some of those who acquiesced in the decision were distrustful of Teer and his professionals. This surfaced in a December 3 MCA meeting when Wendell Wheadon, the first vice-chairman of the MCA, objected to several items in the Phase I document. Wheadon's attack was based on the premise that the document did not accurately reflect target area residents' preferences. Part of the plan implied, he said, that no one in East St. Louis had the capability of assuming administrative or professional positions in the program. Wheadon also contended that the summary of the workshop results was inaccurate, and some plans had not met with the approval of the residents. He proposed a *formal* submission of the Phase II and III reports, with intensive review by MNA residents before submission; suggested that the writers be present at MCA and task force meetings; and urged a review of all plans by committee chairmen, the task force committees, and by the entire MCA membership. A motion to require a formal submission on the next document was easily passed.

Teer's request had been only the first of a long series of similar appeals put before the MNA residents. The crisis of meeting an earlier Phase I deadline was followed by another crisis at submission of the Phase II and III documents. After submission,

[47] Director's report to the East St. Louis City demonstration agency, October 19, 1968.

HUD repeatedly called for revisions in the planning documents, and set one urgent deadline after another.

In early December Teer returned from a national conference of MCA directors with the word that HUD officials were strongly urging an acceleration in planning schedules. "I need not point out to you the reasoning behind such a request," he told the MCA members.[48] His reference was, of course, to the outcome of the November elections. At the director's meeting, HUD officials had encouraged submission of final plans by mid-January —before the inauguration—rather than on February 16, the official end of the first planning year. Teer mentioned in explicit terms HUD's nervousness about its future. "All the directors, along with the federal staff, feel that a united front must be created if the Model Cities program is to survive. Budgetary cuts are already in the making. . . ."[49] On December 9, Teer repeated the HUD call for a stepped up planning schedule and, perhaps to disarm any criticism, he gave the MNA residents the option of keeping the present planning team or recruiting someone else to write Phase II and III. "I assure you that the present team of planners will not be obstructionists. Each is willing at this moment to accept the role of Advisor and Consultant and relinquish the responsibility of writing Phase II and III to whomever you designate."[50] Teer invited criticism so that the planners could make necessary or desired changes, "so long as such criticism and changes do not violate federal guidlines."[51] At a December 17 MCA meeting Teer recommended that East St. Louis engage in a crash program to meet a January 1 submission date suggested by HUD. Teer conveyed (and felt) a sense of great urgency:

> If you are in favor of the crash program, the planning team has agreed to forego all holidays, to put in the necessary hours to get the job done. With your consent, we must send our team to Chicago for a full day of briefing and instructions relative to available programs and how they must be written up. . . .

[48] *Ibid.*, December 3, 1968.
[49] *Ibid.*
[50] *Ibid.*, December 9, 1968.
[51] *Ibid.*

I am asking now if there are any persons you know of, who are willing to forego their holidays and write Federal programs according to the guidelines, to volunteer their services. We must utilize every resource available.

Teer also mentioned that Congressman Price's office had indicated the necessity to get the plans in by the end of the year.

At a special meeting on December 9 the executive board passed a resolution approving a new January 1 submission deadline. The entire planning staff was on hand to explain the necessity for the new deadline and to explain problems of submission. On December 17 the MCA membership also approved the accelerated schedule, and Teer announced a meeting on December 19 to get the last citizen input before the final Phase II write-up. The December 19 meeting, like many others, reflected the new pressures.

In a memo dated December 17, 1968, and addressed to Mendelson, Teer, and others, Stickgold reviewed the development necessitating an accelerated planning schedule and detailed the revised planning schedule to meet the new deadline. Originally, the deadline for submission of the Phases I and II plans had been February 16, the end of the first twelve months of planning activity. Nixon's victory had forced changes. "Given the 45-day review process which HUD has described for us, the period would be completed on February 20, 1969, or exactly one month from the time that the new administration takes office. It is hoped, and considered a good probability, that during this period of time commitments made by HEW and by other divisions of HUD will be honored by the incoming administration. Chicago advises us, however, that there is no guarantee of this."[52] And, Stickgold added, as much as $5-million might be available through other federal agencies under then current budgets and administrative practices if the earlier submission could be made.

As a result of these contingencies, Stickgold said, it would be necessary to alter the citizen participation plans. Originally, the planners had intended to sound out several different groups be-

[52] Memorandum from Arthur Stickgold to Robert Mendelson, Tom Hadd, Fred Teer, and others, December 17, 1968.

fore the final planning document (Phases II and III) was written. Data were to have been obtained from the target area residents making up the subcity organizations, the representatives of agencies who might be administering Model Cities-funded programs, and various political and social leaders in East St. Louis. In addition, a random sample survey of citizen opinion in the Model Cities neighborhoods and a sampling of high school youths had been planned.

Stickgold stated that, because of the new circumstances, the MCA could not "take the luxury of spending two weeks or more" in gathering data from so many sources. One mass meeting would now have to be held to ascertain the opinions of residents and others. Stickgold, in suggesting this plan, added a caveat: "Of prime importance during this entire undertaking . . . will be to communicate the reasons for our rush and the fact that we are still going to honor citizen inputs as the prime input in the Model City program. Under no circumstances should we allow this necessitated rush to make it appear or in fact allow it to become a reality that citizens are no longer being consulted or no longer the prime movers in this program."[53]

Stickgold suggested that a special meeting be held the evening of December 19. Invited would be the "residents who have been active in subcity one and subcity two as participants in the Model City program."[54] Stickgold argued that ascertaining the opinion of this group was probably as reliable though less impressive than the original plans. The setting of the mass meeting would not allow for a "period of negotiation and consensus"; however, this was chiefly important for "cathartic effect" and was not "essential to the operation of the program."[55]

Stickgold suggested a ranking system that would measure the "central tendency" of the residents' responses to a questionnaire that would be distributed at the December 19 meeting. The questionnaire contained a listing, subdivided into ten component areas, of all of the discrete projects recommended by the eleven component citizen committees. These committees had

[53] *Ibid.*
[54] *Ibid.*
[55] *Ibid.*

recommended projects without regard to the cost, in order to come up with "comprehensive" solutions. Now came the task of ranking these projects in order of their importance, to determine which ones could be funded and which ones would have to be "delayed" until future action years.

The December 19 meeting was held in the auditorium of Lincoln Senior High School in East St. Louis—an all Black, approximately ten-year-old school adjoining one of the Model neighborhoods. About 100 target area residents attended. With only a few additions, most of them had been regular participants in Model Cities meetings. They were dwarfed by the 1,500-seat auditorium. A few moments later, however, a larger crowd of about 300 persons came in. These were people not normally involved in Model Cities activities. They were night-school students who happened to be in the building at the time and who had been dismissed from their classes and ushered into the meeting. This was a calculated move; it helped to maximize the number of participants.

Scheduled to begin at 8:00 P.M., the meeting was delayed for one-half hour to give the night school students a chance to file in. After some preliminaries by Fred Teer and Cleveland Chandler, Art Stickgold took the stage and began explaining the procedure for priority-ranking of programs. Five young Blacks came down the center aisle, directly in front of the podium, saying lowly but audibly, "Why you listen to Whitey?" "You must be a bunch of bo niggers, sitting there listening to that shit!" Then, loudly, three of the group turned and faced the audience. "Don't you know this is just a city hall program? You going to let some White hunkey run this thing?" Then to Stickgold, "Get down off that stage, hunkey!" Stickgold, at this point, asserted that a decision about who ran it ought to be left up "to the people here." Immediately he was shoved off the stage, and all five of the group began kicking and beating him. Many in the audience stampeded to the exits in panic. Kermit Jeffers, a Black schoolteacher, rushed up and attacked one of Stickgold's assailants and action momentarily shifted away from Stickgold. Chandler then tried to break up the attack on Jeffers. At that point, all five of the assailants turned on him, driving him up a side aisle until he stumbled backward, hitting his head on the concrete. After a few kicks at Chandler the assailants fled out the back exit of the auditorium. Stickgold, meanwhile, had run into an adjacent darkened classroom. He hid there with the White planning student from the University of Wisconsin, Mary Ellen Ross. Later, Stickgold and Miss Ross sneaked out to his car and "drove like hell to get out of town. I didn't stop for a stop sign, a stop light or anything else." [56]

The day after the incident Teer called Stickgold and other members of the planning staff. Stickgold, though unwilling personally to go back into East St. Louis until the danger could be assessed (and until his wounds healed), pressed for an immediate citizen participation meeting for the purpose of completing the citizen rankings. Teer scheduled one for Christmas Eve, December 24. Robert Mendelson was the only member of the planning staff and one of several Whites to show up. About eighty target area residents attended. This time the meeting was held in the MCA office building, adjacent to city hall and a block from the police station.

Some militants from the south end were visibly and audibly present. Many who attended the meeting were apprehensive about further violence, even though two policemen stood at the back of the room.

After arguments, shouts, and implied threats, Wendell Wheadon went through the entire questionnaire line-by-line, word-by-word with an explanation that lasted for four hours. Either because they were convinced or exhausted, those present at the meeting agreed to distribute the questionnaire to Model Cities' residents, to see that their own were complete, and to return them to the MCA staff. Planners now had the green light to prepare the final planning documents.

Though isolated in the degree and obviousness of the violence, the December 19 meeting could not be regarded as completely unexpected. It was the culmination of severe tension between MCA leaders and militants outside of the program. And it was not the last manifestation of the competition for power in East St. Louis. Model Cities participants were not on

[56] Arthur Stickgold, interview, St. Louis, Missouri, December 20, 1969.

the extreme—it would be more accurate to say they were in the middle, between a political machine on the one hand (city hall) and militant Blacks on the other. Strains resulting from this position were to be felt again and again.

Militant feeling was stronger and more organized than might be suggested by the December 19 assault. Few were willing to commit themselves in such an overt way, but tacit support was widespread. On January 17 a crowd reported by Teer to be composed of 100 people—some of them, he alleged, were MCA members—came to the MCA building and "heaped abuse on me."[57] Teer had been personally confronted and threatened on many occasions, and often carried a gun for his self-protection. Twenty-eight consecutive days of sniping in the summer of 1968 and at least ten brutal murders in the fall and winter were enough to give him cause for concern.

Only a slight upset in the submission schedule for the Phase II and III planning documents was caused by the December 19 incident. A few days of delay, however, was enough to force abandonment of the attempt to submit the plans before Richard Nixon's inauguration, and a new deadline, February 16, the official end of the planning year, was adopted.

At a January 7, 1969, MCA meeting, the planners reviewed the results of the questionnaires completed at the December 24 meeting and the remainder brought in to the MCA staff. Over 400 questionnaires had been evaluated several days earlier with at least 100 not counted in the tally. In one instance, fifty questionnaires were quietly omitted by the planners because they were all obviously filled out by the same person with identical responses and handwriting. Fifty others were apparent duplicates. Each project scheduled for the action year now had money values attached. Planners told residents that they had simply gone down the list of projects in the order of their rank scores until the $2,083,000 East St. Louis Model Cities allocation was exhausted.

Considerable dissatisfaction was aired concerning some of the projects. Education was the only component area not criti-

---

[57] Director's report to the East St. Louis city demonstration agency, January 21, 1969.

cized. Crime and delinquency came under especially heavy attack. Chandler and Teer, however, insisted that the MCA could legally make no changes to the plans on the ground that they had been given a mandate to go ahead in the plan preparation by the people on December 24. A dissatisfied faction, Teer asserted, could not overturn the work of the citizens. Despite loud grumbling, Chandler and Teer prevailed and were able to secure approval for most of the projects.

HUD's concern about the militant opposition was exhibited in a discussion between Ted Robinson (the HUD lead man) and Teer. As reported by Teer, he was advised that the MCA had to become "the official organ of the community." The necessity for getting agency sign-offs and "loyalty and support from residents" was stressed.[58] At the January 21 meeting Teer again asked for the "necessary latitude" and "authority" to get the professional work done.[59]

By the end of January, the Phase II and III document was ready for submission. On January 30 the MCA general membership gave its approval, and on February 2 the executive board did likewise. Following the executive board action, Teer told reporters that he was requesting a city council meeting to approve the plans. Teer hoped for approval by February 5. The mayor put him off, however, until February 11.

At the meeting, Teer and members of his staff filed into the mayor's office to review the plans for the mayor and the council (two council members were present). It was clear that the mayor and commissioners had not read and had little interest in the very lengthy, four-inch-thick document. As he usually did on matters such as these, Mayor Fields followed George Washnis's lead and the commissioners played their usual assenting role to the mayor. Fields frequently "nodded in agreement and commented 'that's fine' and 'I think we need that' " during the brief presentation.[60] The only matter of concern to the mayor was employment. "We have to be careful to follow correct procedures on this," he said.[61] That, of course, was also a main concern

[58] Ibid.
[59] Ibid.
[60] Metro-East Journal, February 12, 1969.
[61] Observer's notes, February 12, 1969.

of the Model Cities representatives, but nothing was said. The meeting ended in agreement and harmony, with the mayor promising approval at the next council meeting, two days later.

After Submission to HUD

On February 19, 1969, three days late, the Phase II and III documents were carried to the Chicago HUD offices. But it was hardly a final step in qualifying for federal funds. In fact, it only initiated an extended series of technical revisions of the plans required by federal officials. The planning staff was formally released on the same day, pending federal review. Not long after the submission, Ted Robinson informed Teer of preliminary federal objections to the East St. Louis plans.

As reported by Teer to the March 4, 1969, MCA meeting, Robinson had expressed three qualifications about East St. Louis's plans: "1. Competent personnel must be on the staff for proper implementation of the programs; 2. Citizens must pull together in a unified manner; 3. The Agency must demonstrate the capability to handle funds in large sums."[62] HUD's signal from the regional office was clear enough, and would be repeated many more times during the ensuing months. HUD was looking for a professionally oriented, administratively sophisticated program that would encounter a minimum of opposition in the local community. Its insistence on proper lines of authority, even to the point of demanding a proper organization chart, also reflected this concern.

By March 19 four federal representatives flew into East St. Louis to give the results of the federal review. They carried with them a long list of recommended changes and set an official deadline for making all the recommended corrections.

In his April 1, 1969, report to the MCA, Teer, after expressing appreciation for the MCA member's permission for him to reassemble the technical team, emphasized the primacy of meeting federal requirements: "Again, I plead with you, let us avoid confrontations, rather should we arbitrate, negotiate, seek com-

[62] Director's report to the East St. Louis city demonstration agency, March 4, 1969.

promise. I am not advocating capitulation, surrender, not in any sense of the word. It has been pointed out to me that acquiring the funds is tantamount to all else."[63] Teer went on to emphasize that the program could probably be changed after funding, if there were dissatisfactions. And he issued a specific warning to dissidents who were questioning his authority: "I would caution against rump meetings in which attempts are being made to revise our program. In my opinion, it would be unwise to structure changes until we are told officially just what needs changing."[64] Those who disagreed with his policy of caution were accused of attempting to sabotage the program.

On April 11, Teer brought the planners together to make the federally mandated changes in the plans. He explained the results of the federal review, and asked them to contribute their time so that the federal requirements could be met. Most of those present agreed. Later, at the April 15 MCA meeting, Teer requested permission to include representatives from local agencies on the revision team. Most were included in name only, however. Two local professionals, Leo Hicks and Wendell Wheadon, took an active part in the revision work.

At the April 15 meeting, Teer was told by several members of the Model Cities executive board that the citizens had little contact with Teer and the staff because of the necessity to get Phase II and III revisions in so soon. Many in the audience shared the same sentiment. Before the complaints became more vociferous, however, Harvey Henderson made an impassioned speech. "If this package is not in by April 30, we can forget everything. In the next two weeks, we must get the technical work done."[65] Teer then expanded on the same theme, discouraging "interference" with the technical work, and warning that the April 30 deadline was imminent:

> We must meet the April 30 deadline if we are to be considered for funding out of the present budget. Defaulted, or unfinished tasks must be arbitrarily re-assigned. In a few instances previously allocated funds must be redirected. I now request authori-

[63] *Ibid.*, April 1, 1969.
[64] *Ibid.*
[65] Observer's notes, April 15, 1969.

zation to effect such transfers in accordance with the collective judgment of the technical review team.

Since the final revision must be re-submitted for agency approval, no programs can be enacted without your knowledge and approval. Because of the critical time factor, I am asking your trust and confidence in our ability to do what is best for our total community in light of your often expressed desires.[66]

On this and many other occasions, Teer requested departures from normal review procedures so as to meet an impending deadline. This had a close parallel to similar appeals in late 1968 and early 1969. In those cases, however, the professionals were not so completely removed from the target area residents. Now the isolation of the staff was almost complete, their reference points being local professionals, each other, and HUD officials.

Like many other "final" deadlines that spring, the April 30 one turned out to be more flexible than it had appeared. Through May and part of June the East St. Louis application was being reviewed and re-reviewed, with each change transmitted typically over the telephone or through private conferences with Teer, Mendelson, or Washnis. Teer consistently appealed for patience from citizen groups through this period, not only, he said, for the sake of meeting deadlines but also to avoid confrontations with HUD officials. He described the relations with HUD as sensitive and tenuous; they could be upset at the slightest provocation. One possibly explosive disagreement illustrated the utility of this position in countering opposition.

At the April 29, 1969, meeting of the MCA, Washnis presented an organization chart which, he indicated, HUD had said would be necessary for approval of East St. Louis's Model City program. Washnis's proposal, backed by Teer, met with loud and vehement objections. Washnis showed a chart that made the MCA directly responsible to the city council, as compared to the chart contained in the original Phase II application which showed the city council sharing power with the MCA executive board. A proposal that the new chart be adopted met vociferous protest. Cleveland Chandler accused Washnis and Teer of "try-

[66] Director's report to the East St. Louis city demonstration agency, April 15, 1969.

ing to pull a fast one; working in secret to weaken citizen participation."[67] Washnis countered that the ultimate power lay in the hands of the citizens, since they could always vote a cut-off of funds any time they did not like a project. The federal government, he pointed out, required the change, although in reality "the power of the CDA depends on the voice of the people which has been very active and which will continue to be so."[68] Will McGaughy, the director of citizen participation, asserted that "as real and sincere as Mr. Washnis is, a working agreement is still needed with the City Council, otherwise the money will get there and will be forgotten."[69] Several more people expressed opposition to the revised chart, charging that it was a disguised attempt to subvert citizen participation. Teer, in his report to the MCA, had anticipated the objections, and had sought to undermine them: "As the Director of the Model City program, I've always followed your directions. Your will is my will. The chart merely indicates that the agency is designed to conform to the federal guidelines, namely that the ultimate responsibility rests with the prime contractor which by statute is the city administration. . . . I sincerely believe that a united agency regardless of structural design can effectively protect the welfare of this community."[70] Teer's explanation was not sufficient, however. Washnis finally agreed to arrange a meeting between the MCA personnel committee and the city council to work out an agreement that would, in effect, formalize everyone's assumption that the new chart was only a paper representation drawn up to satisfy HUD.

On May 5, 1969, the revised Phase II and III document was hand carried by Teer to Chicago and Washington. Again, however, submission was not the end of the line. More criticism came in response to this document. On May 29 the federal regional review team came into East St. Louis. Teer, Will McGaughy, and Washnis met with the federal representatives. On Saturday, May 30, Washnis, Stickgold, Teer, and several others worked in an attempt to rewrite sections of the East St. Louis plans to con-

[67] Observer's notes from April 29, 1969, MCA meeting.
[68] East St. Louis city MCA minutes, April 29, 1969.
[69] Ibid.
[70] Director's report to the East St. Louis MCA, April 29, 1969.

form to the latest HUD desires. On June 3, the revisions of the revisions—now 770 pages as compared to the 319 pages contained in the February 19 submission—were forwarded to the Chicago HUD offices. In his June 3 report to the CDA, Teer reminded the residents of the sensitive nature of the revision period and the need for compliance with HUD's requirements: "Most of the revisions of revisions have been forwarded. We still have numerous items to forward, however. The inter-agency review is extremely thorough and technical requirements are exasperating, but if we hope to stay in the ball park we have no other course open than to comply." And later in the same report: "I have been informed that our program will be formally presented to HUD on June 9. Acceptance, rejection, or additional changes will be made at this top level review. I would urge you not to rock the boat until this decision is made."

Teer's constant warnings that caution was needed were, of course, prompted by his extremely large stake in getting funded. This was the number one goal to which all other considerations had to take second place, and it explained his warnings of dire consequences if the boat was rocked. But his warnings were also designed to undercut complaints that had actually been voiced. Federal officials had been receiving letters from some Model Cities' residents complaining about the lack of citizen participation, the secrecy of the revisions, and some of the substantive changes being made. Ted Robinson expressed to Teer the HUD concern that these kinds of protests not only endangered the East St. Louis program but also made HUD look bad. Teer carried the concern to the residents: "This doesn't show the unanimity we need. Come to *us* [MCA staff] if you have questions"[71]

Only a few professionals were involved in the revision work, and their activities were relatively invisible. A phone call or letter with new HUD instructions, followed by writing assignments, usually to Mendelson or one of the other technicians, was normal. Small meetings among professionals or with HUD representatives were usually held in city hall. Teer, as we have seen, called the revisions "strictly technical"; at all times, he told the MCA members, their desires were being honored.

[71] East St. Louis MCA, remarks at meeting June 3, 1969.

Interest in meetings lagged. Meetings of the task force committees, held every two weeks, were discontinued in March, for lack of anything to do. Citizen participation never recovered from the waiting period. Several incidents during 1969 revealed tension and competition among leaders of the program—but the professionals were so far removed that little chance developed for conflict between them, the residents, and their leaders.

Conclusions

From the decision to apply for Model Cities funds through the first year of the program, planning was characterized by an overriding commitment to obtain federal money for East St. Louis. Washnis, Mendelson, and, at a later date, Teer and other professionals were primarily interested in expanding the federal role in East St. Louis.

Planners wanted redevelopment of East St. Louis and urban renewal, antipoverty, manpower training, and Model Cities programs were perceived in that way. They wanted professionally administered projects achieving measurable goals in the reduction of physical and social disadvantage. To achieve their goal of a reborn community, they were willing to adhere to the bureaucratic guidelines from HUD and other agencies and to satisfy federal demands for a rational planning process.

Model Cities guidelines stressed efficiency, coordination, and a comprehensive approach to planning. Federal officials believed that many of the problems of older American cities were caused by the lack of local administrative competence. Consequently, their demands were to develop efficient structures and systems to carry out plans. Like other grant-in-aid programs, federal concern for Model Cities focused more on form than on substance. To them, organization charts, agency sign-off, and official coordinative mechanisms were indicators of administrative ability.

Lack of clarity in the intent of Model Cities nationally caused conflicts in the East St. Louis program. Initial federal guidelines required that citizen involvement be an essential part of planning and implementation. City halls throughout the country were required to share power and decisionmaking under the

Model Cities concept. Model Cities was conceived, after all, as a partial response to the riots in the cities in the mid-1960s and to the pressures to decentralize local government.

Many of the original East St. Louis Model City planners were in principle (even if not always in practice) committed to citizen participation. Paula Parks had developed community action programs in Carbondale and East St. Louis, while Mendelson and Stickgold had provided technical assistance to neighborhood groups in confrontations with local government. Others, too, shared a philosophical bias in favor of increased representation of the poor in those decisions affecting them.

HUD seemed firmly committed to the notion of comprehensiveness. Model Cities was to be the vehicle which would coordinate all the inputs of federal money into East St. Louis. Local planners were told that federal agencies including HUD would supply four or five times the amount of the Model City supplemental grant. The reverse actually was true. HUD funds for Model Cities far exceeded new grants from other agencies.

Except for a few federal officials like Ted Robinson, the federal bureaucracy was ill-prepared to cope with the politics of Model Cities in East St. Louis and elsewhere. Power struggles between dissident groups, violence, rhetoric, and a general confusion over who represented the poor prompted HUD to increasingly emphasize the professional and reform aspects of the program.

It was apparent to many of the planners, professionals, and even residents in East St. Louis that survival of the program was dependent on the masking of conflict and the appearance of real or imagined consensus. This strategy forced Teer to avoid confrontations and deterred the allocation of resources to conflictual and controversial projects. Only a few were willing to take risks that might lead to a federal decision to withdraw the program.

East St. Louis planners were clearly caught in a dilemma between two ideologies. On the one hand, the planners were encouraged by their own training and by the federal emphasis to rely on rational and logical criteria for judgment while, at the same time, current doctrine dictated a responsiveness to resident participaiton. Model City planners could not push citizen involvement and simultaneously maximize coordination. Co-ordination required professional control and corporatelike man-agement, while citizen involvement included control of jobs and decisions and a de-emphasis of efficiency and cost-effectiveness. Teer, Mendelson, Washnis, and key members of the agency's executive board, among others, recognized this contradiction. After responding to numerous HUD directives and pressure from competing groups within the community, a strategy evolved based not on any doctrine but on pragmatism. First and foremost, the Model Cities money was to be obtained for East St. Louis, for it meant not only the HUD supplementary grant but the promise of far greater allocations from other federal agencies.

Often planners found it extremely difficult to balance the HUD demands with those of the residents. They became com-mitted to neither group, feeling that to do so would have effec-tively eliminated East St. Louis from the Model City program. Had they supported HUD rhetoric about the value of "technical considerations" they would have lost support from the coalition that obtained control of the Model City agency. Had they pushed participation too hard, HUD might have questioned the program and withdrawn support, as happened in the St. Louis, Missouri, program.

Many of those initially involved in Model Cities (Mann, Washnis, Mendelson, and others) had not expected the program either nationally or locally to change so drastically from its original objectives. According to federal explanation, it was to be a demonstration of how entire neighborhoods could be physi-cally rebuilt and socially upgraded within five years. Innovative solutions were to be tried and measured. Those that were suc-cessful would become national urban policy prototypes; those that failed would be discarded. One of the basic premises of the program was that through comprehensive planning—defining problems, establishing goals, developing strategies to reach the goals, and choosing priority programs—the purpose of Model Cities could be reached.

These early objectives became hardly recognizable with the passage of time. When the first guidelines were distributed by

HUD in January, 1967, only ten to fifteen cities were to be se-lected as demonstration cities. As mayors and congressmen from older cities labored to have their constituencies included, the number of cities rose to sixty-three in November, 1967, and to 150 by mid-1968. While the number of cities included in the program increased, Congress sliced funds. What began as a demonstration program reflecting a liberal-reform bias in favor of rational ordering of resources and an innovative approach to programming ended as an operating program influenced by bureaucratic demands for order and coordination and by con-flict between local groups for limited rewards. Thus, the fate of Model Cities was about the same as the fate of many other social welfare measures adopted since the Roosevelt administration.

Planning Doctrine:
Legitimating the Profession

5

The case study literature on urban planning and development reveals no clearly defined ethical or professional commitment among urban planners and development specialists *in practice*.[1] Despite well articulated ideological arguments (which are the main concern of this chapter), urban planners have most often legitimated and implemented the interests of powerful political and economic groups and been concerned with the maintenance needs of the organizations within which they work.[2] These cases

[1] This observation would seem to contradict studies such as Alan Altshuler's *The City Planning Process* (Ithaca: Cornell University Press, 1965) which describe the impact of urban planners' values on their work. However, the projects that planners typically implement seem to reflect a sense of what is pragmatically possible or necessary (given the preferences of powerful political actors) rather than consistent adherence to doctrine. Even in master planning removed from "politics," as Altshuler shows, the planners' values are only imperfectly translated onto paper.

[2] We think the case studies contained in the following literature illustrate this point: Alan Altshuler, *The City Planning Process*; Robert J. Mowitz and Deil S. Wright, *Profile of a Metropolis* (Detroit: Wayne State University Press, 1962); Edward C. Banfield, *Political Influence* (Cambridge, Mass.: Harvard University Press, 1963); Harold Kaplan, *Urban Renewal Politics* (New York: Columbia University Press, 1963); Martin Meyerson and Edward C. Banfield, *Politics, Planning, and the Public Interest* (New York: Free Press, 1964); J. Clarence Davies, III, *Neighborhood Groups and Urban Renewal* (New York: Columbia University Press, 1966); Peter Rossi and Robert A. Dentler, *The Politics of Urban Renewal* (New York: Free Press, 1961).

from East St. Louis are therefore consistent with existing literature, and thus the planning experiences described cannot be
considered exceptional.

Why has this been the common experience, even in the face
of a planning literature which promotes such ideals as comprehensiveness, efficiency, rationality, and projection into the future? In part, the answer can be found by looking at employment
patterns. Urban planners typically are employed in large organizations and bureaucracies like planning agencies, urban
renewal authorities, highway commissions, and consulting firms.
Not surprisingly, the care and feeding of the organizations become paramount to the professionals working in them. In spite
of the values internalized during formal training, professionals
who find themselves in leadership positions are mandated to
pursue pragmatism and learn political acumen. As a result,
politician-professionals like Ed Logue are exemplars of effective
planning and administration. Two questions arise. Assuming
effectiveness to be the highest value, does the planning literature
provide prescriptions for being effective? And assuming, alter-
natively, that the usually stated goals of planning—comprehensiveness, efficiency, rationality, coordination, and so on—are
even more important that effectiveness, does the literature reveal special skills and knowledge to professionals whereby they
can pursue these goals without an excessive adherence to pragmatism? The next two chapters are concerned about whether a
unique professional calling for planners can be identified. Also
whether, if such a calling can be specified, it would help planners to be more "effective" *either* in accomplishing organizational purposes *or* in implementing their own preferences. By
inference, we hope to answer this basic question: would consistent observance of standard planning ideology have helped
professionals in East St. Louis to be more consistent in accomplishing their own values and/or more effective in achieving redevelopment?

Traditional Planning Ideology

For more than half a century, planners have claimed professional
status on the basis of collectively sharing and explicitly pro-

moting a particular set of values. Imbued historically with a missionary fervor, planners have rarely doubted the moral superiority of their own cause. The tendency to equate their own roles, aims, and objectives with righteousness and virtue has had a profound impact upon their professional life. It has made their attachment to certain values virtually unshakable, and has also nurtured a self-image which dominates practically all statements and definitions of their professional role. Thus, in 1963 a prominent planner proclaimed, without embarrassment, that:

> The contemporary planners inherit a proud tradition of service, an egalitarian ethic, and a pragmatic orientation to betterment that are as old as the early social reform movements that spawned the profession. The caretaker of the idea of progress during the long years when it lay in disrepute in respectable quarters, the planner is now being wooed as the Cinderella of the urban ball. The resulting marriage of the social sciences and the planning profession holds out the promise that a new level of intelligence will be merged with a noble purpose, in confronting the problems and opportunities of the day. And then, the payoffs of this new partnership will come, if they come at all, in imaginative social inventions that will increase the city's riches, while distributing them to all the city's people.[3]

Taking on the tasks of saving mankind and ushering in and administering a new utopia, the planners have confidently asked for sufficient power to accomplish their mission. To counteract the unplanned "effects of industrialization and urbanization" the planners' power must be increased, for planning must face the major domestic and international problems of the twentieth century.[4] To undertake these tasks planners must not be hampered by "too little authority and territorial limitations."[5]

Planners' views about how they would exercise power if they held it encourage their yearning for increased authority. In tra-

[3] Melvin M. Webber, "Comprehensive Planning and Social Responsibility," in *Urban Planning and Social Policy*, eds. Bernard J. Frieden and Robert Morris (New York: Basic Books, 1968), p. 22.

[4] Ernest Erber, "Urban Planning in Transition: An Introductory Essay," in *Urban Planning in Transition*, ed. Ernest Erber (New York: Grossman Publishers, 1970), pp. xvi, xvii.

[5] *Ibid.*, p. xvii.

ditional planning doctrine, one of the most sacred assumptions
has been that planners represent and have a unique knowledge
of the public interest. Planners claim a comprehensive viewpoint that allows them to simultaneously benefit all of society
by their actions; in fact, if the planners' claims of comprehensiveness "are to be persuasive, (they) must refer to a special
knowledge of the public interest."[6] Accordingly, the planning
literature is filled with attempts to define and measure what that
interest is. Planners often speak of the "art" of planning, which
requires a "wisdom" or a "special feel" about the public good.
It has been proposed that this becomes increasingly important as
planning and other professional activity acquire greater influence
in a technological world which prizes rationality and efficiency.[7]
With increasingly more power at their hands, planners will, it
is said, be forced to "wrestle with the moral and ethical consequences of the policies they choose and implement."[8] The wisdom of the professionals will become the basis for a responsible
technology.

Planners constitute an identifiable elite not only because they
see themselves as such—note their noblesse oblige sentiments—
but also because they share a core set of values. Their heritage
contains three closely related components: a concern for the
physical environment, a utopian vision, and a political reformer
outlook.[9] These attitudes originated essentially from the class
origins of professional planners:

> Modern city planners began as one of a number of late
> nineteenth-century reform movements, headed by upper and
> upper middle class native Americans who were disturbed about
> the urbanization of their previously agrarian nation, about the
> coming of the poor European immigrants, and about the slums,
> high crime rates, and socialist movements that appeared after
> their arrival. The first planners were hoping that by physical

[6] Alan Altshuler, "The Goals of Comprehensive Planning," *Journal of the American Institute of Planners*, XXXI (August, 1965), p. 3.
[7] Donald N. Michael, "Urban Policy in the Rationalized Society," *Journal of the American Society of Planners*, XXXI (November, 1965), pp. 285–288.
[8] *Ibid.*
[9] David C. Ranney, *Planning and Politics in the Metropolis* (Columbus, Ohio: Charles E. Merrill, 1969), Ch. 2.

planning, they could eliminate the slums and break up the ethnic ghettoes, creating middle-class urban neighborhoods. . . . What the early planners sought, often quite unconsciously, was the City Orderly. Later, as planning became a profession dominated by architects, they also stressed the City Beautiful, and when planning became a commission in, but not of, city government, headed by business leaders, the professionals emphasized the City Efficient.[10]

Because the reform movement provided the rationale for professional planning activities and because legal remedies could most easily be applied to physical features, the "city orderly" was conceived in physical terms. Housing reform started in New York City in the mid-nineteenth century. It led first to the New York City Tenement Housing Acts and then to housing codes which provided the standards for municipal legislation. Early in the twentieth century the housing reformers seized on the idea of zoning as a device to stabilize property values, to establish acceptable population densities, and to guide urban development.

The housing reform movement, with its concern for changing the physical conditions of cities, was an important first step in prompting the formation of the planning profession. New York City housing reformers organized the First National Planning Conference in 1909. In 1910 the American Institute of Architects and the American Society of Landscape Architects (many of whose members were instrumental in housing reform) hosted another planning conference. At this point planners began to assert an independent professional identity, although their attachment to and dependence on reform causes was hardly over.

Most of those professionals who self-consciously labeled themselves "planners" were, by professional training, architects and engineers. Their proposals for changing city life—a concern that had led them to identify with the reformers in the first place —quite predictably reflected their training. Housing reform gave

[10] Herbert Gans, "The Need for Planners Trained in Policy Formulation," in *Urban Planning in Transition,* ed. Ernest Erber (New York: Grossman Publishers, 1970), p. 242.

way to the "city beautiful" movement, with its attendant emphasis on aesthetically pleasing physical structures. This movement appealed to political leaders and nonprofessional reformers as well as to the architect-engineer-planners, and many cities embarked on beautification schemes.

The third and most enduring reform movement expressed the "city efficient" ideal. At the same time that the notion of a separate planning profession was evolving, there was a corresponding growth in the municipal reform movement. Both groups were opposed to machine politics and, to a large extent, became the support for municipal reform.[11]

Corruption and evil in the urban political machines were stressed in the ideology of municipal reform. Developing in response to ethnic migrations to the cities, these machines were functional for the undereducated ethnic populations, providing needed goods and services in the absence of other governmental and private activity. And although they were sometimes functional for business interests, too, the machines were not easily controlled by business, professional, and middle-class groups. The basic and most dependable support for the machines was provided in the low-income ethnic neighborhoods.

The reformers' ideological justification for overturning this system was the claim that machine politics were corrupt, inefficient, and self-serving. By taking politics out of government, the public interest could be served economically and socially. To the reformers progress meant a healthier climate for business interests and a more secure position for middle-class civic leadership.

Not accidentally, reforms such as nonpartisan elections (designed to break the hold of party machines), civil service regulations (to end patronage), and at-large elections (to weaken the machines structurally) redistributed power in favor of the reformers themselves. Business interests and middle-class civic leaders reasserted their political power in the name of the public interest, and goals of the business community often became

[11] Ranney, *Planning and Politics*, p. 24. A concise discussion of the history of urban planning may be found in Ranney's book.

the goals of the planners. "In short, the master planners were advocates for themselves, for the city's business interests, and for the upper- and upper middle-class residents of the community."[12] Another side of the reformer spirit, as commonly interpreted, was a sensitivity for the welfare of members of the working and lower classes [Housing, health, welfare, education, and open-space causes were led by middle-class professionals.[13] These movements were paternalistic, since the professionals and their allies were careful to maintain and consolidate power. Nevertheless, the elite values reflected, at least in theory, a humanitarian concern.]

A particular professional ideology resulted from the values which characterized the growth of the planning elite. At first, when planners were little else but reformers, the reformers' ideology and planners' ideology were one and the same. But the planners soon began developing a distinct set of ideas which were essential in justifying their claim to separate professional status. They were helped in this task by the close relationship between planning ideals and the municipal reformers' goals. Echoing the reformers' call for efficiency and businesslike methods of administration, planning was conceived as a "municipal science." Between 1910 and 1920, conventional planning vocabulary was expanded to include such words and phrases as "system," "efficiency and intelligence," "public control," and "common welfare."[14] By 1917, a textbook written by eighteen authors codified the new planning principles and looked toward "scientific exactness" in running the public business. Loyalty to dominant cultural standards and conventional wisdoms of that period enabled the planning profession to consolidate and grow. Between 1907 and 1917, more than 100 towns and cities undertook comprehensive planning, and in 1913 Massachusetts became the first state to require the establishment of local planning commissions. During that period, half of the fifty largest Ameri-

---

[12] Gans, "The Need for Planners," p. 242.

[13] William L. C. Wheaton and Margaret F. Wheaton, "Identifying the Public Interest: Values and Goals," in *Urban Planning in Transition*, ed. Ernest Erber (New York: Grossman Publishers, 1970), p. 155.

[14] John L. Hancock, "Planners in the Changing American City, 1900–1940," *Journal of the American Institute of Planners*, XXXIII (September, 1967).

can cities created municipal planning commissions, and the first zoning codes were enacted.[15]

Partly owing to their reformer spirit, early planners often revealed a peculiarly audacious attitude concerning their role in society. This attitude has not appreciably softened in the ensuing years. In reviewing the growth of the planning profession, one author commented on the planners' conceptions of their own work: "During the 1920's and into the 1930's, planners became increasingly aware of the uniqueness of their function. They began to inquire whether the basis of their profession was a special knowledge of how cities develop or a special methodology for predicting and controlling purposeful change that had application to all forms of developmental phenomena."[16] Posed in that way, the dilemma was hardly an uncomfortable one.

An attempt to predict and control "purposeful change" was represented in master planning efforts. The Standard City Planning Enabling Act of 1928 described master planning in exceedingly inclusive terms, even by today's standards. A master plan was supposed to provide

> a co-ordinated, adjusted, and harmonious development of the municipality and its environs which will, in accordance with present and future needs, best promote health, safety, morals, order, convenience, prosperity, and general welfare as well as efficiency and economy in the process of development; including, among other things, adequate provisions for traffic, the promotion of safety from fire and other dangers, adequate provision for light and air, the promotion of good civic design and arrangements, wise and efficient expenditure of public funds, and the adequate provision of public utilities and other public requirements.[17]

City planning became institutionalized on the assertion that master planning was needed for the healthy growth and development of the city. Preparation of the master plan legitimized the existence of early planning agencies. Small municipal bud-

[15] *Ibid.*

[16] Erber, "Urban Planning in Transition," p. xviii.

[17] Quoted in Edward C. Banfield and James Q. Wilson, *City Politics* (Cambridge: Harvard University Press, 1963), p. 189.

gets for planning, rather than lack of desire, accounted for the few master plans produced before World War II. Planning agency budgets dictated a narrow focus on zoning ordinances and gathering of limited physical data.[18]

In the postwar period, planners were provided the first opportunities to work in accordance with the master planning idea. In the 1950s master planning received the blessing, at least, of monetary support, and almost all large cities institutionalized full-fledged planning activities. By 1962, 124 of 126 cities of more than 100,000 population included in the *Municipal Yearbook* reported master plans completed or in progress, and all had planning agencies. Over 90 percent of cities of more than 10,000 had planning agencies.

Comprehensiveness as a doctrine frequently dictated the strategies of planning agencies in attracting political support for planning in general, or in building support for particular projects. For example, a case study of St. Paul, Minnesota, found that the planner responsible for preparing the city's master plan was concerned with making it persuasive and universally attractive so that it would guide all future development in the city. To avoid endangering the plan, he was willing to anticipate political reactions and to make revisions in response to protests, because otherwise any possibility of master planning would be doomed.[19] The comprehensive ideal also dictated planning strategies in New York City, Detroit, and Syracuse.[20]

Master planning drew its inspiration from the planners' conviction that planning should encompass all important social, economic, and political factors that impinge on urban growth and development. "To the planner, the importance of the master plan is that it coordinates in space and over time those activities which affect the physical character of the city and which the city government can influence and control. To the planner, then,

[18] *Ibid.*

[19] Alan Altshuler, *The City Planning Process* (Ithaca: Cornell University Press, 1965).

[20] Cf. Wallace Sayre and Herbert Kaufman, *Governing New York City* (New York: Russell Sage Foundation, 1960); Robert J. Mowitz and Deil S. Wright, *Profile of a Metropolis* (Detroit: Wayne State University Press, 1962); and Roscoe C. Martin, and others, *Decisions in Syracuse* (New York: Greenwood Press, 1968).

a plan without reference to a master plan is a contradiction in terms."[21]

Values and assumptions of the early planners have been richly elaborated in the last few years. A recent text on land-use planning heavily implies that virtually nothing should escape the eye of the urban planner.[22] F. Stuart Chapin sketches an orderly, sequential planning process which encompasses the following stages, and more. First a survey of the social, political, and economic environment is conducted to determine the problems that planning can solve. Then, important local groups are consulted in order to formulate planning goals. This step is followed by detailed studies of land-use patterns, the layout and mixture of physical structures, and the history of local land use. Employment patterns and economic characteristics are studied. Attitudes of the local population concerning urban development and planning issues are included as political data. After results of the technical studies are obtained, a plan is devised which recommends future land use and development for the entire city, or even the whole region. Similarly, T. J. Kent holds that master planning is the logical conclusion to more specialized activities by planners.[23] Zoning, project planning, and other activities are part of a larger whole contained in a comprehensive or general plan. All the physical factors are part of the plan along with serious consideration of social and economic characteristics.[24]

Not only has the comprehensiveness doctrine proved to be especially useful in expanding planners' notions of their roles and missions, but the doctrine has extended its influence beyond urban planning. In a 1966 book which is required reading for the admission examination into the American Institute of Planners, Melville Branch maintains that planning occupies the apex of all established disciplines—indeed, that it represents the rational conclusion of all organized knowledge.[25] Because Branch is a respected planner whose contribution to planning theory is

[21] Banfield and Wilson, *City Politics.*

[22] F. Stuart Chapin, *Urban Land Use Planning* (Urbana: University of Illinois Press, 1965).

[23] T. J. Kent, Jr., *The Urban General Plan* (San Francisco: Chandler, 1964).

[24] *Ibid.*, pp. 95–96.

[25] Melville Branch, *Planning: Aspects and Applications* (New York: John Wiley and Sons, 1966).

considered important by other planners, his book merits detailed examination.

Branch equates planning with the use of human faculties of perception and reasoning. He maintains that increasing rationality has allowed the human being to survive, and he explains human progress by referring to a special ability to project into and have a role in the future. Conversely, the human tendency to respond to immediate pressures, external and internal, has been an impediment to advancement. According to Branch, planning, as an independent activity or professional specialty emphasizing rationality and reason, has increased in importance until it has become

> preeminently important in the conduct of human affairs. The accelerated advance of science and technology is creating a society so complex and closely inter-dependent in its many man-made parts that organized forethought is necessary, if only to keep the system functioning. Furthermore, with weapons of mass destruction and the capability of world-wide contamination, our survival, well being, and way of life depend on an even greater extent than they have in the past on wise planning more than any other rational endeavor.[26]

Since Branch equates professional planning with rational thought and action, it is quite appropriate that he consider planning the single most important human endeavor. He places great value on coordination and rationality and decries chance, fate, and lack of reason.[27] No nation, society, or institution, according to Branch, has succeeded without the development of a planning capability.

Planning is important not only because it is the only rational *process* of thought and behavior, but also because, if used properly by wise human beings, it leads to the fulfillment of the general good. "Ignorance, inflexibility, irresolution, custom, selfish interest, politics, socio-economic conditions . . . and forms of planning violating human rights have always acted to slow progress in planning for the general welfare."[28] Because man

[26] *Ibid.*, p. 3.
[27] *Ibid.*, p. 4.
[28] *Ibid.*, p. 5.

has not successfully overcome his "animal behavior"—still giving way to primeval emotions, values, and ethics—his "capacity for rational action is still limited. . . ."[29] Men and women must conquer themselves to take full value of technology.

Branch argues that professional planning can be freed from these human limitations if the proper people are selected as planners. A competent planner must be comprehensive, objective, a consensus finder, and a coordinator. In group planning, "individuality and minority conviction must be preserved when they are appropriate or contributory rather than insistent or disruptive." One must be a "certain kind of person . . . to participate constructively in a group endeavor. . . ." The successful planner must embody many other virtues. He or she must be "genuinely interested, appropriately but persistently inquiring"; and must employ a "constructive mental attitude, analytical approach, and personal balance," and occasionally will have to subordinate "self to the planning problem." He or she has to be receptive to scientific data and "informed judgment," but at the same time must have the "courage of his convictions. . . ." The planner's personal qualities also ideally include self-perception and "extrovertive empathy." Fortunately, points out Branch, psychological testing is developing in sophistication, so that soon it will enable people to select "those best suited temperamentally for planning positions."[30]

Of course, there are professional obligations attached to the planner's role, regardless of his or her own personal characteristics. Overall solutions to human problems must be designed. In fact, the survival of our society is dependent on the activity of comprehensive planning. Branch places a heavy responsibility on planners. With so much at stake, caution must be exercised to reduce the influence of politics, personalities, and subjectivity on comprehensive planning. Only in this way can comprehensive planning continue to "represent indirectly the philosophy for whom it is intended—combined, filtered, and expressed through the many-faceted institutional structures of the democratic process."[31]

[29] *Ibid.*, p. 7.
[30] *Ibid.*, pp. 30–31.
[31] *Ibid.*, pp. 298–310ff. The quotation is found on p. 310.

Consistent with his view of planning and the place of planners, Branch proposes that comprehensive planning be made a separate field of study in academic institutions, one which will integrate all organized disciplines. Practitioners of the new discipline would, presumably, help to strengthen the influence of rationality and reason and reduce the impact of emotional and irrational responses to problems. Stability and minimum risk would be the societal goals of Branch's planners.[32]

Branch's views are not a departure from traditional planning theory so much as a logical extension of the master planning ideal. In the past, utopian planners were necessarily restricted in their vision to discrete metropolitan areas. With increased centralization of programs and services by the national government and accompanying technological advances, the old ideology has been infused with a new vigor by technocratic theorists like Branch.

Probably the least shakable aspect of planners' ideology has been the belief in efficiency and rationality. Planners have long decried the wasteful and inefficient use of resources that results when unplanned development takes place. Ernest Erber has described antiplanning as the basic philosophy of the American creed, which emphasizes rugged individualism and laissez-faire pluralism. Systematic intervention by governmental agencies in the distribution of resources, he asserts, has never characterized the American environment. This heritage has been directly opposed to the "establishment of deliberate goals by public authority."[33] Planning, as a result, was channeled in ways so as not to interfere with "the free play of pluralist market forces."

Many planners impatiently anticipate a more tightly planned, rationalized future society in which their values will receive priority. This literature contends that solutions to urban problems will soon become more rationalized and that society will be increasingly perceived as a closed or exact system: "The most important thread . . . is the *rationalization* of problem solving, an advancing trend for treating the environment analytically, as an exact system, depressing its irregularities and eccentricities as

---

[32] *Ibid.*, p. 316.
[33] Erber, "Urban Planning in Transition," p. xvi.

aspects which cannot be suitably planned. This irreversible trend motivated by many forces in our culture, foreshadows wide-spread change in the nature of future planning."[34] Those factors which cannot be planned will be "depressed" in the name of efficiency and effectiveness.

Donald Michael sees four virtually irresistible "pushes" in the direction of rationalization.[35] The first is the greater complexity in the problems that will have to be tackled. Second, the scale of future problems will require more integrated, inclusive long-range plans. The third push is the need for longer lead time so that programs will "evolve systematically"; also, the greater "application of powerful personalized methods" will be needed to overcome "vested interests" and other political considerations. Fourth, an increased supply of professionals will necessitate mass-produced "excellence and wisdom" and highly standardized training. The new environment resulting from these forces will be dominated by technological hardware and even a new language. This hardware and language will serve as the catalyst for raising human intelligence to higher levels:

> (The) rapport with the computer which will make it possible for the creative person to think in terms of many, many variable, probabilistic, and dynamic relationships, is bound to produce multi-variable, probabilistic, dynamic models of the world that couldn't be invented or evaluated otherwise. And because the thinking will be done in a different environment—the computer-assisted environment—it will produce new types of concepts appropriate to that environment that are not perceivable in other simpler environments.[36]

And there will also exist, according to Michael's prognosis, a unity of knowledge and values where, for example, the differences between Marxism and capitalism will be seen as separate mathematical formulas and not as diametrically opposed doctrines.

Presenting this future as meritorious, Michael's main con-

---

[34] Michael, "Urban Policy in the Rationalized Society," pp. 285–287.
[35] *Ibid.*
[36] Donald Michael, *The Unprepared Society* (New York: Basic Books, 1968), p. 49.

cerns are institutionalized resistance to change and the scarcity of technical talent to effectuate and manage the future society. He counsels us to be institutionally, methodologically, and personally prepared to do the long-range planning which will be essential to cope with social and technological trends, and favors a type of education which will prepare individuals to conform to and welcome these changes.[37] Preparing for the future like this, of course, helps to create it; thus the futurist, if he has influence, can hardly go wrong, since his predictions mandate a course of action which make the predictions come true. Michael does not sidestep this problem, however. Rather, he maintains that we ought to be in the business of self-fulfilling prophecies.[38] Commensurate with this analysis, Michael castigates his potential critics by accusing them, in advance, of being afraid to face the future: "We know from much psychological research that threatening information will be ignored if it is threatening enough. . . . But some people are able to face more intense emotional threats than others, and it is for these people that I write."[39]

Thus Michael's prediction of what the future will be like turns out to be a doctrine favoring the triumph of technological advances over political and "more human" considerations.[40] The computer will encourage simulation, gaming, and replication of reality with attendant growth of data and information systems. Technocratic elites will become increasingly influential, and these people will emphasize rationalized solutions to social problems. Dependence on "fact" as determined by seemingly technical considerations will tend to eliminate the troublesome social issues. Politics and self-interests will be sublimated by more rational and measurable inputs to planning. Increased information and coordination of knowledge will be favored by those who have seen their technical and comprehensive efforts blocked by inhibiting social factors.

All these developments, of course, will be accompanied by a massive growth in the role of government. Direction and coordi-

[37] *Ibid.*, p. 3.
[38] *Ibid.*, pp. 11 and 68.
[39] *Ibid.*, p. 7.
[40] *Ibid.*, p. 7.

nation of all important resources will be the responsibility of the federal government as business and government nearly merge. Rationalized solution of problems will become the predominant governmental activity. Finally, government will become the main device for social control, though this will probably be slowed by elected officials who are "products of the past," by reluctant public constituencies, and by some bureaucrats.[41]

While most planners are probably less clear and inclusive than this in their vision of the future society, the direction of many planners' thinking is similar to that sketched by Michael. An assumption that comprehensive solutions are needed, that resources must be used efficiently, and that decisionmaking must be increasingly rationalized has been and is at the heart of planning ideology.

An assumption closely related to the comprehensiveness-coordination-efficiency doctrine poses the planner as the only neutral participant in decisionmaking. If planners are uniquely comprehensive in their outlook and if they seek rational solutions to problems, it follows logically that they simply amalgamate the values of others. As Branch points out, they must subordinate "self to the planning problem," insisting on rationality as their only value.[42]

The notion of neutrality pervades the planning literature. This is so because neutrality attaches itself so closely to traditional conceptions of the planners' role. Thus, in taking Bernard Frieden to task for suggesting that planners may not always be able to engage in systematic and comprehensive planning in social programs, E. David Stoloff asserts that planners are the only professional group that can claim comprehensiveness and neutrality.

> Comprehensive and integrative approaches are a unique quality of the planning profession. It is clear that neither the housing specialist, nor the land-use specialist, nor the transportation specialist, nor the health specialist, nor the education specialist, can be considered urban planners in situations where a broad strategy involving some or all of these specialties are called for.

[41] *Ibid.*
[42] Branch, *Planning: Aspects and Applications*, p. 30.

There is such a thing as a conflict of interest within the helping professions. The specialist is bound to promote what he knows best and let others provide the countervailing arguments.

There are a number of social planning jobs to be done that professions less well equipped than planning are attempting to do. Planners would be abrogating professional responsibilities to let social policy decisions continue to be the result of the competition between the education, health, recreation, economic development, social work, and other functional specialists and special interests.[43]

As pointed out by Altshuler, views like these would have less credibility were they not implicitly supported by an assumption that planners protect and serve the public interest.[44] Planners have usually viewed themselves as guardians of the public interest, contrasting themselves with other professionals who owe their allegiance to narrower and more clearly defined clients, often found in the private sector. Henry Fagin expressed a more subtle but still illuminating point of view, arguing that the professions and the general public needed to be re-educated to the possibilities of new "exciting urban forms." Such a re-education could lead to the realization of the general good:

For the urban landscape is an inexorable reflection of the urban culture that creates it. The fundamental problem is to create in the consciousness of our culture a vision of what the culture can now create. As the late Henry S. Churchill so eloquently put it:

"A city plan is the expression of the collective purpose of the people who live in it, or it is nothing. For in the last analysis, planning is not just yielding to the momentary pressures of fugitive groups, nor is it even the making of beautiful maps encompassing future hopes. It is something far more subtle; something inherent and ineluctable—the unspun web in the body of the spider."[45]

---

[43] E. David Stoloff, "Competence to Plan Social Strategies," in *Urban Planning in Transition*, ed. Ernest Erber (New York: Grossman Publishers, 1970), p. 296.

[44] Altshuler, *The City Planning Process*, p. 299.

[45] Henry Fagin, "Planning for Future Growth," *Law and Contemporary Problems* (Winter, 1965), p. 24.

Planners see protection of the public interest as their unique calling and obligation. Thus, in writing about planning activities in East St. Louis, Illinois, one planner criticized past planning development as being insensitive to social needs, and suggested as a major guideline for future development that projects be "measured in terms of (their) immediate and ultimate contribution to the needs of the people of East St. Louis."[46] Even those planners who stress the complexity of the city—as most planners do—often speak of one public interest. This may occur for two reasons. First, a notion of several different or private interests contradicts key aspects of planning ideology. And second, planners have their own singular conceptions of the public interest which make up important components of the planners' ideology. These include assumptions concerning the necessity and desirability of efficiency, rationality, planned direction, comprehensiveness, and conserving for the future.

The proposition that the public interest is unitary has come under sustained questioning in the last few years. Some planners, while still holding to the belief of an identifiable general good, have redefined it. Others have recently begun rejecting the idea altogether, and it is conceivable that if this thinking gains esteem, similar notions valued by planners may also come under attack. Erber has posed the problem in unusual clarity in this question:

> The implications of the challenge to the public interest doctrine are clear, direct and serious—and, if true, shattering. If there is no unifying public interest to be served, if the science and art of planning is to be placed in the service of each special interest group in a pluralist society, what happens to the concept of comprehensiveness? Can there be a profession and a discipline of planning without its unique and unifying concept that parts should be designed only in relation to wholes if balanced development is to result?[47]

[46] Seymour Z. Mann, *East St. Louis and the Planning Process—A Philosophical and Operational Statement* (Edwardsville: Southern Illinois University, Public Administration and Metropolitan Affairs, 1966).
[47] Erber, "Urban Planning in Transition," p. xxv.

In fact, the planning literature of the past five years shows a radical redefinition of planners' obligations to political interests. While criticizing planners for being guided by their own middle-class values and for working for powerful economic and political interests, large numbers of planners are calling for the representation of minority viewpoints and of the political interests of disadvantaged populations. Thus, Michael Brooks and Michael Stegman assert that planners ought to work for the ending of poverty and racism, the extension of participatory democracy, and positive social change.[48] In a similar vein, Bernard Frieden says that planners ought to use their resources to press for different priorities when confronted with the political power of city government.[49] Advocacy planning as a movement was built largely on the premise that planners in the past had either been ineffectual or had represented the wrong interests, and that the urban minorities needed professional advocates to help redress the balance. Even these arguments have often represented little more than an extension of the planners' view of himself as the public's guardian; nevertheless, the advocate planners have stated an intention to guard different publics than those represented by planners in the past.

Policy Planning and Advocacy

Within the last decade traditional planning ideology has come under sustained criticism in the professional literature. Three main factors can be identified as stimulating this questioning.

One of the factors has been the turning from physical to policy planning brought about by the changing role of the federal government. The Kennedy and Johnson administrations broke a logjam which had slowed the participation of the federal government in social welfare programs. Nearly 400 urban social programs were enacted between 1960 and 1968. These created

---

[48] Michael Brooks and Michael Stegman, "Urban Social Policy, Race and the Education of Planners," *Journal of the American Institute of Planners*, XXXIV (September, 1968).

[49] Bernard J. Frieden, "New Roles in Social Policy Planning," in *Urban Planning in Transition*, ed. Ernest Erber (New York: Grossman Publishers, 1970), p. 287.

a need for professional talent. It was appropriate that planners, given their perception of their own role and the nature of their work, would eagerly offer themselves for employment in the new market.

A second factor encouraging a questioning of traditional roles was the civil rights movement and the growing unrest of urban minorities. This development occurred at the same time that government expanded social welfare programs (the latter was in large part a response to the new militancy), providing planners with an institutionalized, productive, and profitable outlet for responding to the pressures from below. That planners ought to advocate the interests of particular clients received its classic expression in 1965,[50] and soon advocacy planning became synonymous with planning for and with urban minority groups.

A third factor accounting for dissatisfaction with the traditional definitions of planning was the growing perception among planners that past planned programs had been detrimental to the interests of important segments of the urban population. A new social consciousness about the consequences of such programs as urban renewal and highway building may have been forced on planners by militant groups outside of planning; whatever the impetus for it, it provided fuel for planners' critics.

Changes in the social scene also encouraged literature dealing with the special competencies and attributes of professional planners that asserted their importance in solving new problems. Accused of having focused narrowly on physical aspects of the city, and branded as socially irresponsible by critics outside the profession, planners experienced a crisis in confidence. In reaction, attempts were made to define the profession in ways to guarantee or make obvious planners' continuing relevance and importance.

As new money became available for planning and administration of social programs and as pressures and demands increased from the poor and the Blacks, a revolt took form within the profession. Many planners began to search for a more significant (relevant) role for planning. The danger that they would be-

[50] Paul Davidoff, "Advocacy and Pluralism in Planning," *Journal of the American Institute of Planners*, XXXI (November, 1965).

come unneeded or unwanted provided a powerful stimulus to challenging traditional planning ideology. Quite appropriately, planners attempted to develop a doctrine that would give them an important role in the new social programs. They also tried to appeal to the militant Black minority in the cities. Thus, some planners began to promote policy planning and advocacy.

Melvin Webber, in 1963, was one of the first to explicitly examine the relation between traditional planning theory and the changing social and political environment. Webber's article was a conservative attempt to reassert the utility of traditional planning ideology in a new social setting. It represented the feelings of many planners, but also met with considerable criticism and debate, and helped to initiate continuing controversy concerning the roles and responsibilities of professional planners.[51] Webber argued that planners had always been at the forefront of social reform movements which attempted to attack poverty and accelerate social mobility. Their social reform emphasis on egalitarianism, public service, and progress had produced and nurtured the profession. Planners' natural inclinations were to solve social problems and search for social betterment; they were therefore uniquely qualified, he asserted, to provide leadership for the solution of social problems.

Further, according to Webber, the profession's past emphasis on physical land-use planning was no impediment to a new social responsibility role. Although planners previously had mistakenly assumed that physical environment largely determined social behavior and social problems, it was still true that physical planning was closely linked to social planning. Webber reasserted the traditional concept of the planners' role: "The city planner's responsibilities relate primarily to the physical and locational

[51] Melvin M. Webber, "Comprehensive Planning and Social Responsibility," *Journal of the American Institute of Planners*, XXIX (November, 1963). Webber's paper was first prepared for a 1963 American Institute of Planners Government Relations and Planning Policy Conference. It was the subject of much discussion, and was subsequently published in the AIP journal. Webber's note at the beginning of the article reveals something about the movements within planning at that time: "The lively responses provoked by the conference draft of this essay assure me that it touches upon some sensitive issues that are of deep concern to a great many planners. . . . I do hope that it can serve as a useful foil for a new round of deliberation on the profession's emerging roles and purposes."

aspects of development within a local government's jurisdiction."[52] Performance of this role guaranteed the planner's relevance in solving social problems. Physical locational features were highly related to the quality of social services, the health of local economies, and transportation, employment, and residential patterns.

Another important role for planners was to "integrate larger wholes."[53] By working together, physical and social planners could bring about truly comprehensive planning. New data and new theory would allow planners to engage in social policy that would effectively reach desired social ends. Webber also emphasized the planners' obligation to expand freedom, promote cultural diversity, and to encourage democratic decisionmaking.

Although it did not go far, Webber's essay made a modest bow in the direction of socially sensitive planning. But the formulation fell far short of the responsiveness expected by younger members of the profession. Paul Davidoff's thesis that planners ought to advocate for particular social and political interests, published two years later, contrasts sharply with the earlier, more conservative formulation. Davidoff's article represented an explicit reaction to the racial unrest of the early 1960s and to conservative planning ideology. Protests against social and racial discrimination revealed the need for planners to work toward providing equal opportunities.[54] Questions concerning the justice of the present distribution of social and political resources could not be answered through technical methods, Davidoff maintained. Social attitudes and values largely determine the nature of the questions asked and the solutions proposed. In a democracy, he argued, political conflict is a desirable and necessary aspect of policy development.

Davidoff attacked three important tenets of traditional planning ideology. First, he asserted that planners do not operate as value neutrals and therefore their proposals are biased to achieve predetermined goals. Planners cannot be neutral, he maintained, and rather than hiding their values under a cloak of neutrality,

---

[52] *Ibid.*, p. 233.
[53] *Ibid.*, p. 235.
[54] Davidoff, "Advocacy and Pluralism in Planning," p. 331.

they should openly espouse and advocate them.[55] Second, Davidoff rejected the notion that a uniform public interest could be identified in a complex political system. "Determinations of what serves the public interest, in a society containing many diverse interest groups, are almost always of a highly contentious nature." Therefore, "the right course of action is always a matter of choice, never of fact";[56] public policy merely represents a product of political debate. Third, Davidoff questioned the assumption that a comprehensive plan ought to be devised by a small group of professionals sharing similar viewpoints. Rather, many different values should be represented; criticism and debate should be encouraged. Planning commissions, he held, are obsolete institutions with no constituencies; they discourage democratic planning and the voicing of alternatives, and emphasize unitary planning, usually with a concentration on the physical aspects of the city.[57] Davidoff argued that planners should represent particular clients, and maximize the impact of the clients' values on public policy. Planners would be attracted to those clients whose values most closely matched their own. This sort of pluralist planning would enhance democratic decisionmaking, and in the process policy solutions would be designed which represented the real needs and desires of social and political groups.

Davidoff's article spawned a large advocate planning literature. After 1965, no planning conference was complete without papers and panels dealing with advocate planning. Younger members of the profession found the advocacy concept especially appealing, for it reflected their concerns about the impact of planning on the urban poor and minority groups and their disturbance about the elite status of planners. In the mid-1960s, Planners for Equal Opportunity was formed on the basis of these concerns.

As posed by Davidoff, the concept of advocacy was somewhat neutral with regard to whose interests planners ought to represent. In fact, however, advocacy planning was generally

[55] *Ibid.*, pp. 331–332.
[56] Ibid., p. 332.
[57] *Ibid.*, p. 335.

equated with advocacy for the poor by its proponents and critics alike. Advocacy planning grew from a professed commitment to provide representation to those groups which had been traditionally neglected in the political process. Planners were seeking a new clientele made up of the disadvantaged and Black residents of the inner cities. Past planning had excluded the urban poor and had adversely affected many of them. By the mid-1960s, the poor were making their voice heard, and this was a persuasive rationale for those wanting to champion the interests of this new clientele.

Michael Brooks and Michael Stegman argued that advocate planners should exhibit an ideological commitment in favor of the urban minorities. After documenting the ways in which past planners had worked to the detriment of the Black ghetto minority, Brooks and Stegman reasserted Davidoff's point that all planners were advocates, and that planning schools should train some planners to advocate large institutional interests while training others to advocate for minorities. Minority advocates, they said, must be made sensitive to the complexity of ghetto communities and the planning schools must also recruit and train large numbers of Blacks who have a unique awareness and understanding of ghetto life. Brooks and Stegman also felt that social planners must have ideological commitments to the goals of ending poverty, providing democratic representation in the political process, and assuring equal opportunities for all races.[58]

Antipoverty and Model Cities programs increased the pressure on planners to exhibit a dedication to identifiable values of equality of opportunity and maximum citizen involvement. As the poor became increasingly organized and aggressively active in their demands for a greater share in the allocation of important political and social resources, some planners began to take a new look at the public interest doctrine, with its emphasis on efficiency and effectiveness. Compensatory education, training, and employment were part of a national desire to atone quickly for past injustices toward Blacks. Traditional values of economy-minded planners were shaken and disrupted. As a consequence,

---

[58] Brooks and Stegman, "Urban Social Policy."

planning literature became filled with assertions that planners ought to hold values favoring egalitarianism and participation. Though these assertions (or assumptions) have usually been less explicit than Brooks and Stegman's goals, they underlie much of the advocacy literature. Planners are in search of a new clientele; the search impacts upon how planners view their own work and obligations.

Nevertheless, the most important client of policy and advocate planners is not the urban poor. It is the federal government, along with state and local governmental units which administer federal funds. Social planning has been pushed hardest when underwritten with jobs and money. As planners have eagerly taken advantage of a rapidly growing job market subsidized by federal funds, they have redefined their mission and their ideology. To some extent, social planning doctrine is a defensive reaction to protests against urban renewal, highway building, and other urban development programs which have displaced the urban poor.[59] Hence, it frequently contains rhetorical commitments to protect the poor against governmental abuses. But by far the most powerful ingredient promoting the growth of social and policy planning has simply been the money available for administering federally assisted programs designed to manage troublesome ghetto populations. Social planning represents an attempt by a profession to keep itself relevant, and new jobs in social welfare programs provide the rationale for a much expanded view of what planning entails. The planners' immediate self-interest in gaining a share of the federal largesse has translated into a broadly defined social planning ideology which extolls the virtues and necessities of coordinated, rationalized approaches to social problems. A commitment to traditional planning objectives is everywhere apparent in social planning, as Melville Branch's book well illustrates. In contrast, advocacy planning is built chiefly upon a stated commitment to promote the interests of the poor through political activity.

A major component of the new ideology is its affirmation of the vitality and desirability of pluralist, democratic decision-

[59] John Dyckman, "Social Planning, Social Planners, and Planned Societies," *Journal of the American Institute of Planners*, XXXII (March, 1966).

making—not simply as a value attached to planning but as its most necessary component. This assumption is not consonant with traditional planning notions, for pluralism is "antiplanning" and is the antithesis of comprehensive planning.[60] Belief in pluralism and democracy places emphasis on the *process* of reaching decisions as much as the final decisions. But advocate and social planners are also concerned about outputs (the final decisions)—as their indictment of past planning shows. They have expressed a belief that the best decisions flow from democratic process, not the doctrines and edicts of professionals.[61] This claim is based as much on a judgment of the results of past planning and public policies as upon a normative preference for participatory democracy. Planners, charge the critics, have systematically championed their own class interests, with an emphasis upon property values and the preferences of the privileged, and they have also frequently found their own immediate self-interests paramount. Thus, social programs have failed not for lack of technique or knowledge, but often because of such factors as "leakage of funds to professionals, (the) imposing (of) a colonial status upon the poor, (the) cultivation of dependence . . . unresponsiveness to client interests, and . . . bureaucratic entrenchment."[62] Domination by professionals, this literature tells us, means fewer political interests will be represented, not that public policy will improve. To the advocate planners, the danger of elite monopoly as opposed to social change clearly outweighs the halting progress in pluralistic politics. "The evidence so far implies that the very considerable short-term inefficiencies and exasperations of advocacy are paid for by pressure which they generate for a social policy more sensitive and adaptive to social reality."[63]

An essential aspect of this view is the position that planning is inherently partisan: no plan is neutral, but always benefits some

[60] Erber, "Urban Planning in Transition," pp. xv.
[61] Altshuler, "Decision-Making and the Trend Toward Pluralistic Planning," in *Urban Planning in Transition,* ed. Ernest Erber (New York: Grossman Publishers, 1970), p. 186.
[62] Frances Fox Piven, "Social Planning and Politics," p. 48.
[63] Lisa R. Peattie, "Reflections on Advocacy Planning," *Journal of the American Institute of Planners,* XXXIV (March, 1968), p. 81.

political interests and discriminates against others. No solitary public interest exists in which all social and political groups hold a share, and therefore the concept of serving the entire society is fictional. Planning is an extension of the political system and is political in nature. Planners have the responsibility of making explicit the winners and losers in their proposals.[64]

If planning is partisan—that is, the participants, including planners, pursue their own interests—then it is also political in its involvement in allocating socially valued resources. It is political, because (1) it redistributes wealth, (2) it can be legitimated only by those who hold power, and (3) planners pursue their own self-interests.[65] Planners develop clienteles and constituencies, and attempt to use these to enhance their power. Planners who lack political backing are helpless, and must seek power to be effective.[66] The implication is clear. Planners cannot legitimately claim expert judgment as to what constitutes comprehensive and efficient public policy. Since they cannot espouse a uniquely rational and objective view, they ought to do what other participants in the political arena do: advocate openly for what they think is desirable, and let others do the same.

Irrelevancy of Planning Doctrines

Two dominant ideological strains in the planning profession have been identified. One stresses that planning is properly a neutral, rational, comprehensive activity while the other urges that planning is part of a political process involving choice among available values and clienteles.[67] In the present context, the most relevant question concerning both of the ideologies is

[64] Davidoff, "Advocacy and Pluralism in Planning."

[65] Joseph M. Heikoff, "Urban Politics and Planning," *Bureau of Community Planning Newsletter* (Urbana: University of Illinois, Winter, 1969), pp. 2–5.

[66] *Ibid.*

[67] One could draw finer distinctions than this, of course. Leo Jacobson, for example, identifies six ideological traits among contemporary planners, and envisions an elaborately rich mixture among the six traits. (See his "Toward a Pluralistic Ideology in Planning Education," in Ernest Erber, ed., *Urban Planning in Transition*). It seems to us, however, that five of the six traits he identifies are variants of traditional planning doctrines, with one, which he labels "activist," being the equivalent of our "advocate" category.

this: Do either define a professional role which may be useful in providing guidance to practicing planners? Our answer is an unequivocal "no."

Professional planners have filled volumes attempting to explain and define their work and professional calling. It is not through a lack of effort that utilitarian definitions of the planner's role remain largely absent, but rather that too much self-consciousness has pervaded the literature. Much of the writing has been little more than a defensive attempt to justify a separate professional identity and to defend, preserve, and enhance the status and security of planners. As a result, planning ideology, while performing its prime function of legitimating the profession, has largely failed to fulfill any other purpose. Planners have successfully convinced themselves and constituencies outside the profession of their utility and necessity, but have been largely unable to turn their attention inward—to the task of translating the legitimating instrument into a practicing one.

But the traditional and the advocate doctrines grew out of similar needs and exhibit similar liabilities. Traditional ideology legitimated the profession by espousing the same values as held by dominant social and political groups. Early planners pursued efficiency and rational administration in the name of a municipal science. Reform became professionalized very early in its history, and the values of efficiency and economy have proved extremely durable. These were the same values promoted by business elites during the period of rapid industrialization. These values were transferred freely from the private to public sector. Never seriously challenged until the 1960s, they were almost universally accepted as the defining characteristics of planners and planning. And, as the discussion of the traditional doctrines indicated, the importance of these values for the profession has increased in the last several years in direct proportion to their emphasis in governmental programming. Vast sums for planning from the federal, state, and local governments have reinforced the conventional wisdom summed up in words and phrases like coordination, comprehensive planning, efficient use of resources, rational decisionmaking, and the rational application of technical expertise and knowledge. Traditional doctrines

lend respectability and legitimacy to planners and their proposals precisely because they appeal to the dominant values in
American society.

Advocacy planning, as has been seen, emerged in response to
demands and protests from new political constituencies. It did
not precede the political activity of the 1960s, but rather ad-
justed to it. It was essentially an attempt to redefine the planning role so as to maintain relevance and legitimacy in the eyes
of dissident groups. One need not be cynical to advance this
interpretation. Many of the advocate planners were and are
sincere in their expressions of sympathy for the aims of the
Black and poor minorities and in their challenge to the dominant
values of the profession. Nevertheless, the new doctrine was as
defensive as the old, representing an adjustment to the political
environment within which the profession had to operate.

Only rarely have planners recognized the legitimating role of
their doctrines—perhaps because to do so would endanger the
doctrines' utility. In an unusually perceptive article, however,
John Friedmann has noted the role of ideology in serving the
growth and maintenance needs of the planning profession. In
analyzing the relation between planning and ideology in Chile,
Friedmann drew the distinction between allocative (comprehensive) and innovative (strategic action, pragmatic) planning.
One of the defining characteristics of innovative planning was to
"legitimize new social objectives. . . ."[68] Another of its characteristics was to provide validity and generate support for a specific
proposal rather than rating various proposals on the basis of efficiency and effectiveness. Innovative planning was concerned
with strategy rather than comprehensiveness, unless the latter
was used as a base for rallying support for a plan or action.[69]

Friedmann is exceptionally clear about the uses of ideology in
what he calls innovative planning. When comprehensive planning was undertaken in Chile, it was a tactic, not an end in
itself. Planners, by virtue of their professional reputation and
status, helped lend legitimacy to public policy. In his case study

[68] John Friedmann, "Planning as Innovation: The Chilean Case," *Journal of
the American Institute of Planners*, XXXII (July, 1966), p. 195.
[69] *Ibid.*, p. 196.

planners gave credence to their work by assuming a comprehensive posture. Though they were engaged in "innovative" planning, the ideology of comprehensiveness supported their activities. Under the guise of standard planning ideology, the true nature of the planners' work (innovative planning) was disguised. In the tradition-bound society in which they were involved, this deception made their efforts politically acceptable.[70]

Except for this intentional subterfuge, planning ideology nearly always serves the purposes Friedmann describes. The claim to technical expertise, rationalism, comprehensiveness, and efficiency is perhaps the most important political resource planners have. Planners place the stamp of professional approval and thus legitimate what other people want. Stripped of this resource, planners are left searching for other sources of influence and power. More than any other factor, this may explain the persistence and strength of traditional planning ideology.

While it is difficult to forecast which of the two major doctrines will guide planning in the future, certain recent developments would indicate, on superficial analysis, a movement toward advocacy. The 1970 convention of the American Institute of Planners (AIP) was dominated by activists demanding a more responsive role for planners and was keynoted by Ralph Nader. An increasingly large number of articles questioning traditional planning values is being published by the *Journal of the American Institute of Planners*. Further, a quarterly newsletter called "The Thang" in which planning students stressed issues of ecology, problems of urban minorities, women's rights, and the distribution of power within the planning profession was published for several months under the auspices of the AIP.

But a push toward the advocacy doctrine is not clearly defined. One of the reasons for this is that planners' self-interests and the advocacy idea conflict in practice. Factors both internal and external to the profession continue to encourage a rationalist-comprehensive perspective. Internally, the traditional ideology will continue to attract adherents because like the positivist movement in the social sciences, the rationalist-

---

[70] *Ibid.*, pp. 197–200, 203.

comprehensive idea gives the appearance of linear progression in the acquisition of knowledge and understanding of social, physical, political, and economic phenomena. This notion of progress in the ability to understand increasingly complex phenomena is certainly a compelling logic which planners cannot easily resist.[71]

Even more important for the protection of planners' own interests, the traditional ideology formulates a technical framework within which planners can give force to decisions. Planners have a strong sense of what it is they want to accomplish, and they have been continually frustrated in ordering the world according to their own priorities. Placing decisionmaking on a technical basis gives advantage to those with requisite technical skills not only in portraying alternatives but also in determining goals and means. Frustrations can be overcome by replacing bargaining and compromise among various political interests with narrower conceptions of legitimate participants and issues. The rationalist-comprehensive doctrine helps to impose consensus by restricting the number of competent participants. Since many planners in any case tend to see themselves as representatives of a broader public interest, they can feel justified in excluding from decisions the supposedly more self-seeking members of the body politic.

It should occasion no surprise, therefore, that Rexford Tugwell's call for planning as a fourth branch of national government has been enthusiastically received by practicing planners. Since the 1930s Tugwell has argued that planning should be given official blessing by making it a central and independent activity of government. He has recently resurrected his idea in a proposed U.S. Constitution published by the Center for Democratic Institutions.[72] Under his proposal, the planning function would be promoted as a main concern of government and would be removed from the influence of politics. Tugwell argues that if forced to respond to particular political constituencies, plan-

[71] Whether the appearance of progress represents actual progress or fantasy or a blend of the two is beyond the scope of this discussion.

[72] *The Center Magazine* (Center for the Study of Democratic Institutions), September/October, 1970. See also Rexford Guy Tugwell, *Model for a New Constitution* (Palo Alto: James E. Freel and Associates, 1970).

ners would be unable to protect the general social interest against individual, private interests. As a separate branch of government, long-range national plans would be submitted to the President and the Senate.[73] These plans would attempt to initiate institutional reform and raise the quality of national life. Planners would, among their other duties, assume responsibility for preparation of the annual budget. Israel Stollman, Director of the American Society of Planning Officials, has endorsed the idea of a federal planning agency and emphasized that it "must be a part of our national future."[74]

In addition to forces within the planning profession which favor traditional planning values, there have been external pressures which lead in the same direction. Market demands for certain values and skills have influenced many planners who desire security and professional status. Without a doubt the market has emphasized planners with a commitment to find rational, technical, and comprehensive solutions to public policy or corporate problems.

Continued adherence to traditional norms will seriously hinder the development of a literature describing planners' roles and skills in ways which provide useful prescriptions for professional conduct. Traditional doctrine encourages a divorce between planning and implementation, while the practitioner, if he wants to be effective, must constantly attempt to fuse the two. If he follows traditional professional norms the practicing planner will assume a detached and objective role, thus relegating himself to the job of drawing maps or devising schemes which nobody but himself takes seriously. Effective practitioners must inject themselves into the political process, seeking out allies and devising strategies to give plans force. To be effective, in other words, he must ignore the traditional norms and values of his own profession.

In ideals and in practice, planners have been loathe to consider themselves overt political actors. Thus they have con-

[73] The Senate under Tugwell's constitution would be composed of former chairmen of the federal planning board, past high government officials and appointees of the President, House, and Judiciary.
[74] *Planning*, A Newsletter of the American Society of Planning Officials, Vol. 36, No. II (December, 1970), p. 142.

centrated on the development of master plans, which rarely represent political consensus; or, when they have represented consensus, the goals of the plans have been exceedingly vague.[75] Planners have not seen themselves as "salesmen" for their plans and recommendations.[76] They have preferred to allow the logic and sensibleness of their work to manifest itself and have been extremely reluctant to use political resources to effectuate their plans.[77] It may be that the needs of the profession have simply mandated this tendency, as observed by John Dyckmann: "the prestige of the city planner may hinge on the remoteness of promised results, as with the clergy. But the prestige must be defended on occasion by walling off the operational role of the planner from the world of practical affairs. This segregation of operations is glorified as a rejection of politics."[78] Thus those practicing planners least effectively socialized into traditional professional norms have been most willing to engage in overt political activities.[79]

In principle, the shortcomings of traditional doctrines should not be manifested in advocacy planning. Whereas the old doctrines have encouraged a segregation of planning and politics, the new ideology recommends a fusion between the two. Rejected, too, are the myths concerning the planner's neutrality and regard for the public interest. Despite these challenges to traditional doctrine, it is premature to assume that advocacy doctrine will provide substantially better guidance to professionals. Advocacy theory, like its traditional counterpart, tends to be divorced from practice. Even the frequently expressed notion that advocate planners voice the interests of underprivileged members of society in order to encourage democratic policymaking is questionable. For this rhetoric ignores the pervasive influence

[75] See especially Altshuler, *The City Planning Process.*
[76] Francine F. Rabinovitz, *City Politics and Planning* (New York: Atherton Press, 1969), pp. 12 and 37.
[77] *Ibid.*, pp. 113–138 and 141–144.
[78] Quoted in *ibid.*, pp. 135–136. As our East St. Louis studies show, however, the traditional norms are not necessarily replaced by new ones. Planners who are not highly imbued with planning values may simply act with few clear values. Pragmatism is one of many alternatives to professionally derived values.
[79] John Dyckman, "Social Planning, Social Planners, and Planned Societies," *Journal of the American Institute of Planners,* XXXII (March, 1966), p. 66. Also see Rabinovitz, p. 136, in her discussion of the same qualities.

of the advocates' own values and professional standing: "a central problem of democratic planning . . . is that of preserving an adequate area of individual choice in the face of expert judgments of what is good. Like the planners before them, social planners tend to be the caretakers of other people's interests."[80] In fact, this tendency may be enhanced when planners search around for unrepresented interests, or when they oppose the Establishment, claiming a powerless constituency. Although the advocate has participatory inclinations, he is disqualified by virtue of his professional status from treating other participants as equals. He holds inherent advantages, especially when he advocates for ghetto residents. Despite his intentions, the advocate cannot be a neutral voice for the community:

> Even without administrative power, the advocate planner is a manipulator. The power to conceptualize is a power to manipulate.
>
> He is not and can never be a simple channel through which flow the "interests of the community." Those interests become transformed as they pass into the planner's technical framework. And . . . the advocate planner, like the establishment planner, finds it easier to deal with some issues . . . than with others. . . .[81]

The tendency to be unaware of professional limitations in acting as an advocate for other interests somewhat mirrors the traditional planner's failure to appreciate the extent to which their values have intruded into their work.

Institutional obligations make advocacy ideals extremely difficult to implement. If the professional's ability to purely represent disadvantaged groups has been compromised by virtue of his professional status, it has been dealt a virtual death blow by the terms of his employment. In an important sense, the advocacy literature talks to few planning practitioners who can act upon it. Few planners, including those who call themselves advocates, have the freedom to even select their own clients. They work for municipal, state, and federal planning departments, consulting firms, urban renewal, Model Cities, and anti-

---

[80] Dyckman, "Social Planning," p. 70.
[81] Peattie, "Reflections on Advocacy Planning," pp. 85–86.

poverty agencies, universities, and, unless they are willing to be fired, they conduct their work in accordance with the dictates of their employer. Only in rare instances have public agency, private consulting, or university planners undertaken and sustained advocacy projects. Very often, it appears that the advocacy doctrine reflects little more than a stated moral commitment to end racial discrimination, poverty, and undemocratic politics.

If advocacy or policy planning can be reduced to a set of value commitments, as is often the case, then it is not much help in telling what entitles a planner to claim professional status. When defined as value commitments, advocacy and policy planning becomes as limited as traditional doctrine in describing professional roles. On what professional ground, for example, can a choice be made between efficiency as a value preference as opposed to democratic decisionmaking? Herbert Gans maintains that planners cannot legitimately claim professional recognition if they fail to come to grips with the pressing social problems in our cities.[82] But if such a commitment defines planning, then presumably any socially concerned individual can claim the label "planner."

[82] Herbert Gans, "The Need for Planners."

Toward a Responsible Professional Role

6

Ideology and Practice: The East St. Louis Experience

Our investigation into the professional literature in the last chapter revealed that the East St. Louis experience was predictable given the nature and ideological tendencies of the planning profession. Emerging from the case studies are three significant aspects of planning which provide insights into the connection between professional doctrines and practice: (1) the planners' self-images, (2) their objectives, and (3) the strategies used to carry out their work.

Many of the professionals in East St. Louis tended to regard themselves as outside the political system and detached from individuals and groups vying for political rewards. Their own frequently expressed opposition to the political machine was rarely viewed as "political," and political explanations were uniformly absent in the analysis of other events. The building of city hall bureaucracies was justified in classical professional terminology: efficiency, coordination, and rational administration. When the Negro Unity Planners took over Model Cities, for example, the planners resented the politicizing of the program, even though they generally kept their opposition behind closed doors. Earlier, those fighting against Teer for director, especially East St. Louis and university professionals, argued that he lacked professional qualifications and was attempting to make the post a political one which would serve narrow interests. They were seeking an impartial administrator with a long list of Establishment credentials.

In the case of urban renewal planning, Cannon was skeptical toward a close arrangement with city hall. Actually, he had good reason: failure to keep the politicians at arm's length might have led to pressure for him to hire patronage workers or to provide "special jobs." But aloofness from city hall was not replaced with other alliances. Attempts to court the neighborhoods late in the renewal application process were short-lived and did not reflect a long-term commitment to include neighborhood residents in planning. In a restricted sense, the planning department was nonpolitical, being neither for nor against the status quo in East St. Louis. However, it was also largely isolated from the political system. The department's position was partly the result of a calculated decision by Cannon and it is difficult to speculate whether another position would have been preferable. In fact, there is likelihood that any other position might have been worse in some respects. For example, politicians might have so dominated federal programs as to curtail funding. Federal officials were anxious and eager supporters of professionalism, equating it with "technical competence" as opposed to the self-interest and private gain of the more blatantly political city hall employees. But the consequence of the department's detachment was that planning went on and on in East St. Louis with few tangible results. Planning and planners could remain outside the political system only at considerable cost. Perhaps to have been more intimately connected with powerful political and business interests would have required costs that the professionals were unwilling to pay, namely, policies which would narrowly represent those interests. But the planners, in one sense, by implicitly deciding to be neutral and impartial, failed to work against them and for change. Perhaps ineffectiveness was preferable to working strictly for established interests, but

positive accomplishments were limited despite increasing expenditures for planning personnel and consultants.

Planning goals in East St. Louis generally exhibited three
qualities: grandiose and visionary, general and vague, or unknown and unstated. In all of the planning carried out in the
city, one singular characteristic dominated—promises were
made far beyond the capacity to deliver. Riverfront planners
were unmatched in their utopian schemes for a future East St.
Louis. Their grandiose visions were put forth with no mention
of any obstacles—in fact, practical considerations had to be
swept aside to make the stated goals sound convincing. Cautious
words would have seemed out of place in a public relations and
booster document like the PACE plan. Support for this type of
planning was easy to obtain whether it was from local politicians, citizen groups, financial leaders in the metropolitan area,
or East St. Louis and St. Louis newspapers. The promises made
the sponsors feel good without asking for much in the way of
money, time, or talent. PACE's commitment to East St. Louis
was apparently limited to a share of the cost of a well-paid
consultant who, predictably, came up with a plan representing
the businessmen's notion of civic renaissance. Serious attempts
to implement the plan would have required PACE members to
commit not only money but also time and energy in applying
for funds, lobbying with federal and state politicians, and negotiating extensively with the railroads and local government.
That anyone really expected East St. Louis to be a "new city"
on the basis of elaborate phrases and aesthetic graphics implies
a lack of perception as to the gravity and causes of East St.
Louis's problems. Even the combined actions of public bodies
at the local, state, and federal levels could have had only limited
impact on such significant conditions as the exodus of middle-
income Blacks and Whites to neighboring communities. In many
instances, public authority had very little influence over the
problems in East St. Louis. An accumulation of individual private decisions (and some public actions) had made East St.
Louis a disadvantaged community. If the riverfront planning
showed anything, it was the utility of comprehensive planning

in allowing public and private interests to show much-publicized concern without substantial commitment.

In urban renewal planning and in certain aspects of Model Cities, planning activity persisted without clearly articulated objectives. Rather than programmatic goals, maintenance and enhancement needs repeatedly guided the activities of the planning and urban renewal departments. These needs were especially prominent and visible because both agencies were new and both wanted to build and maintain stable staffs and programs. Since they had been brought into existence as an explicit attempt by federal and local officials to give the city a professional arm, their goals were less to provide internal direction to the city than to satisfy the erratic and painstaking guidelines of federal programs. With the introduction of federal programs into East St. Louis, professionals became increasingly interested in expanding their influence in the administration of large programs. But the new importance for professionals was not accompanied by a coherent view of what planning and redevelopment was to accomplish, except vaguely to "improve the city."

High expectations accompanied the Model Cities grant to East St. Louis. Throughout its first year, Model Cities was seen as the single best hope for the city, and professionals in the program spoke in glowing terms. But by the end of 1968, many of the original aims were forgotten. They were replaced and compromised by one overwhelming pragmatic consideration— how to obtain federal funding for the plan. In reality, it may have been that few of the early goals accurately reflected local conditions and that Model Cities planners had been forced to state virtually impossible objectives. Later on, they certainly were pressured by local and federal demands to divide up limited funds among too many available projects. From the beginning, the setting of overall goals was difficult. To satisfy federal administrators, the MCA reiterated bureaucratic catchwords like "coordination," "comprehensive planning," "problem-solving," "citizen participation," while none of these terms expressed local priorities or created useful strategies. In adopting the catchwords, the professionals in the program were pursuing the only meaningful objective, which was to receive federal money. It was a goal, to be sure, but could hardly be classified as a planning goal.

Because the planning goals in East St. Louis were either absent or exceedingly visionary, it was difficult if not impossible for the planners to devise strategies of implementation. Sometimes implementation was not even seriously considered at all. In riverfront planning, no effort was made to establish a process of redevelopment which was tied to specific actions and individual responsibilities. Grandiose schemes were put forth in an attempt to elicit responses from legislators, bureaucrats, developers, and landowners, and somehow the logic of these plans was to be sufficient to induce a commitment from these various groups. While this could be considered to resemble a strategy, there should have been no surprise at its failure. If the riverfront planners had been highly concerned about redevelopment, they would have made an assessment of the location of important resources, such as money and power, and made a concerted effort to manipulate them. Actual as opposed to possible resources would have attracted their attention. Practical solutions like the subsidization of railroad relocation and the acquisition of funds to purchase and improve the site would have been their main concern. But continued planning seemed more important than marshaling congressional and state support to begin the operational process.

That planners devoted so much time and thinking to large and dramatic solutions reflected the values and commitments of themselves and their sponsors. If the real sources of power had been accurately pinpointed, then the planning would have been based on an appeal to the self-interests of the railroads and federal-state governments. Subsidization of the railroads was an obvious factor, even though a February, 1970, study financed by the Terminal Railroad Association established the feasibility and cost of relocation and determined the economies which would accrue to the railroad through more efficient operations in a new location. It was naive to believe that railroads, in poor financial condition, would move voluntarily or that developers were waiting for riverfront land if only they could be shown

graphically its desirability. Likewise, an accurate assessment of
the state's interest in the riverfront would not have continued
the wishful thinking that the state would automatically join a
riverfront road into the Great River Road. Only political advantage or else a conviction that long-range advantages could
accrue to the state would have been a logical basis for a multi-
million dollar road appropriation by the state legislature. Riverfront planners were attempting to enhance the tax base, increase
commerce in the city, and clean up the backyard of St. Louis.
With these goals in mind they could have pursued alliances
among local, state, and national politicians and private interests
on both sides of the river.

In the Model Cities program, the professionals and amateurs
shared an uneasy relationship. Residents were suspicious of
planners' motives, and frequently accused them of making decisions in secret and failing to accurately reflect residents' desires as expressed in the task force meetings. On the other hand,
residents were helpless to act on their suspicions, because they
had a greater stake in abiding by guidelines than did the professionals. Mostly for this reason, they were easily convinced
by the professionals' doomsday warnings of potential federal
government displeasure. And the professionals' domination also
had the result of directing the substance of planning. Programs
assumed a straightforward delivery-of-services character growing out of the months of negotiation between the HUD regional
office and the MCA administrative leadership.

Bureaucratization of citizen participation proved highly functional for the MCA staff. Most of the actual involvement and
impact that residents had on planning was focused in the MCA
executive board. Though the board frequently vetoed staff recommendations and showed great independence, it was far easier
to meet these demands than those which might have arisen from
a larger, more amorphous group. Meetings of the MCA usually
consisted of communications and proposals from Teer, Mc-
Gaughy, or other MCA staff, and Chandler or a few other members of the executive board. Not infrequently, opposition from
the "grassroots" was heard, but normally this growling was dealt
with through heavy lobbying for staff proposals by executive

board members. Without such assistance, MCA staff on several important occasions would have been extremely restricted in their actions.

Participation became an expression of the needs of the Model Cities organization. At one point, interest-oriented participation —the pursuit of self-interest by competing groups or individuals —was needed for organizational survival.[1] In the late spring and summer of 1968, shortly after Teer was appointed director, the emphasis in citizen participation was to mobilize neighborhood support. Citizen groups were encouraged to organize and exert influence behind Teer, McGaughy, and the planners against city hall and established financial interests which were perceived as threats to the independence of the MCA. The MCA staff needed a base to resist city hall through threats, protests, and militancy.

By the fall of 1968, cooptive participation was needed, with the objective being "to evoke the participant's interest, enthusiasm, and sense of identity with the goals of the enterprise in question," those goals having been determined by higher authorities.[2] Teer had support in the neighborhoods, but those providing it inhibited his ability to negotiate with the federal government and local institutions, thereby threatening the possibility of getting the program funded. HUD was demanding rationality, coordination, and technical decisionmaking—the opposite of making the program more political through citizen participation. Citizen participation was changed to legitimate planning and bureaucratic requirements.

But in spite of the priority eventually given them, the planning objectives were not achieved. By the spring of 1968, support outside of the neighborhoods had been irrevocably lost. The business interests, industry, White and Black politicians, leaders of important public agencies—institutions capable, in principle, of making comprehensive planning and coordination possible—had been replaced by the neighborhood groups. Racial and social changes were taking place in East St. Louis and

[1] Peter Bachrach and Morton S. Baratz, *Power and Poverty—Theory and Practice* (New York: Oxford University Press, 1970), pp. 204–206.
[2] *Ibid.*, pp. 206–208.

the neighborhoods provided the base for these changes, while Model Cities supplied the resources for continuing political activity (compromising to the extent necessary to satisfy the federal emphasis on planning). At times, the professionals in the program were not aware that the neighborhood groups had replaced the established interests. They talked and believed in citizen participation, but seemed ready to counsel absolute submission to federal dictums, whatever the price.

Two explanations may be offered for their failure to come to terms with this contradiction. First, it was difficult for them to break the habit of regarding the program as a way of bringing rational bureaucracy to city government. In the original proposal, Washnis had wanted a physically redeveloped city with efficient and competent management. Mendelson and Mann wanted the same thing, plus expanded employment and income opportunities. They were never as comfortable with an "irrational" and "political" citizen participation as they were with a simple and quiet planning process. Thus they became the wolves within—the impartial technicians, carrying out instructions, giving advice, and in the process encouraging a conservative strategy with respect to the federal government's demands. Anything asked for by federal officials, no matter how contradictory or absurd, was immediately acceded to. And the second explanation is that the planners were caught in the middle. Though willing to do any sensible thing, they simply did not know what their goals were or who they were serving. Very soon, the professionals became disenchanted with federal requirements, which were confusing, contradictory, and dedicated to form in the guise of logic. Issues became obscured and conflicts difficult to resolve because they operated in the absence of any guiding priorities. Unable to understand or know their own values or to select appropriate allies to help them effectuate a course of action, they fell to aimless pragmatism.

A lack of clear objectives likewise pervaded East St. Louis's urban renewal planning. Work on the GNRP was not dictated by internal direction, but rather by the availability of federal funds. This was also the case in the work on the NDP. Once committed to the NDP, work to prepare the proposal was guided by agency needs and not by strategic or value priorities. It appeared that the planning and urban renewal professionals regarded urban renewal to be so sufficiently self-justifying that unilateral action in obtaining a program was warranted. And unilateral action was obviously the most sensible way to facilitate a rapid application. Going to the neighborhoods did not represent a commitment to citizen participation but rather a symbolic attempt to be responsive to the "people" and to avoid major confrontations over the proposals. Two values, two different priorities, were in conflict. Theoretically, selection between the two would determine whether the planners would choose to advocate for ghetto residents or whether they would pursue redevelopment using every means possible to implement it, including domination over neighborhood groups. But the conflict was not perceived by the professionals.

Our case studies show a rather insulated group of professionals frequently pursuing their own values and self-interests without being aware of doing so. They tended to promise much, but refused or were unable to utilize political strategies to forge coalitions of power sufficient to accomplish their purposes. And the more grandiose their visions, the further removed they were from the resources necessary to effectuate their plans. It would be improper to blame a common planning ideology for these tendencies; the studies do not clearly show that. But the East St. Louis experience seemed to reflect the values and priorities advanced in the planning literature. Perhaps more important, the literature provides little advice as to how planning could have been different.

A Responsible Professional Role: Some Considerations

One could argue that planning has been less harmful when it deals in abstractions and supposedly satisfies all societal interests than when it has been effective in representing Establishment groups in programs such as highway building, public housing, urban renewal, and Model Cities. A cynical position might hold, for example, that the professionals' ineffectiveness in East St. Louis was the best that could be hoped for. Riverfront renewal would likely have served narrow financial interests, while urban renewal might only have reduced the supply of low-cost housing and disrupted the lives of residents, as it has in many other cities. More authority and power by professionals in Model Cities might have made that program even further removed from the neighborhoods. Yet this type of analysis avoids an important issue. As was pointed out in the previous chapter, the growing strength of technocratic and elitist ideology over the past decade offers planners and professional managers the possibility of long-sought-for power and authority. How planners will use this power is a significant question, especially if they continue to believe that their own values are inherently superior to those held by other social and political groups. The consequences of professional autonomy and increased power are almost certainly not going to be a maximation of the public interest, however the latter is to be defined. Rather, the professionals' own interests will become increasingly paramount and pervasive. In the next few pages, the inherent conflicts between autonomous professionals and their clients are considered.

In his role as a helping professional, the planner instructs, informs, advises, provides technical assistance, and is often seen as a guardian over certain values which he tries to impart to others.[3] As a result, he enjoys a built-in advantage over his client. For example, he normally has more information, expertise, experience, and formal training than the client. Of course client resources vary enormously in planning situations. A governmental unit or private corporation may contract with a city planner and have very specific measures of the planner's performance. Conversely, citizen representatives on an antipoverty board typically have a minimum capacity, educationally or politically, to dictate any terms at all to the professional, or to provide him with guidance. Even in the circumstance when the client's resources are considerable, the professional, by virtue of

---

[3] We wish to thank William R. Caspary of the Department of Political Science, Washington University, for allowing us to elaborate on several of his ideas contained in his paper, "Sharing Power in Tutelary Relationships" (unpublished).

his claim to expertise and his control over the services needed by the client, may wield considerable power and leverage.

The professional's resources are usually sufficient to place him in a dominant position. This superiority is enhanced when the client believes that the professional's training and knowledge give him the right to dictate the terms of the professional-client relationship. One important ingredient of the relationship is the determination of the recipient's self-interest. Commonly the professional decides the interest of the recipient, often without the client's definition of his own interest. Imposition of the professional's view in this way has been the norm with relation to welfare recipients and in housing and urban renewal programs. Planners have frequently been able to dictate the best interests of powerful clients, too. Planning departments have engaged in master planning because the professionals were successful in convincing city officials that this was the highest priority in planning. Once the plans were produced, of course, they tended to be ignored, but the planners nevertheless assured themselves and their clients that comprehensive planning was useful and necessary.

The professional's usefulness to the client is limited by several factors, including his own inherent self-interest, quality and extent of knowledge, and conflicts of values between the professional and client. Often the helping professional fails to acknowledge, even to himself, a self-interest which conflicts with that of the recipient.[4] When a conflict of interest is perceived, the client's interest may be dismissed as illegitimate, as when the planner elevates the "public interest" against the "narrow, partisan" interests of politicians or even other professionals. Planners have assumed their values to be universally shared and appreciated. Thus, they have usually depended upon the logic, sensibleness, and beauty of their proposals to be sufficient to rally support and power to insure implementation. When the

[4] For especially insightful comments on the relationship between professional communities and nonprofessionals, see William J. Goode, "Community Within A Community: The Professions," *American Sociological Review*, XXII (April, 1957).

proposals failed to generate resources, planners blamed "special interests" and "politics" for getting in the way and obstructing plan recommendations. In these instances the professional's calling is considered, by its nature, to be beneficial to the recipient. Consequently, it is a contradiction in terms to speak of a conflict of interest. Planners, of course, are not alone in this; many other professions have also erected elaborate doctrines to permit the professional's values to prevail.

Of primary importance to the practitioner are the professional and personal needs which influence the attraction of particular kinds of clients. This need encourages the professional to minimize the importance of real and potential conflicts of goals and commitments with the client. It also encourages the creation of philosophies and priorities which enhance the prestige and perceived necessity for the professional's services. For example, planners tend to create plans that reflect the values and training of the planners and that mandate further planning activities for implementation.

Even if the professional's personal interests do not conflict with the recipient, the professional may be limited by institutional interests in choosing what courses of action he can pursue in his client's behalf. Few members of any of the helping professions are free from institutional restraints. Social workers both follow and devise rules in providing welfare assistance which heighten their own advantage and lead to manipulation and coercion of clients, legal aid lawyers choose cases carefully so as not to engender overwhelming controversy, and public schoolteachers, if they value their jobs, are careful about using too much controversial material in classrooms. The professional's institutional interests are often as important (or identical with) the previously mentioned personal interests in limiting his freedom to serve the recipient.

Probably the most common clash of interests between professional and client concerns the extent to which the professional makes use of all available resources on the client's behalf. Professionals tend to concentrate in those areas where there is the most to gain in such rewards as money, status, and psychic satisfaction. This tendency is, of course, tempered by the professional's ethics as well as by the state of the market in the desired commodity, so that in serving individual clients the professional must make calculations as to the amount of time and energy to expend for the client. The structure of rewards is extremely important in this calculation. Lawyers tend to be better lawyers when their clients are wealthy or their cases bring acclaim or prestige. University professors frequently emphasize publishing rather than teaching. And planners are predisposed to large, well-publicized projects which entail primarily written reports in preference to activity demanding substantial monetary and political investment.

Though a practitioner claims expertise, there is no guarantee that it will automatically be used when requested. Application of training and knowledge requires time, energy, and sometimes considerable expense. He must conduct research, must communicate findings to the recipient of his services, and must often persuade the recipient to accept the results. There is no automatic application of expertise when a professional accepts an obligation. Use of professional skills depends primarily upon personal and institutional commitment and values, the calculation of rewards, and the client's status and resources. For clients to predict the utility of the professional, they must know the professional's training and expertise and assess the chances that those credentials will be put to maximum use. Several factors may limit the quality of the practitioner's training or expertise, so far as it applies to the client. One is the state of theories and methods of the practitioner's profession. If these are consistent and clearly defined, professionals' credentials will reliably reveal their competence and values. But if the theories and methods are not well developed, it may be difficult to determine just what the practitioner can supply. The importance of this point in the case of planning is obvious, for not only are the theories and methods of planning in dispute, but also there is doubt in some quarters that any even exist. Thus, the profession is generally unable to define and enforce professional norms and skills.

Another limitation in the quality of service available to prospective clients may occur when a professional attempts to apply general knowledge in specific situations. Experts may find difficulty in applying their training in novel situations. This problem is compounded when a gap exists between the experiences and values of the practitioner and the client. Thus professors who are acknowledged experts in their disciplines may find it difficult to communicate with undergraduates. Architects and planners, largely owing to their middle-class backgrounds rather than the extent of their expertise, may unwittingly destroy functional inner city neighborhoods. Social workers and manpower specialists may devise training programs which neither lead to employment nor encourage economic independence. Institutionalization of citizen participation in federal urban programs partly reflects the inability of technical experts to understand the problems and politics of low-income communities. Professionals may be well qualified to design solutions without understanding the problem while the reverse can be true for the client. Expertise is not automatically translated into service for the recipient.

The professional's usefulness is severely compromised when he disagrees sharply with his actual or prospective client. Such a disagreement is almost always present when the client groups are attempting to bring fundamental change. If the professional could be an objective appraiser of alternatives, if all important value determinations could be left in the hands of the client, then little conflict would be present. But one can scarcely conceive of a professional role that is not saturated with value commitments. The practitioner's goals and attitudes consistently intrude due both to his institutional and personal self-interests and his social class background. His ability to use his own philosophy and principles to manipulate his client is maximized when the latter lacks a perception of his own self-interests and objectives or lacks resources to successfully compete with the professional. In guiding or perhaps dictating the best interests of the client, the professional defines part of the task as educating the client as to proper values. That professionals traditionally choose this course rather than a break in the relationship reflects the importance they frequently place on persuading others to accept their values.

The previous discussion raises a basic question concerning the distribution of power in the professional-client relationship. Groups advocating democratic decisionmaking have become increasingly concerned about arbitrary control by technocratic elites over decisionmaking and public policy. As indicated earlier, a strong technocratic tendency exists within the planning profession. Some planners, like Branch, Michael, and, to a degree, Tugwell, explicitly argue for increasing technical-professional leadership while others favor it without having worked out arguments in its behalf. But planners are hardly alone in this regard. Strategies designed to enhance the power and prestige of their members probably dominate all professions in the United States.

In the face of this aspect of professional life, a significant issue is how to insure that the client can assume control or at least share in controlling the professional-client relationship. There is no alternative to guarding against abuses of professionals' power except to put power in the hands of the client. Professionals can hardly be expected to criticize abuse which arises from pursuit of personal self-interest and values. Only the client can judge such abuse. It may constitute a negative rather than a positive power; nevertheless, clients are the only ones fully committed to their interests.

Client power in the relationship is dependent on various factors. One is how well clients know what they want and the ability of the professional to supply it. Another is the degree of available client options. Many times the options are few and clients cannot withdraw from professional-client relationships without jeopardizing their own interests, such as the loss of an antipoverty or Model Cities grant, or, in a negative sense, the imposition of urban renewal without suitable housing options. The supposed voluntarism of clients can and often does become a trap: "love it or leave it."

A third variable determining recipient power is command over key political resources. In the case of the East St. Louis Model Cities, for example, when clients of the program combined with other Blacks in the city, it became very difficult for professionals not to work with the recipient coalition. The number of options had been expanded through the accumulation of political resources. They were in a position to bargain with the professionals who had conceived the program because continued existence of the local Model Cities program was dependent upon client support.

A fourth factor which is somewhat independent of the previous three is the mode and extent of participation by the recipients in making decisions both concerning their interests and concerning the contractual relationship. Recipients without prior resources do not develop skills and political options unless they are given a share of the power. This was, in fact, part of the rationale underlying citizen participation in federal programs of the 1960s.

In the last analysis, development of independent political power is probably the only way that recipients can redistribute the power in professional-client relationships. Professionals find it difficult to give up power, and the frustration of sharing power is rarely welcomed. In city after city professionals in education, transportation, housing, and urban renewal are having their judgments questioned by heretofore silent groups which will be affected by these decisions. In those places where the political resources have been strong, highways have been blocked and innovative school programs attempted.

Like the members of other professions, planners have been reluctant to share power with those on the outside. Any change which provides greater power to the recipient at the expense of the professional is usually forced on the latter. Over the past ten years the growing strength of minority groups has precipitated a questioning of standard planning ideology. This questioning has arisen simultaneously with trends in the direction of increased power, autonomy, and insulation of professional elites. It is difficult to predict the outcome of the struggle over the distribution of power between professional elites and militant groups advocating rapid political change. Professionalism is inherently conservative in this context. But the issue need not be whether the professions are dismantled or not. A somewhat restricted role still allows considerable autonomy and prerogative for those who can make legitimate claims to special knowledge and expertise. The critical test, of course, is whether what is offered by the professional is actually needed and sought after. Only nonprofessionals can decide that. Whether they have the chance or not is purely a matter of political power.

Our suggestion that the definition of the planner's role be decided largely through the client's preferences is quite conservative when compared to others. David Gurin, for example, holds the viewpoint that "the necessity for that hybrid—the professional city planner—is questionable."[5] Gurin charges that planners have used the ethos of their profession as a cover for the exercise of entrepreneurial power and that their proposals, in the name of the public interest, have consistently benefited bankers, realtors, construction firms, and downtown business interests. He wants city planning changed into a social movement rather than a profession, with its practitioners working within communities which articulate their own rights and goals. Gurin backs away from the suggestion of totally dismantling the professional role, however, and speaks instead of professionals who will "practice their specialties in terms of overall community aspirations."[6]

Similar proposals have been pushed by planners discontented with the conservative tendencies of their profession. Alan S. Kravitz has suggested a "liberatory planning" which, he says, would pragmatically root out the rhetoric and dogmas which have supported a conservative, elitist, and technological mentality emphasizing competition and high material productivity. Kravitz's "liberation" planning promotes:

> . . . a new, participatory utopianism that would radicalize individuals by enabling them to create new possibilities beyond those defined as "feasible" by traditional political, economic, or even technological constraints. It would create a demand for the equalization of power and the decentralization and democratization of authority by focusing on the development of new life styles based on individual and shared awareness of authentic intentions rather than externally determined wants. . . . People would become the planners; planning would be *by* the people

[5] David Gurin, "City Planning: Professionals and Protestors," paper presented at the Conference on Radicals in the Professions (Ann Arbor, Mich., July 14–16, 1967), p. 6.
[6] *Ibid.*

with the professional serving as the catalyst or "actualizer" of a communal planning process.[7]

He further argues that the new planning would express a "power to the people" ethic and would best be carried out in small communities. David Ranney expands on Kravitz's suggestion, calling on professionals to organize communes which will provide free or at-cost services to clients who cannot normally afford professional help.[8] In all these cases, a continuation of the professional planning role is assumed, even though the primary commitment is presumably the achievement of equality and community, not technical expertise as such. The logic of Kravitz's position, in particular, would make planners fulltime guerrillas using whatever tactics seem effective, including violence, for attacking existing social and political arrangements. It appears that the desire to maintain professional identity and power ("catalyst" or "actualizer" of a communal planning process) conflicts directly with the expressed revolutionary goals. If radical planners find it difficult to advise abandonment of the professional role, then it cannot be expected that the majority of the profession, even the sizable proportion who are deeply dissatisfied with past planning, will seriously entertain such a suggestion. Most planners are constrained by their own self-interest and/or their conviction about the legitimacy and utility of the planning function. Partly for this reason, our proposed strategy for changing the profession is directed toward the limited goal of breaking down professional autonomy. Our decision to support this limited objective is also influenced by the belief that professionals with skills in administration and budgeting who have an understanding of public policies and their consequences now play, and in the future will play, useful and necessary roles. Their utility, however, would be enormously enhanced if the entrepreneurial and expansive tendencies of pro-

[7] Alan S. Kravitz, "Mandarinism: Planning as Handmaiden to Conservative Politics," in Thad L. Beyle and George T. Lathrop, eds., *Planning and Politics: Uneasy Partnership* (New York: Odyssey Press, 1970), pp. 266–267.

[8] David C. Ranney, "Self Defeating Planning: A Critique of City Planning and Some Proposals for Change" (graduate program in Urban and Regional Planning, University of Iowa, unpublished).

fessionalism could be tempered. How, in practice, could this be accomplished?

It is clear that not much can be accomplished to this end within the profession. Planners are constrained by career and institutional pressures to remain essentially loyal to the profession, even if they call themselves radical and especially if they call themselves liberal or conservative. Traditionally, the profession has discovered and successfully utilized the central values of the social and political order, thus virtually guaranteeing not only professional survival but also increasing influence and authority. And in the final analysis, hardly any planners, even the most radical ones, will seriously consider implementing proposals which fundamentally threaten their livelihood and social status.

Possibilities of changing the profession from within are further complicated by the wide differences in occupations among planners. Academicians, private entrepreneurs, redevelopment specialists, bureaucrats, and consultants are all included in the classification of professional planner. And neither the planning literature nor our own experiences indicate that the profession is ready for basic change of the type that gives greater power to the clients of planning. And even a call for client power does not assure basic change, since it can be turned to conservative ends. Thad Beyle and George Lathrop, for example, advocate putting planning at the service of politicians to make it more effective.[9] Obviously, such a position is not so much strategic analysis as a judgment in favor of the legitimacy of those who govern. Beyle and Lathrop choose to support existing institutions. And if planners are encouraged merely to make a "choice" among values,[10] such will be the result most of the time. As independent cadres of program managers and administrators assuming more and more control over important social and political institutions, planners can hardly be expected to engage in introspection and

<hr/>

[9] Thad L. Beyle and George T. Lathrop, "Planning and Politics: On Grounds of Incompatibility?," in Beyle and Lathrop, eds., *Planning and Politics: Uneasy Partnership* (New York: Odyssey Press, 1970), p. 9.

[10] Paul Davidoff and Thomas A. Reiner, "A Choice Theory of Planning," *Journal of the American Institute of Planners*, XXVIII (May, 1962).

self-criticism against their own actions. Encouraging choice by professionals does not attack the basic problem, which has been their autonomy from the groups which they supposedly serve.

The expansionist tendencies of professional organizations and bureaucracies will be moderated, if at all, by pressures applied from outside, not from within, professionally dominated institutions. Problems in checking professional domination are similar to the problems faced by consumers challenging corporate power. Change mainly comes through increases in the political power of consumers, not through the good intentions or moral virtues of corporate managers and stockholders. To be strategically effective, those challenging professional elitism need to look for allies outside the professions and need to be concerned with developing skills and political strategies which can be used to force professionals to represent different political interests.[11] This Nader strategy is appropriate whether the target be corporate irresponsibility or professional arrogance. If, as in the past, planning continues to react to and not initiate change, then alterations in the environment within which planning takes place would seem to be the most effective way to make changes within the profession. Little will be altered in how planners perceive themselves or in what they do until those who are affected by their work are able to participate in deciding the priorities and values of planning activities.

---

[11] For an excellent review of the failures of radicals to effectuate change within the American Political Science Association, see Alan Wolfe, "Unthinking About the Thinkable: Reflections on the Failure of the Caucus for a New Political Science," *Politics and Society* (May, 1971). Wolfe castigates the radicals within political science for focusing upon changes within their own organization, rather than forging alliances and working with those outside the profession.

Selected Bibliography

East St. Louis

Altes, Jane. *East St. Louis, the End of a Decade.* Edwardsville: Southern Illinois University, Regional and Urban Development Studies and Services, January, 1970.

Cannon, Jamie. "Up Against the Wall in East St. Louis." *St. Louis Construction Record,* May 13, 1969.

Economic Study for Community Renewal Program, East St. Louis, Illinois. Washington, D.C.: Robert Davenport Associates, Inc., 1968.

The Future of Tourism in East St. Louis (Including Three Feasibility Studies). Washington, D.C.: Checchi and Co., August, 1966.

Mendelson, Robert E. *Housing—An East St. Louis Challenge.* Edwardsville: Southern Illinois University, Public Administration and Metropolitan Affairs Program, 1966.

————; Tudor, William; Ferguson, Sally; and Junz, Sophie. *East St. Louis—Studied and Restudied.* Edwardsville: Southern Illinois University, March, 1969.

Meranto, Philip. "Negro Majorities and Political Power: The Defeat of an All Negro Ticket in East St. Louis." Unpublished paper, 1968.

National Commission on Urban Problems. Hearings—Detroit, East St. Louis, St. Louis, Washington, D.C., Vol. 5, 247–315. Washington, D.C.: Government Printing Office, 1967.

Organization and Management of the Government of East St. Louis. Report to the City Council of East St. Louis, Ill., February, 1961. Carbondale: Southern Illinois University, Local Government Center, 1961.

The "Pace" Plan for East St. Louis, Illinois. St. Louis: Schwarz and Van Hoefen, Architects, 1966.

Ranney, David C. *Fiscal Crisis in East St. Louis.* Edwardsville, Ill.: Southern Illinois University, Public Administration and Metropolitan Affairs, February, 1967.

Rudwick, Elliott M. *Race Riot at East St. Louis, July 2, 1917.* Carbondale, Ill.: Southern Illinois University Press, 1964.

Schusky, Jane. *Employment and Unemployment in East St. Louis.* Edwardsville, Ill.: Southern Illinois University, Public Administration and Metropolitan Affairs, 1964.

U.S. Department of Interior, National Park Service. *The East St. Louis, Illinois Waterfront: Historical Background,* by John W. Bond. Washington, D.C.: Government Printing Office, 1969.

Planning

Altshuler, Alan A. *The City Planning Process: A Political Analysis.* Ithaca, N.Y.: Cornell University Press, 1966.

————. "The Goals of Comprehensive Planning." *Journal of the American Institute of Planners,* XXXI (August, 1965).

Banfield, Edward C. *Political Influence.* Glencoe, Ill.: The Free Press, 1961.

Bellush, Jewel, and Murray Hausknecht, eds. *Urban Renewal: People, Politics, and Planning.* Garden City, N.Y.: Anchor Books, 1967.

Beyle, Thad L., and George T. Lathrop. *Planning and Politics: Uneasy Partnership.* New York: The Odyssey Press, 1970.

Boguslaw, Robert. *The New Utopians.* Englewood Cliffs, N.J.: Prentice-Hall, 1965.

Bolan, Richard S. "Emerging Views of Planning." *Journal of the American Institute of Planners,* XXXIII (July, 1967).

Branch, Melville. *Planning: Aspects and Applications.* New York: John Wiley and Sons, 1966.

Brooks, Michael. *Social Planning and City Planning.* American Society of Planning Officials, 1970.

———— and Michael Stegman. "Urban Social Policy, Race, and the Education of Planners." *Journal of the American Institute of Planners,* XXXIV (September, 1968).

Chapin, F. Stuart. *Urban Land Use Planning*. Urbana, Ill.: University of Illinois Press, 1965.

Davidoff, Paul. "Advocacy and Pluralism in Planning." *Journal of the American Institute of Planners*, XXXI (November, 1965).

———— and Thomas A. Reiner. "A Choice Theory of Planning." *Journal of the American Institute of Planners*, XXVIII (March, 1962).

Davies, J. Clarence, III. *Neighborhood Groups and Urban Renewal*. New York: Columbia University Press, 1966.

Dyckman, John. "Social Planning, Social Planners, and Planned Societies." *Journal of the American Institute of Planners*, XXXII (March, 1966).

Erber, Ernest, ed. *Urban Planning in Transition*. New York: Grossman Publishers, 1970.

Fagin, Henry. "Planning for Future Growth." *Law and Contemporary Problems*. Winter, 1965.

Frieden, Bernard J. "Toward Equality of Urban Opportunity." *Journal of the American Institute of Planners*, XXXI (November, 1965).

————. "The Changing Prospects for Social Planning." *Journal of the American Institute of Planners*, XXXIII (September, 1967).

———— and Robert Morris, eds., *Urban Planning and Social Policy*. New York: Basic Books, 1968.

Friedmann, John. "Planning as Innovation: The Chilean Case." *Journal of the American Institute of Planners*, XXXII (July, 1966).

Gans, Herbert J. *People and Plans*. New York: Basic Books, 1968.

Goodman, Robert. *After the Planners*. New York: Simon & Schuster, 1971.

Greer, Scott. *Urban Renewal and American Cities*. Indianapolis: Bobbs-Merrill, 1967.

Hancock, John. "Planners in the Changing American City, 1900–1940." *Journal of the American Institute of Planners*, XXXIII (September, 1967).

Heikoff, Joseph M. "Urban Politics and Planning." *Bureau of Community Planning Newsletter*. Urbana, Ill.: University of Illinois, Winter, 1969.

Holleb, Doris B. *Social and Economic Information for Urban Planning*. Chicago: The Center for Urban Studies of the University of Chicago, 1969, Vol. 1.

Kahn, Alfred. *Theory and Practice of Social Planning*. New York: Russell Sage Foundation, 1969.

Kaplan, Harold. *Urban Renewal Politics*. New York: Columbia University Press, 1963.

Kent, T. J., Jr. *The Urban General Plan*. San Francisco: Chandler Publishing Co., 1964.

Martin, Roscoe C., *et.al. Decisions in Syracuse*. New York: Greenwood Press, 1968.

Meyerson, Martin. *The Conscience of Cities*. New York: George Braziller, 1970.

—— and Edward C. Banfield. *Politics, Planning and the Public Interest*, Glencoe, Ill.: The Free Press, 1965.

Michael, Donald. *The Unprepared Society*. New York: Basic Books, 1968.

——. "Urban Policy in the Rationalized Society." *Journal of the American Institute of Planners*, XXXI (November, 1965).

Mowitz, Robert J., and Deil S. Wright. *Profile of a Metropolis*. Detroit: Wayne State University Press, 1962.

Peattie, Lisa. "Reflections on Advocacy Planning." *Journal of the American Institute of Planners*, XXXIV (March, 1968).

Perloff, Harvey S. *Education for Planning: City, State and Regional*. Baltimore: John Hopkins Press, 1957.

Rabinovitz, Francine. *City Politics and Planning*. New York: Atherton Press, 1969.

Ranney, David C. *Planning and Politics in the Metropolis*. Columbus, Ohio: Charles E. Merrill Publishing Co., 1969.

Rein, Martin. "Social Planning: The Search for Legitimacy." Ed. Daniel Moynihan. *Toward a National Urban Policy*. New York: Basic Books, 1970.

Rossi, Peter, and Robert A. Dentler. *The Politics of Urban Renewal*. New York: The Free Press, 1961.

Sayre, Wallace, and Herbert Kaufman. *Governing New York City*. New York: Russell Sage Foundation, 1960.

Scott, Mellier. *American City Planning Since 1890*. Berkeley: University of California Press, 1969.

Stafford, Walter W., and Ladner, Joyce. "Comprehensive Planning and Racism." *Journal of the American Institute of Planners*, XXXV (March, 1969).

Tugwell, Rexford Guy. *Model for a New Constitution*. Palo Alto: James E. Freel and Associates, 1971.

Webber, Melvin M. "Comprehensive Planning and Social Responsibility." *Journal of the American Institute of Planners*, XXIX (November, 1963).

Index

Valley: area of prostitution, 9–10
Vice (East St. Louis): prostitution, 9; gambling, 10

Ware, Jefferson: riverfront planner, 114; Model Cities directorship, 135–137
Washnis, George: reform recommendations, 29–30; relationship with Fields, 30; conflict with Denman, 51–54; Model Cities work, 119, 120, 121, 122, 123; trip to HUD, 123; Model Cities staffing, 125; reconvenes Model Cities, 129; planning revisions, 134, 170–171; involved in GNRP, 146; aids Model Cities, 153–154; seeks Model Cities approval, 169–170; goals for Model Cities, 218. *See* Administrative assistant to mayor

Webber, Melvin: planners tradition, 178; on social planning, 196–197
Wheadon, Wendell: attacks Model Cities planning, 159; chairs meeting, 164; revises plan, 168
Wiggins Ferry Company. *See* Terminal Railroad Association
Williams, Dakin: in senate race, 28
Williams, George: HUD official, 119–120
Williams, James E., Mayor: election results, 3; primary campaign, 34–37; reform candidate, 38–40; Republican support, 38–39; promise from state, 108; questions riverfront planning, 117

Zerweck, Louis P.: suit against Terminal Railroad Association, 74–75